"This is definitely a needed book on a long-ignored topic. The chapters cover a diverse range of topics—all needed for the spectrum of parenting issues—not just for parents with different needs but also for children of different ages and developmental levels. It should be distributed widely and read by depressed parents as well as their family members, mental health professionals, and advocates."

—Carol Thiessen Mowbray, Ph.D., Professor and
Associate Dean of Research, School of Social Work,
University of Michigan

"This comprehensive manual helps depressed parents understand their illness, manage their moods, deal with the stresses of child-rearing and household management, maintain positive relationships with their children, and effectively negotiate the outside world. Based on careful research and nourished by the ideas and personal accounts of research participants, this valuable book offers a step-by-step guide to help parents recognize their own strengths and enhance their coping and parenting skills."

—Harriet P. Lefley, Ph.D., Professor of Psychiatry and
Behavioral Sciences, University of Miami School of
Medicine, Miami, FL

"Parents who've experienced depression have actively participated in the preparation of this resource guide and their first-person accounts give examples of difficult situations that many parents will recognize as well as successful strategies they've used to overcome them. The experts on living with depression and caring for children are those doing it—the parents, and this guide acknowledges that, and provides a valuable resource for parents who read it."

—Vicki Cowling, social worker and psychologist,
Melbourne, Australia

Parenting Well When You're Depressed

A Complete Resource for Maintaining a Healthy Family

JOANNE NICHOLSON, PH.D.

ALEXIS D. HENRY, SC.D.

JONATHAN C. CLAYFIELD, M.A.

SUSAN M. PHILLIPS

NEW HARBINGER PUBLICATIONS, INC.

Publisher's Note

This publication is designed to provide accurate and authoritative information in regard to the subject matter covered. It is sold with the understanding that the publisher is not engaged in rendering psychological, financial, legal, or other professional services. If expert assistance or counseling is needed, the services of a competent professional should be sought.

Distributed in the U.S.A. by Publishers Group West; in Canada by Raincoast Books; in Great Britain by Airlift Book Company, Ltd.; in South Africa by Real Books, Ltd.; in Australia by Boobook; and in New Zealand by Tandem Press.

Copyright © 2001 by Joanne Nicholson, Alexis D. Henry, Jonathan C. Clayfield, and Susan M. Phillips
New Harbinger Publications, Inc.
5674 Shattuck Avenue
Oakland, CA 94609

Cover design by Poulson/Gluck Design
Edited by Carole Honeychurch
Text design by Michele Waters

Library of Congress number: 01-132280
ISBN 1-57224-251-5 Paperback

Printed in the United States of America

New Harbinger Publications' Web site address: www.newharbinger.com

03   02   01

10   9   8   7   6   5   4   3   2   1

First printing

To parents and children living with depression

To Larry Stier, whose courage, commitment and organizational skills keep us on track

To Lucinda Sloan Mallen, whose conviction that "parents with mental illness want to be the best parents they can be" inspires us every day

Contents

Acknowledgments

This book is the product of years of work with many stakeholders—parents, family members, service providers, policy makers and researchers. Our work groups became an intervention, as we all grew in our understanding of the challenges facing families living with depression. We are reluctant to name each person who participated in the work group process for several reasons. Many are living with mental illness and the choice to disclose their participation and perhaps, by implication, their illness, is theirs alone. Others have asked that we not use their names, evidence that the stigma of mental illness is real and felt. And, lastly, the list is so long, we might mistakenly miss someone. So, to those very important people who contributed so much to our work groups—we thank you.

Many friends and colleagues reviewed drafts of chapters and generously gave of their experiences and expertise. We want to acknowledge the contributions of Marinna A. Banks, Sara R. Barney, Peter P. Berkery, Kathleen Biebel, Vivian B. Brown, Elaine Campbell, Tryne Costa, Jonathan Delman, Marsha Langer Ellison, Albert Grudzinskas, Ming Ming He, Lila Maier, Lucinda Sloan Mallen, Shery Mead, Dee Meaney, Missy Nicholson, Larry Richards, Mark Rodasta, Nancy Rollins, Roberta G. Sands, Melanie Shaw, Susan Sheperd, Mary Sidoti, Jodi Utter, Tyra Walker, Carol Wheeler, Anne Whitman, Wendy Woodfield, and Gina Yarbrough. Thanks, too, to our endorsers, whose kind words were very rewarding to us.

Our research staff has been graced by the efforts of many research assistants and student interns from universities, colleges, and local high schools. To them we offer our gratitude for their hours of transcribing tapes, building databases, taking notes in work groups, retrieving articles from the library, and being generally essential to our efforts. They include Patricia Andrews, Tom Bocian, Carolann Clevesy, Bruce Gillespie, Linda Gordon, Frances Gray, Danielle

Grignon, Taisha Jesse, Delbert Kimball, Jr., Cory Larkin, Eunice Marigliano, Maria Marsh, Ben Mullin, Stephanie Page, Laura Perkins, Robert Pichette, Christina Puleo, Robert Recko, Mandy Richards, Helen Shore, Dena Simons, Cheryl Spinney, Linda Spiridigliozi, Tara St. Germain, Lawrence Stier, Mary Thomas, Julia Vera, Marie Walters, Eric Wish, and Robert Young.

Our clubhouse colleagues have opened their doors to us, providing member and staff time and assistance, essential space and snacks for meetings and, most importantly, opportunities to try things out in the "real world." Our clubhouse consortium includes the members and staff of Atlantic House, Charles Webster Potter Place, Crossroads at the Larches, Elliot House, Employment Options, Inc., Friends Together, Genesis Club, Inc., Point After Club, Renaissance Club, and Stepping Forward. A special thanks goes to Toni Wolf, the Family Project, and all the present and past staff and members at Employment Options, Inc., in Marlborough, Massachusetts. Toni's leadership in developing services for families in the clubhouse environment, and her professional and personal support for this project have been significant.

This project was developed under a grant (#H133G970079) from the National Institute on Disability and Rehabilitation Research, U.S. Department of Education. NIDRR and our project officer, Roseann Rafferty, are active proponents of the participation of individuals with disabilities in the development of new products and technology. While the contents of this book do not necessarily represent the views of NIDRR or the Department of Education, and are not endorsed by the Federal Government, this book would not be in your hands without their vision of the full participation of individuals with disabilities in family life. Other federal partners have made major contributions to our efforts to bring attention to the issues of parents living with illness and their families. These include Judith Katz-Leavy and Susan Salasin from the Substance Abuse and Mental Health Services Administration, Center for Mental Health Services, and Gina Tesauro, from the National Cancer Institute. They have convinced us that it is possible to make a positive contribution to change, to improve the quality of life for families living with multiple challenges. The Massachusetts Department of Mental Health also is an active supporter of the parents' projects, under the leadership of Commissioner Marylou Sudders, past Deputy Commissioner Paul Barreira, and Director of Policy Development Joan Kerzner. They have been instrumental in paving the way for work of national significance in Massachusetts.

We want to thank our friends and colleagues at the University of Massachusetts Medical School Center for Mental Health Services Research, who generously made resources available to us. And special thanks goes to our own families, who make living the vision possible.

Introduction

Parents have a wide range of skill levels. Some parents are "naturals," with instincts that allow them to meet their children's needs without any thought at all. Other parents struggle to find ways to be comfortable with their children and themselves. Over the course of your lifetime, your ability to parent may be compromised by many factors, including accidents, injuries, and ill health. Depression is one of these factors.

According to the U.S. Surgeon General's Report on Mental Health, mood disorders, including depression and bipolar disorder, are significant causes of disability the world over (U.S. Department of Health and Human Services 1999). Almost one-fourth of American women and 15 percent of men in this country will cope with depression and other associated disorders (like anxiety and substance abuse) during their lifetimes (Kessler et al. 1997). The majority of these women and men are parents.

A significant body of research indicates that children may be affected by their parents' depression (Oyserman et al. 2000). Mothers with depression tend to be less responsive to their children and to express more sadness and irritability (Goodman and Brumley 1990). They think more negative thoughts and evaluate themselves poorly as mothers (Taylor and Ingram 1990). Consequently, their children's functioning may suffer. They may develop negative self-concepts, too, and the likelihood that they will become depressed or develop other emotional or behavioral problems increases for a variety of reasons (Hammen 1997). Other circumstances likely to occur along with depression, like marital conflict and poor family communication, can affect children negatively (Downey and Coyne 1990). The severity of a parent's depression, how often a parent is depressed, the age of a child when his parent is depressed, and whether that parent seeks and benefits from treatment all affect outcomes for children, too. In addition, there may be a biological component to depression that runs in families.

Fortunately, many people with depression respond well to treatment. Psychiatric medication, psychotherapy, or a combination of these tends to help many people. Untreated depression contributes to poor quality of life, missed days at work, and parenting difficulties. Seeking treatment is key to successful parenting when you're depressed.

Who We Are

We're a group of researchers and practitioners based at the University of Massachusetts Medical School, in the Department of Psychiatry. We represent several disciplines including psychology, occupational therapy, psychiatric rehabilitation, and counseling. We have a combined total of over fifty years of clinical experience working with adults, children, and families living with mental illness. We are parents who have coped with mental illness and substance abuse in our own families. Our children range in age from sixteen months to twenty-something. We have grandchildren. We personally have dealt with divorce and stepfamily issues, chronic and terminal illnesses, hospitalizations, children with special needs, and elderly parents. We bring a wide range of skills and life experiences to the preparation of this book.

The Parenting Options Project

Our group was funded for three years by the National Institute on Disability and Rehabilitation Research and the Massachusetts Department of Mental Health to develop skill training materials for parents with a group of key stakeholders in the community called "The Parenting Options Project." Our partners included parents and family members, community service providers, psychiatric rehabilitation clubhouse staff and members, mental health and child welfare agency administrators, and policy makers. Relevant topics for this book were suggested in research conducted by the Parents' Project Team at the UMMS Center for Mental Health Services Research over the past ten years. Work groups of stakeholders met to expand and refine topics and to develop the contents for each chapter. Parents wrote personal accounts and came up with activities for examining their values and attitudes and learning and practicing skills. Chapters were reviewed by mental health services consumers, providers, and researchers from across the country, to ensure they would be relevant to parents living in different geographic areas and to different cultural and ethnic groups.

This book, therefore, is based on a firm foundation of research, conducted by our group and other scientists across the country. In our work groups, we took this scientific knowledge a step further to provide practical solutions to the basic challenges of parenting when parents are living with depression. There are not a lot of specific scientific references in the book chapters, because very few people have taken the research findings and applied them in this way. If you are interested in learning more about research studies that have suggested the needs of parents with depression and their children or that have contributed to strategies for intervening, contact us at the University of Massachusetts Medical School Center for Mental Health Services Research.

We Believe in Growth and Change

We believe that parenting is a significant role for adults, and that parents want to do the best job they can. The range of skill levels among parents with depression is no different from that among parents in general. There are some parents diagnosed with depression who do terrific jobs with no help at all; there are some who would benefit from education, skills training, and the development of supports at home and in the community.

We believe proven strategies for behavior change, rehabilitation, and recovery offer hope to parents with depression who want to be better parents. Behavioral approaches have been found to be effective in parent training (Taylor and Biglan 1998). The psychiatric rehabilitation approach is effective in helping adults with mental illness achieve better functioning in work and social roles (Mueser, Drake, and Bond 1997). Cognitive behavioral strategies are useful in treating depression (U.S. Department of Health and Human Services 1999). We borrow techniques from all three "tool bags" and take them a step further in this book, providing opportunities for parents with depression to examine their values and attitudes and modify their thoughts and behavior.

We believe in a strengths-based approach—that is, you start with people's strengths and build on them. Therefore, we assume you have strengths to bring to the task of parenting. One of the first steps to becoming the best parent you can is to look at your thoughts about yourself and the world around you. You may not believe you have any strengths at all! Many of our chapters begin with an opportunity to examine your thoughts and, if they are primarily negative, develop some positive beliefs about yourself and your family.

We believe you are capable of changing your thoughts and behavior and improving your parenting skills even if you are depressed. In these chapters, you will have opportunities to look at your current habits and patterns and to set goals for changing these to lead to a healthier lifestyle. Adults who are functioning as well as possible themselves are better parents. We'll encourage you to become a keen observer of your children, to understand what is normal for their ages and stages of development, and to tailor your interactions with them to meet their needs. We provide suggestions for fun growth activities for you and your children and encourage you to practice them together. The more you tune in to the positives in yourself and your children, the better your relationships with them will be!

Who Is This Book For?

Anyone can use this book, depressed or not, parent or not, if you want to improve the way you relate to children. It is targeted to parents with depression, though we know depression rarely occurs alone. If you are depressed, you may be anxious, too. You may use substances to help yourself feel better. You may have a parent who is an alcoholic, or perhaps you suffered abuse as a child. This book will be useful to any individual coping with an illness or life circumstance that is compromising his or her ability to parent.

Both mothers and fathers will benefit from this book. Depression is not just a women's issue, and neither is parenting. Many men are actively involved in caring for children and may be living with mental illness as well. You will notice we have tried to alternate our use of male and female pronouns so the book will be relevant to all. So, for example, we refer to parents and children as him or her, as randomly as possible.

How to Use This Book

One way to start is by completing the self-assessment on this and the following pages. Identify your strengths and the areas you would like to work on. You can read the book through from front cover to back, or go directly to the chapters that correspond with your goals. You may find it most useful to begin with the areas you identify as your priorities for change.

You may read this book on your own, together with a friend, or with members of a parents' group. Your therapist may be helpful to you in going over some of the material. Certain activities are suitable for role-play. You may want to find a friend or group member to act out these role-play exercises. Several activities involve talking with your children about specific issues. You may want to try these encounters on your own with them, or involve your partner, co-parent, or another family member.

Parenting Strengths & Goals

Here is a list of things that you may need to do as a parent. For each one that applies to you, *circle* the answer that describes you best.	This is a strength of mine.	I do this okay.	I'd like help with this.	Does not apply.	Check items to work on.
1. Manage everyday household tasks (chapter 1)	Strength	Okay	Help	NA	
2. Plan and prepare healthy meals (chapter 4)	Strength	Okay	Help	NA	

3. Understand the relationship between my mood and spending (chapter 3)	Strength	Okay	Help	NA
4. Manage my family's budget (chapter 3)	Strength	Okay	Help	NA
5. Set appropriate limits with my child (chapter 7)	Strength	Okay	Help	NA
6. Have positive interactions with my child (chapter 11)	Strength	Okay	Help	NA
7. Have a pleasant routine with my child (chapter 7)	Strength	Okay	Help	NA
8. Find fun things to do with my child (chapter 8)	Strength	Okay	Help	NA
9. Secure adequate child care for my child (chapter 2)	Strength	Okay	Help	NA
10. Balance work or school, and parenting (chapter 2)	Strength	Okay	Help	NA
11. Know what to do when my child has problems (chapter 9)	Strength	Okay	Help	NA
12. Identify my child's strengths (chapter 7)	Strength	Okay	Help	NA
13. Make mealtimes pleasant for my family (chapter 4)	Strength	Okay	Help	NA
14. Know my legal options as a parent (chapter 10)	Strength	Okay	Help	NA
15. Get help for myself, if I need it (chapter 1)	Strength	Okay	Help	NA
16. Talk with my child about my situation or worries (chapter 6)	Strength	Okay	Help	NA
17. Keep in touch with my child living with others (chapter 11)	Strength	Okay	Help	NA
18. Maintain a substance-free lifestyle (chapter 1)	Strength	Okay	Help	NA
19. Know how my child prefers to communicate (chapter 6)	Strength	Okay	Help	NA

Here is a list of things that you may need to do as a parent. For each one that applies to you, *circle* the answer that describes you best.	This is a strength of mine.	I do this okay.	I'd like help with this.	Does not apply.	Check items to work on.
20. Have good relationships with my child's other parent or caregivers (chapter 11)	Strength	Okay	Help	NA	
21. Express anger without hurting anyone (chapter 5)	Strength	Okay	Help	NA	
22. Cope with the custody determination process (chapter 10)	Strength	Okay	Help	NA	
23. Make time for my own leisure interests (chapter 8)	Strength	Okay	Help	NA	
24. Manage stress in healthy ways (chapter 5)	Strength	Okay	Help	NA	
25. Cope with bad things that have happened to me in my life (chapter 5)	Strength	Okay	Help	NA	
26. Get special services and supports for myself and my children (chapter 9)	Strength	Okay	Help	NA	

We encourage several strategies consistently throughout the book.

- **Observe.** Change starts with seeing how things are to begin with. We encourage you to observe yourself and your children and to become an expert in the way things are now.

- **Record.** Make lists, keep notes, or write in a journal. Jotting down events, thoughts, and feelings helps you establish what we call a "baseline," that is, a reading of where you are now, so you can identify strengths and problems clearly and set goals realistically to make improvements.

- **Experiment.** As you begin to make changes, allow yourself to take a few risks. Try a new strategy, perhaps one you've never imagined yourself trying before. Novelty is often very effective with children. They expect you to be the same old boring mom or dad. A different approach may just get their attention and provide the opportunity for them to respond in a new, improved way. There are no right or wrong answers to the activities or questions in this book. See what works for you!

- **Practice, practice, practice.** New skills usually do not come naturally. If they did, you would not have to learn them, you would just sort of discover them on your own. Old habits die hard, as the expression goes.

And you will probably miss the mark the first few times you try. Don't give up. New skills are worth the time and effort. You and your children will benefit.

- **If you feel you can't do it for yourself, do it for your children.** When people are depressed, they tend to feel that nothing will ever help, that they are incapable of being successful at anything, and that they don't deserve to feel better. If you can't get motivated to make changes for yourself, make them for your children. You deserve to enjoy the benefits of parenting, and your children deserve to have you be the best possible parent you can be.

- **Go at your own pace.** Don't sit down and read this book in one sitting. If you are depressed right now, choose your goals carefully, saving your energy for the most important tasks. When you're feeling well, it's easy to think you don't have to focus on making changes. On the contrary—the time to dig in and make changes is when you are feeling well! That's when you'll have the energy and ability to make the effort.

- **Reward yourself and your children.** Even the smallest change in the positive direction is worth a reward—a few words of praise, a pat on the back, a trip to the ice cream parlor. Look for the positive, grab on to it, and wave it boldly for all to see. You have to accentuate the positive to eliminate the negative!

We're Looking for Feedback

Our group is dedicated to making research findings useful to you. We have a long-term commitment to parents with mental illness and their families. We provide training and consultation to a wide variety of policy makers, providers, and consumer organizations. We actively advocate for the rights of individuals with mental illness and, particularly, those who are parents. We believe that by serving parents, we are contributing to better lives for children.

We would like to hear from you. If there are things about the book you like or not, topics you would like expanded or you think have been missed, please contact us. Our goal is to help you be the best parent you can be.

Chapter 1

Managing Your Mood and the Demands of Parenting

Meeting the day-to-day expectations and demands of parenting is a challenge for anyone. Parenting when you're living with depression can be more than challenging—it can be overwhelming. And feeling overwhelmed can lead you to feel like a failure, becoming even more depressed. While the rest of this book addresses ways to meet the challenges of parenting, to enhance your relationships with your children and be the best parent you can be, this chapter really focuses on *you*. Taking care of yourself is one of the most important things you can do as a parent. Your children need you to be as well as possible. In this chapter, we discuss depression and the many treatment options. We do not endorse any one treatment, because different things work for different people. We focus on positive ways to meet some of the day-to-day challenges of parenting with depression and on ways to work toward a healthy lifestyle. We address the issue of substance abuse, a common problem for many people with depression. And we discuss the special issue of pregnancy and depression.

Throughout this chapter and this book, we present strategies for managing the many challenges facing you as a parent. We might suggest that you make plans, get information, or try new activities or approaches to solving problems. We make these suggestions knowing that when you are really depressed it's difficult, sometimes impossible, to face problems or try new things. Some of the things we suggest might be useful to try when you are depressed. But others will be things that are probably best tried when you are feeling better. (It is important not to make major decisions or plans that can affect your family, your children, or your health when you are feeling your worst.) Many of the strategies involve planning ahead to manage during times you're not feeling so well.

Depression: What Is It?

Major depression is one of the most common mental illnesses. It occurs world-wide, and effects people of all racial, ethnic, and social backgrounds. About 15 percent of the U.S. population will experience depression at some point in their lives, and women are even more likely to get depression (as many as 25 percent) (Kaplan and Sadock 1998). As a parent coping with depression, you are not alone! Depression can begin at any point in life, but most often begins between the ages of twenty and fifty.

Although almost everyone has felt depressed ("down" or "blue") at some point, the occasional blues are not the same as major depression. For most people, occasional feelings of being down pass fairly quickly. People can often do something to help themselves feel better. Major depression is different. Major depression has been described as a "whole body" illness, affecting a person's body, mood, and thoughts. And it doesn't pass quickly. People with major depression cannot just "pull themselves together" and feel better.

There are some specific symptoms that mental health professionals agree characterize major depression. A person with major depression will have either a depressed mood or a loss of interest or pleasure in all or almost all activities for at least two weeks (American Psychiatric Association 1994). The depressed mood and/or loss of interest occurs all day or most of the day. People with depression also will have at least some of the following symptoms:

- Appetite loss and/or weight loss, or overeating with weight gain;

- Sleep problems, such as sleeping all the time, or being unable to fall asleep or stay asleep;

- Irritability or restlessness;

- Fatigue or loss of energy, being "slowed down";

- Feeling worthless, helpless, hopeless, or guilty;

- Difficulty concentrating, remembering, or making decisions; and

- Frequent thoughts of death, suicidal ideas or plans, or suicide attempts.

You may know these symptoms by different names. You may describe your-self or, unfortunately, others may describe you as "a compulsive overeater," "lazy," "useless," "forgetful," "morbid," "seeing the cup as half empty," or as a "pessimist." Symptoms will vary among people but usually are severe enough to cause the person to be distressed and to interfere with important areas of life, like work, school, parenting, homemaking, socializing, and having fun.

No one really knows what causes depression. For most people, depression is probably the result of a combination of biological, genetic, and psychosocial fac-tors. Some people seem to develop depression in response to stressful events in their lives, while others can develop depression without any clear reason. Regardless of the causes, there have been many advances in the treatment of depression in recent years, in addition to the development of extremely useful self-help strategies. Most people with depression do benefit from treatment, typi-cally a combination of some form of medical treatment such as medication, and psychotherapy or "talking therapy" (American Psychiatric Association 2000). These treatments may complement strategies you try on your own or with the help of peers, family members, or a partner.

Unfortunately, not everyone with depression gets help. Some people do not seek out treatment, perhaps because they feel hopeless and that nothing will make a difference. Or perhaps they think asking for help is a sign of weakness, or they assume everyone feels the way they do. These ideas are simply the depres-sion talking! If you have some or all of the symptoms listed above, and you have never received any help for them, put this book down and call your doctor. Your primary-care physician or family doctor may know quite a lot about depression or can refer you to a psychiatrist, if necessary.

Knowing Yourself

Take a moment to consider the symptoms of depression listed above. You may never have thought of yourself as "officially" depressed before. Perhaps you picked up this book because you are trying to figure out why you are grouchy with your children all the time, or you are feeling exhausted, or like you can't seem to get anything done, or just plain old "down in the dumps." To label some-one with depression is only useful to the extent that it allows people, and particu-larly health care providers, to understand how someone might be feeling and what to do about it. A diagnosis can suggest a particular course of effective treat-ment. Acknowledging that you're depressed is not the end of the journey—it's only the beginning.

The first step in the journey is to make your own diagnosis, if you will. Take a few minutes to jot down how you would describe yourself. Do some of the symptoms listed above describe you? Include them on your list, or write down how you feel in your own words. Think about how you feel today and how you usually feel. Also consider how long you have felt this way, and whether you have ever felt this way before.

Don't let this task make you feel worse. If you find that most of the words you use to describe yourself seem negative, take heart! This is probably a symptom of your depression and not a true picture of the "real" you. People who are depressed often have negative or distorted thoughts. Changing these thoughts, which is something we'll work on together, will lead you down the path to wellness. There are many strategies you can try on your own that are meant to complement the treatment recommendations of your professional health care provider.

Depression Can Come and Go

Some people can have one period of serious depression in their lives and never get depressed again. But more often people have repeated bouts of depression. It's possible to have a long stretch of time when you are feeling well but then get depressed again. It can happen even when you're taking medications or seeing a therapist regularly, and it can happen even when things seem to be going well in your life. If you've been living with depression or bipolar disorder for a long time, you've probably had this experience.

If you have had repeated episodes of depression, then you probably have a sense of when your depression is getting worse and what events in your life might trigger depression. It can be helpful to make a list of the warning signs that indicate you're getting depressed. You can also develop an "action plan" of steps to take when you see these warning signs happening. Your action plan can include anything that you think might help—talking to a family member, calling a friend, taking a walk, listening to music, meditating, contacting your therapist. It is helpful to think about these things when you are feeling better, so you can prepare in advance for times when you're feeling worse.

Warning Signs—When I Am Getting Depressed

1. _____

2. _____

3. _____

Action Plan—Steps to Take When My Depression Is Getting Worse

1. _____

2. _____

3. _____

Share this list with important people in your life—your partner or spouse, family, friends, and other supportive people. Involve them in thinking through steps you can take if your depression is worsening. Resources that can help you both monitor how you are feeling and plan for when symptoms get worse are the *Wellness Recovery Action Plan* and other books by Mary Ellen Copeland, listed in the Resources section near the end of this book.

Depression and Parenting

Depression most often occurs between the ages of twenty and fifty—just the ages when most people are having and raising children! So coping with depression while trying to raise children is a common challenge. Sharon, a single mom, describes how she meets the demands of parenting when she is feeling depressed:

> *It is hard to understand what is happening when your depression acts up. There are a lot of things that can happen to you that can make it hard to know what is right or wrong. Your mind jumps around, and it seems like you have no time to think things out.*
>
> *When I wake up feeling depressed, I really feel caught off guard. I know I have to get the kids off to school. That means I have to get up and get breakfast ready, make sure they are getting ready, that they're wearing clothes that are appropriate, and that they have their homework in their backpacks, and other things like that. But, when I'm depressed, I feel too tired to move, I have a headache, I feel alone. I don't want them to miss school, but I have to admit that sometimes it happens.*
>
> *When I'm depressed like this, I try to just focus on one step at a time and keep my mind on the kids. I try to push away the negative feelings that are holding me back from getting things done and think about what's most important. I want to make a good start to the day for both the kids and me. Sometimes this is really hard to do, but I'm a parent, and this is what I have to do.*
>
> *Here's what I do when I'm feeling down. Sometimes I just try to stop, take a deep breath, and start over. I shut the door to my bedroom and tell the kids I'll be out in fifteen minutes. I sit on my bed and breathe deeply with short, clean breaths. I try to relax (not enough to fall asleep again), then I get up, stretch, take a shower, and then look into the mirror and say to myself, "I have kids who depend on me and I love them, so I have to start the day off right for them." I get dressed, go downstairs, and start breakfast, and when the kids show up at the table, I smile and say "good morning." If the morning starts out good for them and for me, I can make it through the rest of the day.*

Many parents worry about the impact of their depression on their children. You may feel like a failure if you don't have the energy to make a home-cooked meal or sew a Halloween costume. It may take all your energy to get to the baseball game; coaching the team would be out of the question. You may feel you are disappointing your entire family by not participating fully in holiday preparations or birthday parties. Parents with depression often worry that their illness is causing their children's bad behavior or low grades, or they feel blamed by others or blame themselves for their children's shortcomings, as well as their own.

While your depression is probably not directly causing your children's bad behavior or low grades, it would be beneficial to them if you had the energy and emotional resources available to help them make improvements. You can turn your worries into the motivation you will need to make changes. Even if, when you are depressed, you think you're worthless and don't deserve to feel better, the fact is your children deserve your best efforts!

Getting the Help You Need

The good news about depression is that many treatments are available, and most people who get treatment are helped. The hopeless feelings that come with depression can make this a hard thing to remember! Again, let your caring and concerns for your children motivate you to seek the best help you can get.

Finding a Physician or Psychiatrist Who Is Right for You

Your primary-care physician or family doctor is an important resource and the first person most people call or see when they're not feeling well. Many people seek help and obtain treatment for depression from their primary-care physician. Primary-care physicians are familiar with depression, can prescribe appropriate medications, and make treatment recommendations. In addition, your health insurance or managed care organization may require you to set up a first appointment with your primary-care physician before a referral to a specialist like a psychiatrist can be made.

A psychiatrist is a medical doctor who has special training that allows him or her to understand both the physical and mental aspects of emotional problems. A psychiatrist can make a specific diagnosis based on your current symptoms, your past history and, sometimes, other tests or evaluations. In addition, because psychiatrists are physicians, they can prescribe medications. In some states, psychiatric nurse practitioners can also prescribe medications for treating depression.

If you've never seen a psychiatrist, you might feel uncomfortable about the idea. Just the fact that you need to see her may confirm your suspicion that you really are "crazy." Many people feel this way. It's important to remember that a psychiatrist is just like any other medical doctor with expertise in a particular area. You wouldn't hesitate to see a heart specialist if you had a heart condition or a diabetes specialist if you had diabetes. It's the same with depression.

It is important to feel comfortable with the psychiatrist you're seeing. There are several questions you may wish to ask him on the first visit.

- Are you board certified in psychiatry?

- What experience do you have treating depression?

- How will you go about deciding which treatment is right for me?

- What are the risks and benefits of different treatments?

- What are your opinions about psychotherapy?

- What type of therapy do you do?

- What hospitals do you use?

- What insurance do you accept?

- Do you have appointment times during the day when my children are in school?

- If not, is there a playroom where my children can wait during my appointments?

If the psychiatrist doesn't answer questions such as these to your satisfaction or seems annoyed by your questions, maybe he isn't right for you. People are often assigned a psychiatrist when they are hospitalized. If this is your situation, can you talk openly with her? Remember, if you don't feel comfortable with the person you're assigned or referred to, you can select another. If you don't have a psychiatrist or think you might want to change from your current psychiatrist, you have several options. A good first step is to talk with your primary-care physician. If you have a psychotherapist, talk with her about a psychiatrist she might recommend.

Medications

One of the most common approaches to the treatment of depression is medication. While there are no medications that "cure" depression, medications are successful in alleviating the symptoms of depression for many people. Our goal is not to give you advice about medications—what to take or how to take it—but rather to review some of the common medications for depression, their benefits, and their side effects.

Today there are many different types of antidepressant medications that can help treat the symptoms of depression. Serptonin-specific reuptake inhibitors (SSRIs) are the type most often used to treat depression. Other types of medications for depression include tricyclic and tetracyclic antidepressants (TCAs), and monoamine oxidase reuptake inhibitors (MAOIs). Researchers believe that, in many cases, depression is caused by a low supply of certain brain chemicals (neurotransmitters such as serotonin or norepinephrine). In general, each of the three different types of antidepressants (SSRIs, TCAs, and MAOIs) works by increasing the amount of these chemicals in the brain.

People often need to take an antidepressant for several weeks before they begin to notice any real improvement. Most experts agree that a fair trial of any antidepressant should last for at least four to eight weeks (American Psychiatric Association 2000). Antidepressants are often first helpful in improving the appetite and sleep problems common in depression, followed by an increase in energy, and then an improvement in mood. But waiting for an antidepressant to work can be frustrating. It's important to make sure you give an antidepressant enough time, at a high enough dose, to see if it will really work for you. Because there are so many antidepressants to choose from, if one medicine doesn't work for you, it's likely that another one will. However, the transition from one antidepressant to another is time consuming, and you can sometimes feel worse in the process (Thase and Rush as cited in U.S. Department of Health and Human Services 1999, p. 265). Having good, open communication with your doctor or nurse practitioner is essential when you're trying any new medications, particularly if you require adjustments in type or dose.

All antidepressants have some negative side effects, although the SSRIs tend to have fewer side effects than the other two types. Some of the common side effects of antidepressants include feeling sedated, dizzy or agitated, having nausea, diarrhea, or constipation, dry mouth, blurred vision, weight gain, or sexual dysfunction. Make sure to let your doctor or nurse practitioner know if you are having side effects, especially if you're considering stopping the medicine because of the side effects. In many cases, you can decrease unpleasant side effects by adjusting the dose or time of day you take the medication or by switching medications. But you and your health care provider should make changes together. Don't adjust medications without talking to him first!

You cannot become addicted to antidepressant medications. However, almost all antidepressants can be dangerous if you take more than the amount prescribed. If you have children in the house, make sure to keep any medicine out of their reach in order to prevent an accidental overdose.

Questions to Ask Your Doctor About Medications

- What is the medication for? How will it help me?

- When and how often should I take it?

- When will it start to work? How long will I need to take it for?

- What are the side effects I should watch for?

- Will the medication affect my ability to take care of my child or do other everyday activities?

- Are there any dangers to taking the medication?

- What happens if this medication doesn't work?

- What should I do if my child accidentally takes the medication?

Electroconvulsive Therapy (ECT)

Another treatment that may be recommended for depression is electroconvulsive therapy (ECT; also sometimes called "shock treatments"). The use of ECT is controversial, but some people with depression have been helped by it (Rudorfer, Henry and Sackeim 1997). ECT may be recommended as a last resort when medications have failed for people who have depression and psychosis (disturbed thinking or hallucinations), who are severely suicidal, or who have a medical condition that makes using medicines difficult or impossible (U.S. Department of Health and Human Services 1999).

When administered, ECT causes seizure activity in the brain. ECT is usually performed in a hospital, although it can be done on an outpatient basis. The major side effects of ECT are confusion and memory loss. Virtually all individuals experience confusion immediately after an ECT treatment. The impact of ECT on memory impairment and mental functioning are highly variable and may be permanent and severe. Anyone considering ECT must carefully weigh the benefits and risks and should consult with advocates, family, or friends, as well as the treatment team in making the decision.

Psychotherapy

Many people with depression are treated with a combination of medications and psychotherapy. There are several different types of psychotherapy. Many practitioners use a combination of approaches. Strategies may include supportive listening and feedback, clarifying values and correcting distorted thinking, and assigning activities and homework designed to provide opportunities to change your thoughts and behavior. Research suggests that, for people with severe or recurrent depression, a combination of medication and psychotherapy is more effective than either treatment alone (American Psychiatric Association 2000; U.S. Department of Health and Human Services 1999).

A psychiatrist, psychologist, social worker, psychiatric nurse practitioner, or other counseling professional, preferably licensed or registered in your state, can provide psychotherapy. You may receive psychotherapy and prescriptions for medication from the same person, that is, your psychiatrist or psychiatric nurse practitioner. Or one individual, a primary-care physician, psychiatrist, or nurse practitioner may prescribe your medications, while your psychotherapy is provided by another. The questions suggested above for choosing a psychiatrist also apply to choosing a therapist. It's important to feel comfortable with the person treating you. It is appropriate and wise to change therapists if the person you are seeing doesn't feel like a good match for you.

Hospitalization

Most people are treated for depression on an outpatient basis and may never go into the hospital. There are times, however, when a person's depression is so long lasting or debilitating that he needs to be hospitalized. These days, hospitalizations are typically very short, lasting from three to ten days. It is easy to think of going into the hospital as representing weakness or failure on your part. Try to remember that the decision to go into the hospital can be a positive, responsible step. You're doing something to keep yourself healthy, which is the most important thing you can do for your children.

If you are a parent with depression, making the decision to go into the hospital can be very difficult. You may put off going into the hospital and getting the treatment you need because of your worries about who will care for your children or how they will be affected by your absence. If you are a single parent without a partner in the home, this decision can be even more difficult, as your caregiver options may be more limited.

The time to make a plan for when you need to be hospitalized is when you're feeling well. If you have a spouse or partner, you should discuss what you would like to have happen with your children while you are gone. If you are separated or divorced from your children's other parent and have a good relationship, then that parent may be the person best suited to care for your children. However, if your relationship with your children's other parent is poor or nonexistent, you need to make alternative arrangements. Your children's grandparents, your siblings, other family members, or close friends may be good choices. Have a conversation with your partner, trusted friends, or family members, and make your wishes known to them.

Things to Consider

- Will my children stay at home with a caretaker, or will they need to go to the home of the caretaker?

- If my children need to stay in someone else's home, are there things they can take with them to increase their comfort, like favorite blankets, stuffed animals, or pets?

- Can my children continue their normal routines, including school and after-school activities?

- What alternative arrangements need to be made for transportation to school, dance class, or Cub Scouts?

- What should I tell my children about my being hospitalized?

Chapter 7, "Communicating with Children About Depression," is an important chapter to review. It has many suggestions for how to talk with your children about issues like hospitalization.

If you do go into the hospital, you might wonder whether it's a good idea for your children to visit you there. In most situations, it is probably fine and, in fact, reassuring to your children to see you. Your children need to know that you're okay, and that the hospital is not a bad or scary place, but a good place where you are getting help. And it may be reassuring to you and facilitate your recovery to know that your children are doing well in your absence.

Managing the Day-to-Day Stress of Parenting

No doubt about it—parenting is a stressful job! Couple the ever-changing demands children make with the daily challenges of keeping a home going—cooking, shopping, laundry, housekeeping, bill paying—and it can all be pretty overwhelming. If you're faced with all of these normal demands, perhaps also holding down a job outside the home, *and* dealing with depression, you have even more responsibility. Your days and weeks may include treatment appointments with several providers and perhaps an occasional hospitalization, as well as the numerous routine activities of most parents.

Your Daily Demands

The first step toward feeling less overwhelmed and more successful in meeting everyday demands is to understand what you're trying to accomplish and in what amount of time. It's rare that any of us takes a moment to think through how we spend our time on a typical day. We're usually too busy! The point of completing the following chart is to give yourself a moment to reflect on what you do each day. Pick a typical weekday and record your activities for that day, accounting for all twenty-four hours. Include the time you might spend relaxing, napping, or sleeping. You can do this for a single day or track your time use over several days.

My Typical Day

12:00 midnight	12:00 noon
1:00 A.M.	1:00 P.M.
2:00 A.M	2:00 P.M.
3:00 A.M.	3:00 P.M.
4:00 A.M.	4:00 P.M.
5:00 A.M.	5:00 P.M.
6:00 A.M.	6:00 P.M.
7:00 A.M.	7:00 P.M.
8:00 A.M.	8:00 P.M.
9:00 A.M.	9:00 P.M.
10:00 A.M.	10:00 P.M.
11:00 a.m.	11:00 p.m.

While this is a simple exercise, it can be very revealing. Look at the activities you try to accomplish in a typical day, and look at how much time you're devoting to different activities over the course of a week. What activities take the bulk of your time? Are there activities you wish you could devote more time to? Are there times of the day or certain activities that are really stressful for you? Overall, are you satisfied with how you are spending your time? Do you have the time you want to have with your children or your spouse or partner? Do you have enough time for yourself? Or, do you feel that you don't have enough interesting or meaningful activity in your day? Are you feeling overwhelmed by your daily routine?

Once you've really thought about how you spend your time, think about your priorities. What are the things that really *need* to be done? Are there things you can let go of or do less often? Think about what you can accomplish when you're feeling well, and what it's like when you are feeling depressed. What are the essentials, the minimum you still need to be able to do even when you are depressed?

You might ask other members of your family, like your spouse or partner, or your children if they are old enough, to track their time use over a few days. When you've all had a chance to do this, sit down and talk together. What are the priorities of each individual in the family? What are the needs that you all have in common, like fixing meals or doing laundry? As a family, decide what activities need to done around the home, how often they need to be done, and who can do them. One way to accomplish more is to delegate!

Household Responsibilities

Needs to Be Done	How Often	Person Responsible

Of course, you may have activities that don't happen in the home or involve other family members. Again, what are your priorities? What do you need to do? What do you want to do? It's difficult to think about taking time for yourself when you're a parent. Set a goal. Identify the first step. Changes don't have to happen all at once, so start small. Plan two hours a week when you're going to do something for yourself.

Childcare Needs—Not Just for Work

Even if you're not working outside the home there may be times when you need childcare. Consider whether you might need childcare for the following activities.

- **Appointments.** Do you have doctors' appointments, therapy sessions, or other regularly scheduled appointments where your child can't accompany you?

- **Treatment programs.** Do you attend a day treatment program or self-help group like Alcoholics Anonymous?

- **Hospitalizations.** Making emergency plans for childcare in the event of a hospitalization can alleviate further stress for both you and your family.

- **Legal situations.** If you have to go to court, but your child is not required to attend, childcare can free you from the stress of a bored or disruptive child.

- **Self-care.** Using childcare can provide you with the break that you need to rest, relax, and meet your own needs to stay healthy; it can make you a better parent.

Consider the twenty-four-hour time chart you and other family members just completed. Note everyone's schedule, including work, school, activities, therapy appointments, or any other times you and your family will be out of the house. Are there times that you and your family would benefit from the help of a person who regularly provided childcare? For example, you might have a therapy appointment every Thursday afternoon or would like to have Tuesday morning free for errands. Maybe Friday afternoons would be a good time to meet your personal needs. You might even want someone who could come in to help your child with homework while you get dinner ready. The point is to think about childcare as a possible tool to manage the demands of home life. Finding and using adequate childcare can be a way to cope with all of the priorities in your life. As one mother with depression noted,

> *Childcare has really helped me out and has been great for my*
> *three-year-old. I have him attending day care two times per week, which*
> *allows me time to take care of my own needs—therapy appointments, time*
> *for relaxation, and so on. My son benefits from playing with kids his own*
> *age, doing art projects, and being read to. He looks forward to going each*
> *week and has actually asked me if he could attend day care more often.*

Working Toward a Healthy Lifestyle

Certainly, staying as healthy as possible is one of the most important things you can do as a parent. As a parent with depression, it's really important to recognize that keeping yourself well and taking time for yourself and your health needs is good for both you and your children. In earlier sections, we've talked about the common treatments for depression. But, in addition to medications and therapy, there are lifestyle choices you can make that may help you. These strategies are not a substitute for comprehensive professional treatment of depression. And the cruel truth about depression is that sometimes it recurs, even if you are doing everything you can to stay healthy. But, to gain the most depression-free day-to-day experience you can, it's important to create a supportive, healthy lifestyle.

The Importance of Friends

Depression is an isolating illness. Depression makes you think other people don't want to have anything to do with you. Many people feel a sense of shame about having depression or that it's a sign of weakness or a personal failing. The general stigma that exists in society about mental illness can intensify these feelings; they become stigma turned inward. Luckily, we live in an era of ever increasing openness about the realities of depression. Many well-known people have "come out" about their own struggles with depression—Tipper Gore, Mike Wallace, and others. The more open we are about mental illness, the less stigma there will be.

If you feel you have to hide your depression from the people around you, it makes it hard to build real supports for yourself. Because depression is so common, most people have some firsthand experience with it. If they haven't experienced it directly, they might know a family member, close friend, coworker, or neighbor who has struggled with depression. If you take the risk to tell someone, you might find it wasn't much of a risk at all. The person you tell might just then tell you about her personal experience. This is not to say that you need to tell everyone you encounter in your daily life about your depression. But, if you can have at least a few friends who know and understand, then you don't have to hide or explain when you're feeling depressed or having a bad day. You can be yourself. And that can help a lot.

We all need friends. Friendships are one of the most important supports anyone can have. Because depression is an isolating illness, you might not feel that you have many friends, or the idea of making new friends might seem overwhelming. If you are at home with young children, your opportunities to meet friends might be limited. It may take some effort, but look into programs and services in your community. Self-help groups are an organized way of meeting other people. If you attend a place of worship, you may meet people through fellowship activities, in addition to the spiritual support you may find. Community centers and libraries often sponsor activities where people gather and get to know each other. Activities at your child's school can be a place to meet other parents.

Play and Leisure

At every age, people need to play. Play in adulthood involves participation in hobbies, sports, and other recreational activities. Our leisure activities are ones that we choose to do. They are not obligatory activities, like work or parenting. Leisure activities allow us a respite from work, and they can be an important source of satisfaction in our lives. We do them for enjoyment, for relaxation, and for stress reduction. They allow us to express ourselves, and they allow us to grow physically, mentally, and creatively. Shared leisure activities often provide the foundations of friendships or a strong partnership.

Many adults give their recreation low priority. In meeting their children's needs and managing their activities, parents often put aside their own need for leisure. It's hard to find the time. Some leisure activities cost more money than we can afford. And when you're depressed, your leisure activities are probably one of the first things you stop doing. It's important to set aside some time in your week for leisure activities, as they are an important tool in maintaining your health.

Using the chart below, fill in activities that you have enjoyed in each category. Solitary activities include things you do by yourself, like reading and listening to music. Creative activities may include painting, cooking, gardening, or knitting. Physical activities may include team sports, hiking, or swimming. Social activities might include playing cards or going to the movies with friends. There are no right or wrong answers. Just list activities in categories in a way that makes sense to you. If you're depressed, list activities you've enjoyed when you're feeling well.

My Leisure Interests

Solitary Activities	Creative Activities	Physical Activities	Social Activities

Now, circle the leisure activities that you've most enjoyed. Go back and look over the daily schedule you completed earlier in this chapter. Make a commitment to setting aside time each week in your schedule for two of these activities. Maybe it's only an hour or two a week, but it is important to both you and your children to prioritize these.

Regular Exercise

Research shows that regular exercise is important to good health. Many people with depression find exercise a helpful way to maintain or improve their moods. Walking is one of the least expensive and best forms of regular exercise you can do. Start with a distance that is comfortable for you—it might be a block, it might be a mile. Set aside twenty to thirty minutes three times a week and take a walk by yourself, with a partner or friend, or with your children.

Other forms of regular exercise can include swimming, running, or biking. Many people find yoga to be both an invigorating and stress relieving form of exercise. Yoga classes can often be found at community centers, adult education centers, and local YMCAs.

Diet

In addition to regular exercise, good eating habits are important to overall health. Food is often very connected to our emotions and moods. We use food to celebrate when we are feeling good, and we use food to soothe ourselves when we're feeling depressed or anxious. Try to be mindful of the ways you use food in relation to your moods. Are there changes you want to make to your eating habits to maintain health? Chapter 4, "Feeding Your Family and Yourself," discusses healthy eating habits for you and your family.

Sleep

Getting a good night's sleep and having good regular sleep habits are really important to keeping yourself on an even keel. Sleep disturbance is very common in depression. It's also common during parenthood! Having an infant or young child almost certainly means your sleep is going to be disrupted. And waiting for your teenager to come home at night with the car has disrupted the sleep of many parents.

The age at which infants begin to sleep through the night varies tremendously. If you have an infant who still needs feeding in the middle of the night, remember that this won't last forever. Trading off middle of the night feedings with your spouse or partner can help you both get through this time. If you are a breast-feeding mom, you can try to pump enough breast milk to store for your partner to use in middle of the night feedings. You can also make the decision to use a bottle for nighttime feedings.

Most parents confront the issue of a child who isn't sleeping through the night at some point. Many children have periods when they don't sleep well. If your young child isn't sleeping through the night at an age when you think he or she should, consult your pediatrician. There are a lot of approaches you can take to solve your child's sleep problem.

Lots of other things, besides children, affect your sleep. Anxiety, stressful events in your life, your activity level, medications, alcohol, caffeine, and nicotine can all have an impact on your sleep. Some of these things are easier to control than others. But there are strategies you can try to help you fall asleep, stay asleep, and get the sleep you need.

- Go to bed and wake up at about the same time each day, weekdays and weekends. The recommendation of eight hours of sleep a night actually seems to be good for most people.

- Think about the place where you sleep. Are light and noise kept to a minimum? Make sure the room is not too cold, not too hot.

- A high level of activity near bedtime can affect your ability to fall asleep. Intense work late in the evening and even exercise can make it difficult to "settle down" physically and mentally.

- Obviously, caffeine and nicotine are both stimulants and can keep you awake. Avoid cigarettes, coffee, tea, soda, and chocolate later in the day.

- Your mother was right—warm milk and a hot bath before bed can help you relax.

- If you can't fall asleep or fall back to sleep after a period of time, get out of bed. Some people find it useful to keep a small notebook by the bed in which to write your "worries." Read a book until you feel sleepy. Many experts recommend not watching TV in bed.

- Some antidepressants can disrupt sleep if they are taken late in the day. If you think this may be a problem for you, talk with your doctor about changing your medication schedule.

Sleep problems can be a sign of a recurrence of depression. If you have persistent sleep problems, whether too much or too little, talk with your primary-care doctor or mental health professional.

Drugs, Alcohol, and Tobacco

Using nonprescription drugs, drinking, or smoking is not the way to stay healthy. Many people, with and without depression, struggle with substance use and abuse. It can be easy for someone to say, "I'm going to cut back on my drinking, stop smoking, or quit using drugs." Doing it is much more difficult. Depression and substance abuse frequently go hand in hand, so it's important that you know right from the start that your experience is not uncommon and that it is treatable. For some, using substances is a way of self-medicating a depression that either has not been diagnosed or is too difficult to face. Some people use drugs and alcohol because of a stressful home situation, because they want to avoid their problems, or because their medication is not very effective or has uncomfortable side effects. Others may feel their illness prevents them from "fitting in" socially with others, and the drugs and alcohol reduce their social anxiety, allowing them to feel good.

Unfortunately, drinking and taking drugs to cope with depression almost always create more problems, like losing your job, divorce, and financial difficulties. Getting help for a substance-use problem may reveal an underlying mental illness. This was the case for Bob, who discovered that his addiction to drugs had been masking his depression for many years.

> *A lot of things happened to me when I gave up drinking and drugs. I moved into a sober house where I met a lot of nice people. I attended Alcoholics Anonymous meetings on a daily basis where I met with other sober people. Surprisingly, after I got sober, I found out that I also have depression. Now I take medication daily to help control my symptoms.*

If you're using substances, it can be hard to tell if the symptoms or problems you experience are due to depression or to the alcohol or drugs you use. And treating your condition effectively can be difficult. For example, isolation and withdrawal can be symptoms of depression or of substance abuse—or both. Even doctors and mental-health counselors have a hard time distinguishing between symptoms of depression and symptoms that result from drug or alcohol use. Your mental-health professional may request that you abstain from substance use while in her care, so that she can make a more accurate diagnosis and prescribe the best course of treatment.

Substance abusers often deny, conceal, rationalize, and blame others when it comes to their abuse problems; it's a symptom of the disease. Though it may be hard for you to seek help, it is important to remember that the sooner you get help, the better your chances are for recovery. Seeing your mental health professional is a good first step. You can get information about treatment in your area from your primary-care doctor, psychiatrist, or counselor. Treatment information is also available through your local Yellow Pages. If you decide to seek help, ask to see a professional who specializes in both mental health and substance-abuse problems; not all health-care providers are aware of the way these different issues interact.

Using Substances When Taking Psychiatric Medications

Mixing alcohol and drugs with prescribed medication is a bad idea. You may not only ensure that the treatment you take for depression is less effective, but you may run the risk of a dangerous interaction (Kaplan and Sadock 1998). Alcohol, for example, can prevent certain antidepressants from being absorbed properly. Some psychiatric medications can increase the intoxicating effects of alcohol, increasing the loss of coordination and the chance of accidents. Most psychiatric medications come with specific warnings against using alcohol while taking them; the health consequences are just too great.

Even though there may be no specific warnings against taking psychiatric medications while using illegal drugs, it's safe to say that combining your medications with any of these substances will have unpredictable, harmful, and even lethal consequences. Inform your doctor about your drug or alcohol use so she can make a safe decision regarding the choice of your medication.

The Special Challenge of Pregnancy

Whether it's your first baby or not, deciding to have a baby or finding yourself pregnant raises questions and concerns. How will the baby change my life? Will I be able to manage? How will a new baby affect my relationship with my spouse or partner or my other children? If you are a person with depression, having a baby brings with it another whole set of considerations. Whether you are a prospective mom or dad, a primary consideration is to make sure that both mom and baby are healthy during a pregnancy.

If you are thinking about becoming pregnant or if you are pregnant already, and you are taking medication for depression, one of the important questions you have probably already asked yourself is whether you should continue to take medication during your pregnancy. This is an important decision, one that should be made after careful consideration and open discussions with either your primary-care physician or psychiatrist and your obstetrician. While conventional wisdom tells us that a developing baby is always better off if a pregnant woman takes no medications during the pregnancy, this is not always the case. If you have had repeated episodes of serious depression, going off medications means you have a good chance of getting depressed again. And a recurrence of depression can put both you and your baby at risk. If you are depressed during pregnancy, you may not gain enough weight because of poor appetite, which means your baby might get inadequate nutrition and be at risk for low birth weight. Pregnant women with untreated depression may have more complications at delivery (Grush and Cohen 1998). And, of course, the most serious consequence of an untreated depression is an increased risk of suicide. Alice, who has struggled for many years with depression, shares her story about making the decision to have second baby.

> The decision to become pregnant for a second time was not easy. And it was not hasty; there are almost nine years between my two children. In the years following my first child's birth, my illness became very disruptive, and I required hospitalization two different times. The good that came out of that difficult time is that I began working with a wonderful psychiatrist and, after a great deal of experimentation, was able to find a combination of

medications that seems to work for me. I also joined a church, which has become a huge source of support and comfort to me.

Having finally achieved a semblance of balance in my life, I was extremely worried about the prospect of risking another pregnancy, not to mention adding the stresses of raising a second child. My husband, while he very much wanted a second child, was very understanding of the extraordinary risk it would be for me. We weighed the pros and cons of trying for a second child for years, and I wish I could say that our decision to go ahead was based on some very rational thinking. But the fact is, we decided to take a leap of faith. If it was meant to be, it would happen, and we would find a way to cope. At the time, I was rapidly approaching my fortieth birthday, so part of our decision was driven by the knowledge that our biological "window" would be closing soon.

Once I became pregnant I expressed my desire to taper off medications, both for the health of the fetus and so that I would be able to breastfeed. My doctor advised strongly against it, but agreed to help guide me through my decision. In retrospect, I wish I had heeded his advice, because going off my meds was a terrible decision. I fell into the worst depression I have ever experienced. The first trimester of my pregnancy was a nightmare. I agreed to go back on my medication, and by the fourth month was coming out of the depression. My doctors, both my psychiatrist and my obstetrician, were very encouraging in their belief that the baby would be fine and that the benefit of keeping myself healthy far outweighed the risk of using medications during pregnancy.

I gave birth to a beautiful, healthy baby boy right on his due date, and I have yet to feel any regret about my decision. I can't overemphasize how important my support system has been in making this possible for me—my family and friends have always been there to help. When I had so much trouble following my first pregnancy, no one, including my closest family members, knew the extent to which I was struggling. One of the best things I have done over the past nine years is to get better at letting people know what my limitations are and to learn to accept help.

Research conducted over the last ten years suggests that it is possible for a pregnant woman to remain on certain antidepressant medications and not put her developing baby at risk (Nulman et al. 1997; Wisner, Gelenberg, Leonard, Zarin, and Frank 1999). However, there may be some complications that come with taking particular antidepressants. Another thing to keep in mind is that little is known about over-the-counter treatments for depression, such as St. John's wort, and their use during pregnancy. With good prenatal care, good communication between you and your doctors, and careful management of the pregnancy and delivery, these complicated issues can be managed. The most important thing is to make sure that you talk openly with your health-care providers during this special time.

Steps Toward Wellness

This chapter provides you with information on depression. If, after reading this chapter, you aren't sure you have depression or require additional information, contact your primary-care physician, therapist, or psychiatrist for an accurate diagnosis and appropriate treatment recommendations. Great resources describe strategies for managing your depression as a complement to, but not a substitute for, seeking professional treatment. Some are listed in Resources near the end of this book. Parenting can be stressful, and when you add living with depression, it can seem overwhelming. Begin to take control when you are feeling better to prepare for times when you're feeling worse. You can provide a meaningful and productive lifestyle for both you and your children if you obtain the professional help you need and take steps toward health and wellness.

Chapter 2

Balancing Work, Parenting, and Wellness

For working parents, life is a juggling act. You are on the run from morning until night, taking the children to school or the baby-sitter's, getting meals on the table, and trying to spend some "quality" time with your family. At the same time, you're dealing with a demanding supervisor or responding to crises at work. Some days are probably harder than others. Perhaps your child is sick, you have to work overtime to meet a deadline, or you're just having a bad day in terms of your mood. It's easy to feel overwhelmed and guilty and that you're failing both at home and at work.

Something working and parenting have in common is that other people expect things of us. This can be good and bad. When you are depressed, the feeling that you've disappointed others can make you feel guilty and even more depressed. On the other hand, knowing others are counting on you can help you rally and get yourself going. Sometimes, when you are really down, knowing someone else needs you may be the one thing that gets you out of bed.

People with depression often get conflicting messages about work from important people in their lives—partners, family members, friends, and even mental-health professionals. You may have been told you are "too sick" to work, or that a job would be "too much stress" for you to handle. Many people with depression *do* work and find it a source of structure, satisfaction, and meaning in their lives, something that contributes to their health and wellness. If you aren't employed outside the home, you may have been told you are "lazy," or "irresponsible," or "taking advantage of the system," especially if you receive disability benefits or public assistance. If you are not working, perhaps you have made a wise decision, based on the needs of you and your family at this time.

Balancing a job, your family's needs, and your mental health is something that takes effort every day. To manage the work and parenting juggling act, it helps if you know your priorities, know what compromises you can and should make, and know when it's okay to say "no." In chapter 1, we suggested completing a twenty-four-hour chart to track your time use on a daily basis, and over the course of a few days. If you didn't complete the chart before, do it now. What activities take the bulk of your time and energy? What are your priorities at work and at home? Do you have the time and energy to meet your obligations? You may need to make adjustments or accommodations, at work or at home, to balance everything and stay as healthy as possible.

Believing in Yourself

Believing that you *can* handle the expectations of parenting and work while maintaining a healthy lifestyle can actually help you cope with those demands. It can be difficult to have a positive attitude, especially if you are feeling overwhelmed by your responsibilities. Some people find the use of self-affirmations a helpful strategy. Affirmations are small, positive statements that you repeat to yourself many times each day to help remind yourself of something or to change the way you think. The most powerful affirmations begin with "I am" statements. They should always be linked to positive views of you, never negative ones. Through continuous use, these messages can eventually become part of your self-image. Here are a few examples of positive affirmations:

- I am confident of my ability to do my job.

- I am a good and patient parent.

- I am a good person.

Write your own affirmations:

I am _____

I can _____

Write others on additional sheets of paper. Keep the list next to your bed and review your affirmations each morning and evening. Add one new affirmation to the list every day. Read the list out loud. Really believe in yourself!

Work or School—Yes or No?

If you're not currently working, you might be thinking about returning to work, or going to school to learn new skills. Before you look for a job or decide to go to school, it's a good idea to consider the demands this will make on you. Consider again how you and your family will meet the daily demands of family life.

The Pros and Cons of Working

For many people, having a job is about more than just earning money; finding the right job can give you a sense of self-esteem and a new purpose in life. In addition, a job can give structure to your day, a new network of friends, a sense of identity and belonging, and a chance to be a role model for your children. Of course, just like everything in life, there is a down side to working. Working gives you less time in the day to do the other things you want and need to do. Working when you are depressed can be difficult. You need to think carefully about how much you can take on and stay healthy. When you have a family to take care of, it's easy to become overburdened, with too much to do and not enough time to do it.

The competing demands of work and family life make guilt an almost certainty. Your third-grader's school concert may be scheduled just on the day and at the time you have an important work obligation. What will you do? You will feel guilty, no matter what you do. Realizing this ahead of time and knowing what your priorities are can help.

Another important consideration is your current financial situation. If you receive disability payments through Social Security Disability Insurance (SSDI) or Supplemental Security Income (SSI) because of depression or another disabling condition, you need to know the impact that returning to work may have on both the cash and health insurance benefits you receive through these programs. Your therapist or case manager should be able to help you get this information. Chapter 3, "Managing Household Finances," contains information on these programs. You can also contact the Social Security Administration at their Web site.

Before pursuing work or school, consider your reasons for making this change, and the potential impact on your family and your health.

Why work or go to school?

- Are your reasons primarily financial? Do you need to support your family, and how much do you need to earn? How will working affect your family's financial situation?

- Are your reasons social in nature? Being at home all day with young children can be isolating. Are you looking for increased interaction with other adults?

- Are you considering returning to work or school for the sense of purpose you might derive? Do you feel the need to be productive and make a contribution outside the home? What kind of experience would satisfy this need?

- Are your reasons based on somebody else's expectations? Has a family member or friend told you that this is what you should be doing with your life now? Is this good advice for you? Remember, only you can truly know what is right for you.

How will working or going to school affect you?

- What symptoms of depression are most difficult to cope with? What situations make these symptoms worse? If your symptoms interfere with work, how will you manage?

- What times of day are you at your best? Are you better off working in the morning, because that is when you have the most energy? Or would a job later in the day be better?

- Finally, talk with your therapist or psychiatrist about returning to work or school. Some psychiatrists or therapists have very conservative views about work and believe that you should only go to work or school if you are "totally well." But there is a growing recognition of the importance of meaningful, productive activity in promoting recovery from mental illness.

Explore Your Feelings About Work or School

Consider the situations below and how they make you feel—concerned or confident. Visualize yourself in each situation. Put a check mark in the concerned or confident column. Once you have completed the activity, think about your answers. Talk to others in similar situations; you may find many people share your concerns. Getting a sense of which parts of pursuing a job or school worry you most can help you set goals to address these concerns.

The following ideas make me feel . . .	Concerned	Confident
Searching for a job or applying to school	_____	_____
Putting my résumé together	_____	_____
Going for an interview	_____	_____
Trying to find childcare	_____	_____
Learning a new job	_____	_____

Taking a class	_____	_____
Being with coworkers or fellow students	_____	_____
Experiencing symptoms at work or school	_____	_____
Disclosing my depression at work or school	_____	_____
Asking for accommodations at work or school	_____	_____
Supporting my family financially	_____	_____
Trying to juggle all my roles	_____	_____
Trying a new and different career	_____	_____
Meeting my family's needs while working	_____	_____

Finding the Right Job Is Important

Everyone does better in a job that is a good match for his skills, personality, and needs. It is easier to find a perfect match if you have a lot of marketable skills or if the economy is good and jobs are plentiful. But even if this is not the situation, the right job can enhance your mental health, and the wrong job can make it worse.

Sybil, a mother of two who has had depression for many years, shares her experience with "wrong" and "right" jobs.

When my younger child was small I went back to school part-time and earned my master's degree in elementary education. Like many mothers, I thought that a classroom job, with summers and school vacations off, would fit well with my children's schedule. After student teaching, I was offered a job as a long-term substitute teacher in the same urban school where I trained. Thinking it would be a good way to break into the job market, I accepted.

The teaching job turned out to be way more stressful than I ever imagined. Granted, substitute teaching is stressful with or without a mental illness. Still, it became clear very quickly that this was not a good fit. The kids were great, but there were so many of them, with such extensive and unrelenting needs, that there was never time to catch my breath. Even during break times, I found the teacher's lounge to be an unsettling place. Teaching, unfortunately, is not given the high status it deserves as a profession, and the dissatisfaction the teachers were all feeling was a constant source of stress. Eventually, in the middle of a semester, I was overcome by the stress of the job and needed to take time off. I never went back.

Several months later I returned to the field that I was employed in before my children were born. A former colleague had recommended me for a fund development position with a large health care system. While fund-raising has its own pressures, I work in a large, light-filled private office, with a small staff of wonderful, supportive people with whom I have felt comfortable disclosing my illness. It has been a wonderful experience. When I am feeling good, I'm very productive. And when I am suffering, it has been okay to close my door and take a break, or go for a walk. My coworkers understand that I am working within these limits, and couldn't be more supportive. It has made all the difference in the world to be working in a calm, supportive, physically appealing environment.

Looking back, I think it was good that I had the teaching experience. It was hard at the time, but I came out of it knowing a lot more about what sort of things about a job work best for me, and what I can and cannot tolerate.

Factoring Your Family's Needs into Your Decisions

Before you make a decision about work or school, consider your family's needs. There are many questions you may ask yourself. If you have young children, who will care for them while you're working? Will leaving them in somebody else's care make you feeling anxious or guilty? How will they react? Do you have older children who attend school? Are they old enough to care for themselves after school if nobody else is available? If not, what kind of support or supervision will they need? What will happen in emergencies? Can you develop a plan to deal with an emergency situation in case you're not at home? How much physical and emotional energy will you have to meet both work and family needs? Is your family supportive of your return to work? How will your family manage if you are home less?

Below are two brief stories about parents who made different decisions about going to work when their children were young. Fran shares,

I knew that when my son was young, I did not want to work. He was my one and only; his childhood was the most important thing in my life, something I didn't want to miss because there would never be another opportunity to be a mom to him. I realized that working would have been a major drawback to my experience of motherhood. I also knew that, because of my depression, I would have been unable to cope with more than one role in life at that particular time. I would not have been able to be a good worker, because I would be constantly thinking about my son.

Mary has had a different experience.

Even though I have a mental illness, I like to work. It gives me a sense of structure and energizes me so that I actually have more energy for both my job and for my work at home. While I still do a lot, my children really help with the daily household chores. My children are very curious about what I do at work; having them ask questions about it has given us many opportunities to talk together as a family.

Looking for a Family-Friendly Employer

Many employers are becoming more family friendly as increasing numbers of parents with young children enter the workforce. A family-friendly employer is one who takes the needs of parents and their children into consideration by allowing for family emergencies, such as a sick child, snow days, or a childcare provider who quits. A family-friendly employer may offer flexible work hours; day care at the workplace or vouchers to help parents pay for day care elsewhere; a referral service to help you find childcare; and parental or family leave. You can ask about these benefits during a job interview. Many employers post benefits on their Web sites, so you can find out this information before applying for a job.

Making Accommodations at Home

As a working parent, developing a regular routine for you and your family can help you manage daily responsibilities. Remember, a workable routine is one that helps keep things going and is fairly consistent but is still flexible enough to deal with the unexpected.

Managing the Daily Routine

For most families, there are times of the day or days of the week that are more stressful than others. Weekday mornings can be especially hectic. You may be trying to get ready for work and get your children off to school or to childcare all within a short period of time. Building some structure into the morning routine can help things go more smoothly. For example, you might begin to expect your first-grader to lay out her school clothes the night before and get dressed by herself in the morning. You can help her pick clothes that are appropriate for the weather and for school activities, but if her outfit is not one you would choose to wear yourself, that's okay. As she begins to develop a sense of independence and responsibility, you might be able to finish that cup of coffee or spend five more minutes in the bathroom!

Preparing breakfasts and packing lunches are common morning tasks. Keep breakfasts simple—cold cereal and a warm hug from you are just as nutritious as something more elaborate. Instant oatmeal in the microwave takes ninety seconds. Your spouse or partner might pack tomorrow's lunches for everyone in the family at night after dinner, or you might decide that the easiest thing is for your children to buy lunch at school. Talk with your family to figure out the shortcuts that will work best for your family.

The hours between 4:00 P.M. and bedtime can also be activity filled. Parents usually face getting dinner on the table, children may have homework or after-school activities, there's bath time, maybe a story before bed, and getting ready for the next day. Involve all family members in figuring out who takes on what responsibilities. Perhaps you and your spouse or partner can trade off making dinner and helping with homework. You might hire a neighborhood teenager to help your second-grader with homework while you cook dinner. A calendar in the kitchen listing family members' activities can help keep things organized. Chore charts for children can help them remember to pick up their toys or brush their teeth before bed.

One of the realities of depression is that your mood and energy level can vary during the day. Mornings may be the time that your mood is worse or your energy is low, or you may find the end of the day more difficult. You may be on medication that makes you groggy when you first wake up or makes you sleepy in the early evenings. Let family members know what times of the day may be more difficult for you and think together about how to manage during these times. If mornings are particularly difficult, you may be able to make adjustments in your work schedule so that you only have to concentrate on getting the children off to school. After they are on their way, you can take the time you need to get ready. If you think that your medications make it difficult to handle parenting or work responsibilities at any point during the day, talk this over with your physician or nurse practitioner. Medication adjustments may help.

For most of us, the weekends are less hectic. If your weekends can be more relaxed, then let them be! An extra hour of sleep or cuddling in bed and reading a book to your child on a Saturday morning can make up for the stress of the weekdays. Working parents often spend weekend days on activities like grocery shopping or housecleaning. In this way, weekends can become just as stressful as weekdays. On the days you don't have to work or your children don't have to go to school, take advantage of the free time to enjoy being together. Again, think about what is really important to your family. What really needs to get done? If you need to grocery shop, can you make it a fun outing? What can be put off until tomorrow? It's not procrastinating, it's prioritizing!

Coping with Unexpected Events and Emergencies

No matter how well you plan ahead, unexpected events and emergencies can happen at any time and come in all shapes and sizes, from a child missing the morning school bus, to a sick baby keeping you up most of the night. While you can't always control events, you can get better at controlling your reactions to them. Looking at the positive side of things can help. Instead of focusing on the sleep you missed, remember you were there for your baby when he needed you.

One way to cope with unexpected events is to have a plan ready for when they occur. Think now about what you will do when the school nurse calls you to pick up your sick child or your child's school has a snow day. Even though you don't know when, you can be pretty sure these events *will* occur at some time. If your child misses the bus, are you able to drive him to school and still get to work on time? What are other solutions? Perhaps your neighbor, who always drives her child to the same school, is happy to take your child along on that day. Getting to know the parents of your child's schoolmates can help you in these situations.

Develop a plan with your spouse or partner to handle these events. If your child's other parent doesn't live with you, is he or she close enough to be involved in these situations? If you are raising your children alone, try to involve a family member or trusted friend.

Finally, know your employer's policies regarding the use of sick, personal, and vacation time so you will know how to draw on these when the unexpected happens. Some employers will allow you to use your accrued sick time to stay at home with a sick child. Depending on your job, you may be able to work at home for the day or even bring your child to work with you.

Making Accommodations at Work

Even if you're doing well and your mood is generally on an even keel, when you have depression it's not uncommon to have "bad days." You may feel down, your energy level might be low, or you might have trouble concentrating. It can be difficult to get work done on days like this, but there may be things that you can do at work to manage. If you have a job that has a variety of tasks you need to accomplish and at least some degree of flexibility in how and when you get them done, you can take advantage of this if you're having a "bad day." All of us make choices about which tasks are going to have our time and attention, and we base these choices on our priorities and on our energy level on a particular day. What are your work priorities? What absolutely must get done? On a bad day, spend time on routine, everyday tasks. If you can, set aside the things that require a lot of creativity or concentration. Don't feel guilty about doing this. Your coworker or boss who is getting over the flu is probably doing the same thing! Other strategies for managing work tasks that most people use include appointment books, "to do" lists, and "cue cards" to remember complicated procedures. Strategies like this can help you stay organized. Sometimes it helps to get out and take a walk or close your office door and meditate.

If you have the kind of job where there is little variety to the tasks or the tasks are fairly inflexible, then you have less control over what you do at work. But even in this situation there are some things you can do. For example, make sure you take the breaks you are entitled to. If you work in a noisy environment and find it difficult to concentrate, ask your supervisor if you can do your work in a different area or wear headphones so you can listen to soft music.

Flexible Jobs

Traditional nine-to-five jobs are no longer the only ones available. Increasingly, employers offer options for part-time, "flex-time," or "job sharing." Flex-time jobs have flexible working hours, often at times other than regular business hours. A flex-time job might allow you to arrive earlier or later than normal so you can see your child off in the morning or be home when your child returns from school. Job sharing is similar to working part-time; two workers share the duties of one full-time position. In addition, if you "telecommute," you can work at home or other locations. This is an option for those whose work can be done on the computer.

Taking Time Off from Work

Make sure you know your employer's benefits and policies regarding the use of sick, vacation, and family-leave time. While it is never a good idea to misuse sick days since you may need them later, it's important to realize that taking a day for your "mental health" is just as legitimate as taking a day for the flu. If you're unable to get to work for several days in a row, your depression may be worsening. It's a good idea to call your doctor or therapist.

If you're unable to work for an extended period because of depression or other reasons such as a child's illness, you need to let your employer know what is happening. Especially if you have a job you like, you want to have good communication with your employer before you are in a situation where you've used all of your paid sick or vacation leave or your job is in jeopardy. If your employer has fifty or more employees, then, under federal law, you may be entitled to take up to twelve weeks of unpaid leave in a twelve-month period without fear of losing your job or any benefits. The Family Medical Leave Act allows you to take this time to meet your own health needs or to care for a family member. Make sure you know whether this law covers your employer.

Disclosing a Psychiatric Disability in the Workplace

The federal Americans with Disabilities Act (ADA) was passed in 1990. Title I of the ADA requires employers with fifteen or more employees to provide qualified individuals with disabilities, including mental illnesses like depression, with equal opportunity to benefit from employment. The law prohibits discrimination in recruiting, hiring, training, promoting, and compensating people with disabilities. The law also requires employers to make "reasonable accommodations" for workers with disabilities. Reasonable accommodations can vary from one workplace to another, and what is "reasonable" for one employer might not be "reasonable" for another. While accommodations can be made to help an otherwise qualified worker do a job, the law regarding reasonable accommodations does not require employers to change job requirements or lower job standards. A disabled worker who receives accommodations still has to be able to do the job she was hired to do.

Letting Your Employer Know You Have Depression

To be eligible for accommodations, a worker must disclose a disability to an employer. Because a disability due to a mental illness is often "invisible," the decision to disclose is up to you and is a complex one. Only you can decide whether and how much to tell an employer about your depression. On the positive side, telling your employer about your depression is the only way to protect your legal right to workplace accommodations that might help you. And, because depression is so common, you might find your employer is very understanding and supportive. On the other hand, the reality is that discrimination against people with disabilities of all types exists, and this is particularly true of mental illness. So, disclosing is not risk free. While you cannot be fired for merely disclosing a mental illness, you may find that your opportunities in the work setting have become limited. Make sure you think this decision through before you disclose. Talk over the pros and cons with a trusted friend or therapist. How will you feel about sharing this information? If you feel it's not safe to disclose, maybe this isn't the job for you.

Disclosing a disability does not mean you must or should tell everybody. One thing to think about is the timing of your disclosure. If you have been working for a while and things are going well, and you don't require accommodations, you might elect not to say anything. On the other hand, you might decide to inform the Human Resources Department at your workplace that you have a potentially disabling condition and, thus, be eligible for accommodations if needed, but ask them not to inform your supervisor at this time. However, if you recognize that you are having significant difficulty at work, such as problems concentrating or decreased energy, or if you are missing a lot of work, then this is the time to let your employer know about your depression. If you don't feel comfortable starting with your immediate supervisor, you might begin by telling someone in the human resources department. If your company has an Employee Assistance Program, go there for advice. Ultimately, your supervisor will most likely need to know, since she will be most directly involved in providing the accommodations you might need.

Reasonable Accommodations

If you disclose your mental illness and request "reasonable" accommodations, your employer will likely ask how depression might interfere with your job performance and what accommodations you will need. Unlike the typical accommodations made for people with physical disabilities, like a wheelchair ramp, accommodations for people with mental illness are often very individualized but very simple and inexpensive. You should think ahead about what would be most helpful. You may want to talk to your therapist or doctor about this and ask for her thoughts. These are some suggestions for coping with depression on the job and typical accommodations you and your employer might make.

- A flexible or reduced work schedule

- Workspace changes to decrease distractions

- More frequent breaks

- Getting instructions in writing

- More frequent meetings with a supervisor to get help managing assignments

- Time for doctor or therapist appointments

An excellent resource on the ADA and reasonable accommodations for both people with mental illness and employers is the Web site for the Center for Psychiatric Rehabilitation at Boston University. (See "Resources" at the end of this book.)

Childcare Options

Working or returning to school may require you to find childcare for your children. If you're a new parent or have never used childcare before, you might wonder if your child is ready to be cared for by someone else. Perhaps you have an older child and are unsure whether he or she is ready to be left alone. There are many types of childcare appropriate for a wide range of ages, maturity levels, and abilities. However, when choosing childcare, the most important thing to remember is that your child is an individual; he or she may not feel comfortable or safe in situations that may be appropriate for other children. You can gauge your young child's readiness by asking how he or she feels about going to a day care center. With very young children, you might want to take them on a visit to see how they react. In the case of a baby or infant, it is more important to gauge the quality of emotional attention they will receive, as well as how safe they will be in that environment. Older children and teens may have definite opinions about after-school programs, and it may take some negotiating to agree on an acceptable site.

Can I Leave My Child By Herself?

Sometimes you have no other choice but to allow an older child to take care of herself when you're not available. In households where there is more than one child, the older child may also have to care for younger siblings after school or during vacations. Before you consider this alternative it is important to assess the maturity level of your child to ensure that she will be safe while you're not there, and that she is capable of caring for your younger children. Even if she is normally sensible and trustworthy, she may not be capable of using her best judgment in emergency situations. Young children, or those with emotional or behavioral issues, may be easily confused, frightened, or unable to act logically, even in normal circumstances. If you were neglected as a young child and had no choice but to look after yourself, you might find it difficult to assess your own child's ability to care for himself or whether it's appropriate. This was Joan's experience from her recollection of being left alone as a child.

> *I still have a hard time leaving my thirteen-year-old daughter by herself for one to two hours, a few days a week, while I work. I can remember how scary it was when my mother would go through these bouts of depression, when she would be passed out for hours from drinking alcohol, leaving me to care for my younger brother. I guess the only good things to come out of those experiences is that I learned how to take care of myself at an early age, I learned that using alcohol to deal with depression doesn't work, and I have a strong relationship with my brother. I'm concerned about being a good role model for my daughter, and I'm also more cautious and careful with my daughter to make sure she knows what to do and how to reach me in case of an emergency.*

If you're faced with the prospect of leaving your child unattended, the following questions can help you evaluate your child's maturity level and whether this is a safe option to consider. Can your child lock and unlock doors? Use the telephone? Prepare a snack, get juice or water, or open a can of food? Recite his or her name, telephone number, and address? Tell time? Follow directions? Read and understand written messages? Feel confident about being home alone? Be able to handle problems or ask for help? Understand dangers—like not talking to strangers or opening the door to strangers. Is your child safe in your home environment? Is your home in a safe area? Will your child be able to walk home alone, or will he or she need an escort? Does your home contain any dangerous weapons, fire hazards, or medications? Can you make your home safe?

Depending on your child's age and ability, you should consider setting some general ground rules around the following areas to help him cope with the responsibility of being alone:

- Visits from friends

- Use of television and/or the Internet

- Answering the door or phone

- Going outside

- Using appliances

- Completion of homework

- Dealing with squabbles among brothers and sisters

Even if you have decided your child is mature enough to be left alone, it's important to realize that there is still some risk to being a latchkey child. Keeping your child safe includes staying in contact with him or her while you're absent, ensuring they know what to do in an emergency situation, and building a relationship in which it is easy to talk about maintaining safety.

The following activity will help you and your child develop an emergency plan together, as well as provide a theme for family discussions about the importance of staying safe. Fill out the form below and keep it posted where everyone in the family can easily see it. Make sure it is updated every six months, and encourage your children to take notice of it, and discuss possible emergencies that may occur.

A "Safe-at-Home" Plan

Parent contact phone numbers: **Work** _____

                                       Mobile Phone _____

                                       Other _____

Neighbors/relatives phone numbers: _____

Local Police: _____

Fire Department: _____

Hospital: _____

Other important phone numbers: _____

Use the space below to plan a routine for days when your child will be home alone.

_____

_____

_____

_____

_____

Use the space below to plan for possible emergencies and how your child can cope.

_____

_____

_____

_____

_____

Formal Child Care Arrangements for Young Children

Preschool children need to be in a safe environment that is well supervised and stimulates their minds to help them learn and grow. Leaving a preschool-age or young child at home alone does not meet these requirements and may even be considered as neglect.

- **In-home care.** An in-home caregiver is someone who comes to, or lives in, your home. This can be very expensive, although it may be the most comfortable for very young children and babies. It can also be an ideal alternative for children who have difficulty socializing or have special physical, mental, or emotional needs.

- **Family day care.** Family day care takes place in the home of a caregiver; they usually take only a small number of children and may not be licensed. If you decide on this option, it will be up to you to monitor and ensure the safety and comfort of your child.

- **Center-based care.** This includes day care centers, nursery schools, preschools, preparatory programs for school, parent cooperatives, work-place and college-care programs, and other non-home based care. They are usually licensed and have an organized, school-like atmosphere and may care for a lot of children; if too much noise or activity makes you or your child uncomfortable, this may not be a good option.

- **Au pairs and nannies.** Au pairs are foreign students who perform childcare as part of a cultural educational exchange. Nannies differ in that they are professionals who work full-time caring for children in your home. They can be hired through agencies found in the Yellow Pages, but can be very expensive and, because they frequently live in your home, might cause concerns about privacy.

Informal Childcare Options for Young Children

Because most formal childcare options can be expensive or may not be available in your area, you might need to consider these other informal child care options.

- **Baby-sitters.** Teenage baby-sitters are a good short-term option; when you need to go out in the evening or weekend or need somebody to meet your child's school bus, they can be a very affordable choice. Be sure to check their references and whether they have any training, like a first aid course. You could also monitor them until you feel you can trust them with your child.

- **Develop a childcare networking system.** A childcare networking system is an arrangement you make with other local parents to collectively care for all your children. You could involve family, friends, neighbors, or members of your church or psychosocial rehabilitation clubhouse program. You could also develop cooperative arrangements with other parents with a similar need for day care in your area by advertising in a local store or newspaper. An example of a networking arrangement would be one in which, if you worked three days a week, you could help look after another mother's child as well as your own on the days you're not working; the other mother would then care for your child while you work. A networking system involving many sets of parents and children could become quite complicated and may involve caring for several children at once, so it's important that you keep your own limits and health in mind. It is also important to remember that even very young children need to be read to, listened to, and held; informal arrangements for childcare therefore need to be very carefully arranged. You must be able to trust a network parent before you leave your children with her. Ask yourself if your child will be safe and healthy, and provided with the right amount of attention and stimulating activities that will help her socialize and grow.

Childcare Options for Older Children: After-School Programs

If you picture childcare as just for preschoolers and imagine your children are too old to benefit, you might be unaware of the variety of after-school and vacation programs that are available. After-school programs can be a great option for older children; they range in price or may even be free, are usually supervised, and allow children to further their interests in a wide variety of subjects, sports, and activities. Schools, churches, boys and girls clubs, "Y"s, public agencies, libraries, city recreation departments, local colleges, and clubs can run them. They are fairly easy to find, as most of them actively seek participants. Look for letters from school, notices in local newspapers, or postings in health clinics, at the library, in clubhouses, or social service centers. You could also ask other parents if they know of any good programs.

Relying on Relatives

An obvious solution to finding childcare may be to ask your relatives for help, especially if they live close to you and have expressed an interest in helping. Relatives of all ages are a popular childcare alternative because you know them and were either raised by them or helped raise them. However, before you ask for their help it's a good idea to consider the following points.

- Your relative may not want to look after your children every day or may be physically incapable due to age or poor health. Looking after children is hard work. It is unfair to expect a relative to care for your children just because you are related.

- Your relative may have other things to do or be too young to act responsibly all the time, and therefore may not be consistent or reliable.

- Your relative may not have the facilities or knowledge to be able to stimulate your child's mind and growth. This may be particularly true for younger relatives who have not had children, or older relatives who did not raise children of their own.

- If your relative is aware of your depression and regards you unfavorably because of it, she may undermine your authority as a parent.

- Your relative may have poor health habits, like smoking or drinking, and could put your child's health at risk.

- A serious concern for any parent with mental illness, whose childhood family relationships were difficult or abusive, should be whether placing their own child with those same relatives or in that same environment will put their child at risk. Remember, as a parent it's your responsibility to keep your child safe.

Though using relatives for childcare may seem like a really good option, there are some down sides to consider, too. As one single mother with depression points out, having a relative help you out has its good and bad points.

I currently live with my mom, which is good when it comes to having someone readily available to care for my six-year-old daughter. She is actually a better caretaker to my daughter than she was to me when I was growing up. Yet, it's also tough living with my mom because I always feel like my parenting is constantly being scrutinized. My mom openly worries that I may not be able to care for my daughter if and when I get my own place to live. I realize that she has reason to have such worries given my history of bipolar illness, but I'm managing my illness much better. Her criticisms certainly don't give me much confidence in my own ability to parent.

Before you consider a relative as an option for childcare, use the following exercise to help you think about whether asking certain relatives for help will be a good choice for you and your children. You may need to use additional pages if you're considering more relatives.

Relatives Who Might Help

Possible Relative	Pros	Cons
1st Choice _____	_____	_____
	_____	_____
	_____	_____
2nd Choice _____	_____	_____
	_____	_____
	_____	_____

Finding Childcare Help for Emergencies

There are times when you may not be able to use your usual childcare arrangements, such as when your child is sick and is not allowed to attend day care because he or she might spread the illness, or your childcare provider becomes sick and has nobody to fill in. School may be cancelled because of snow, or a program may be shut down due to lack of interest. Any number of emergencies can occur, but there are only two basic options that you will need to consider in order to prepare for such childcare emergencies:

- **Stay home yourself.** If you're working, you could use your sick days, personal days, vacation days, or try and work out an arrangement with your boss in order to take care of your child. You could also ask a spouse or partner to take turns caring for your child, or you could rearrange appointments for another day. However, because your health must also be a priority, you should take care not to miss essential medical visits or treatment appointments, or use up time you might need for your own health and well-being.

- **Find someone else to help.** Relatives can be an obvious choice in an emergency, but you could also find another local family who uses in-home care and make arrangements with them to take your child in an emergency, with the understanding that you will take care of their children if they need help. You could also get together with a group of mothers and agree to rotate your children among you when an emergency that affects you all crops up, such as a school snow day. The company you work for may also be able to recommend an alternative childcare provider in the event of an emergency.

Making plans to cope with a personal emergency can help you and your family feel less stressed. Personal emergencies can take many forms, from having a sudden appointment to requiring hospitalization, and may require assistance with childcare from a couple of hours to several weeks. Depending on how long you are going to need the care, it's a good idea to make a variety of plans for different types of situations. The consequences of not making emergency childcare arrangements can be serious if it means you will be leaving a child without adequate supervision.

Developing an Action Plan

This activity will help you develop a plan of action for obtaining childcare in the event of an emergency. It might take a while for you to gather this information, but it will be worth it to provide you and your family with a blueprint for coping during a difficult time. It is important, in order to make this a real working plan of action, to involve those you will be listing in creating the plan. You want to know if they can be counted on to help you and where they can be reached at all times. Once you have completed the plan, you should also discuss it with your children if they are old enough and your partner, relatives, or those you live with, so they can put it into action when necessary. Post a copy where it's easy to find, and make a point of updating it every few months.

Emergency Childcare Action Plan

This emergency plan is for (child's name): _____

If my child needs to miss time at school or from other activities, please contact:

Childcare provider/School: _____ at _____

After-school program/Activity program: _____ at _____

Other :_____ at _____

Name	Address	Phone Number

For emergency childcare for a few hours, contact:

_____ _____ _____

_____ _____ _____

_____ _____ _____

_____ _____ _____

For emergency childcare for overnight, contact:

_____ _____ _____

_____ _____ _____

_____ _____ _____

_____ _____ _____

For long-term emergency childcare (like a weekend or week), contact:

_____ _____ _____

_____ _____ _____

_____ _____ _____

_____ _____ _____

A Final Note About Childcare

Being away from your child while you're working or in school can be difficult. There are small things you can do to stay connected with your child when you are apart that will allay her concerns as well as your own. If your child is at your home or the home of a childcare provider, a quick phone call might make you both feel good. Little notes in your child's backpack can let him know you're thinking about him while you are working. At the end of the day when you are together again, share your day with your children. Let them know what your day has been like and find out what happened to them when you were apart. These conversations can enhance family life.

When a parent has an illness that seriously affects his ability to function or develop relationships, it becomes easy to rely on children to help around the house, for emotional support, or to provide companionship. If you had a difficult childhood you might be overly worried about your child's safety. Perhaps you find it difficult to trust another person or are fearful about what might happen if you're not watching your child every minute. Having somebody else care for your children might leave you feeling alone, sad, anxious, or even angry. Gradually learning to let go of your children, no matter how young or old they are, is a difficult but important lesson for *all* parents. However, this release is essential, as it allows your children to learn independence, so they can become self-sufficient adults. You can learn to cope with these feelings by talking to a therapist or a good friend about how you feel and the worries you have, or by starting a new activity that will help you refocus some energy into *self*-discovery and learning about what *you* want out of life. Children learn through modeling, so if you show yourself to be an independent and caring adult, your children will probably follow in your footsteps.

It's Up to You

Only you and your family can determine whether balancing work and parenting is beneficial for you and enhances your well-being or contributes to your stress and depression. Find a job that seems like a good fit and make the necessary adjustments at home and at work, so you are supported in being successful. Good childcare, which both you and your children are comfortable with, will go a long way toward a positive experience for everyone.

Chapter 3

Managing Household Finances

Money affects almost every aspect of life. If you are like many people, there never seems to be enough of it. As a result, few of us are without money worries. Financial difficulties can make you feel depressed. Financial stresses can lead to relationship problems with your partner and children, divorce, loss of custody, a lower standard of living, or even bankruptcy. Likewise, depression and manic depression can contribute to your financial difficulties. Medications can be costly. This can add to your worries if you have a limited or fixed income or if your illness limits you to working part-time or prevents you from working altogether. You may lose track of your money, go on uncontrollable spending sprees, miss work, or even lose your job entirely due to your illness. Parents with depression often face a greater challenge than most in meeting their family's financial needs.

When you're living with depression, even the smallest financial setback can seem overwhelming. How do you overcome your depression and manage your finances at the same time? Although managing your money may seem like an impossible task, you can take control by learning to tackle your money problems one step at a time. What if you need help managing your finances? You may have major trust issues when it comes to using a banking institution or feel ashamed or humiliated about asking your partner or other members of your family to become involved in your finances. It's important to sometimes set your own feelings aside to do what's best for your family.

In this chapter, you will move step by step to explore your values and attitudes about money, determine where your money goes, use a budget as a management tool, develop strategies for coping with emergencies and preventing crises, and deal directly with your children about money. Once you understand how your spending behavior influences your mood and vice versa and determine your specific financial issues, you can learn to anticipate and plan to avoid future problems, teaching your children lifelong skills in the process.

What Money Means to You

Your values and attitudes affect your behavior. They provide the framework for your decisions about life goals and influence what you're willing to do to achieve them. They affect how you feel about yourself when you evaluate yourself against a certain set of standards. Your values and attitudes about money and feelings about yourself are influenced by many factors. Your parents may have communicated their values and attitudes to you. Your partner and other people you respect may also have a great impact. The society and culture you live in are big factors. We are bombarded on a daily basis by media messages about products we "must" have to appear successful or to enjoy life to its fullest. Your children may be influenced by these messages as well, demanding the latest toy or video game they have seen advertised on television.

When you value money highly as a symbol of personal worth, losing control of your finances can create negative feelings of self-worth and trigger symptoms of depression. Your perception of how others view you may affect how you feel, particularly if they seem to be judging you against their own standards of success and you seem to fall short. As a parent, you may be vulnerable to feeling like a failure if you cannot afford the designer blue jeans or sneakers your children seem to desperately desire. Focusing on financial failures can send you plummeting into depression, and make your recovery all the more difficult.

As William explained,

> I can always remember as a child how my parents used to argue about money, or the lack of it. Having enough money meant having some semblance of harmony and happiness in my family. My family was also big on appearing as though they had more money than they actually did. The message I learned early on was that earning a lot of money equaled success, and that without money you were a failure.
>
> As an adult, I can realistically see how this attitude toward money is unhealthy, and that there are more important things in life. Yet, my gut tells me that I need money to feel good about myself. Living paycheck to

paycheck, as my wife and I do right now, often makes me feel like a loser. I sometimes get so depressed that I can't move, can't sleep, and often find myself feeling hopeless and crying in the middle of the night. The only thing that seems to help, after I get my stubborn pride out of the way, is sharing my worries with my wife and my counselor. I look at my children and see so much hope and happiness in their eyes. I don't want my kids to have the same attitude about money as I do.

It's important to remember that, even though you may feel others look at you as "less of a person" because you don't have much money, feelings are not facts. Focusing on negative thoughts and feelings can only lead to more stress and a worsening of your depression. Try to acknowledge that you are doing your best, focusing instead on what you can do to take control of the situation. If you have trouble gathering and focusing your energies on helping yourself, do it for your children.

Being depressed can influence your feelings and thoughts about money and, consequently, your behavior. How you feel and what you do about making money, saving money, and paying your bills on time may change drastically. You may lose interest in your financial responsibilities entirely and not want to be bothered handling money or paying your bills. You may be able to leave paying bills to your partner, or even your children, but this may not be possible in all instances. And it may not be appropriate, depending on the age and maturity level of your child, to depend on her to manage household finances.

If your depression is disabling, you may only be able to work part-time, if at all, and your income may be reduced until you no longer have the resources to pay all your bills. Stan, who is a husband and father, described his experience.

While unemployed, my income was reduced, and eventually I had no income. Limited income created severe credit problems. This made my depression worse, and I could no longer face these problems. I turned all finances over to my wife. I had no idea, nor did I care, what bills were being paid.

You may go on a spending spree in a manic state, buying things for yourself, your children, or your home in an effort to help yourself feel better. Unfortunately, you may end up deeply in debt. The good credit record you worked long and hard to establish may become tarnished, and you might not even care. Or, as your financial difficulties snowball, you may become even more depressed, confused, and angry about your situation. Creditors may contact you more frequently until they seem to be or actually do become harassing. You may lose your temper when creditors call. This anger will, in most cases, be directed not only at the creditors, but also at your family. You may even blame your spending on your children, justifying your behavior to yourself and others by claiming you were only trying to make them happy.

Taking the First Step

The first step in managing your money is to think about what money means to you and why. It's not a good idea to begin to evaluate your feelings about money or your financial status when you are severely depressed. You may want to wait until you feel well to answer the following questions.

What Money Means to Me

How does your lifestyle reflect your values and attitudes about money?

_____

_____

What is your biggest worry about money?

_____

_____

How do your mood and how you feel about yourself influence your spending?

_____

_____

How does your spending affect your mood and how you feel about yourself?

_____

_____

Do you wish for or purchase things you really can't afford? In what circumstances?

_____

_____

Are there times when you argue with family members about money? Describe a time.

_____

_____

Do you feel you have control of your money? Are there times when you don't?

_____

_____

If you have a limited or fixed income, how does it affect how you feel about yourself? How do others view you?

_____

_____

What are the most important things in life to you?

_____

_____

After answering these questions, you will probably discover that how you feel about money is closely related to your feelings about and relationships with your children. For example, you would not be alone as a parent if your biggest worry about money was providing for your children's present or future needs, like a good education. You would certainly be in good company if you realized that you often fight with your children about money, especially if they are teenagers with seemingly endless needs for new clothes, entertainment, and gas money for the car. And many parents, with and without depression, might consider their children's well-being to be the most important thing in life to them.

You may decide that you or your family members place far too much importance on money. If this is the case, you may need to re-examine your beliefs about money to see if they are healthy and realistic. You may want to test your beliefs by sharing them with a trusted friend or counselor, with your partner and children during a "family meeting" or, if you're participating in a parents' group, with the group members. Your depression can be made far worse if your beliefs about the importance of money are distorted.

If, on the other hand, you discover you couldn't care less about your money situation, you may need to examine these beliefs as well. This other extreme may reflect the hopelessness and powerlessness you feel because of your illness. Again, your beliefs can be tested to see if they are serving you well when you share them with others whose opinions you value.

Where Does Your Money Go?

The next step you need to take is to determine where your money goes, to become aware of what you are spending and why. You probably have a certain number of fixed expenses each month—a rent or mortgage payment, for example. You also have many expenses that vary each month. If you are like most people, you may think you have some idea of what these variable expenses are and how much you spend. On the other hand, many people have no idea what they spend on a day-to-day basis for incidentals—coffee on the way to work or cosmetics on that quick trip into the drug store. Parents are especially prone to handing out cash to children for sodas, candy, or renting videos, and not paying much attention to how that adds up over time.

Some people find that spending money temporarily soothes them when they feel depressed, only to regret later having spent money they couldn't really spare. They may buy something for their children to feel more adequate or powerful as parents and then feel worse because their children don't seem to appreciate what they've done or understand the sacrifices they've made. Others find they are inclined to spend money when they feel overexcited or manic. If these scenarios sound a little too familiar, you may want to think about better ways to manage your mood. For example, read a book, go for a walk, call a friend, or do something creative.

Some people can justify spending money on their children, when they might not spend it on themselves. While it's important, at times, to prioritize children's needs, take the time to question your motives. Do your children really need the item or activity you are about to pay for, or are you trying to make up for your bad moods or times when you have been irritable or unavailable to them? Indulging your children can be fun and feeling capable of indulging them can be empowering. If you are trying to manage your finances and control your spending, be sure you are spending for the right reasons.

Keeping Track

It's a good idea to keep a running log of your daily expenses for a week or a month to get a better handle on where your money goes. Decide ahead of time how long you will keep your expense log. Create a list in a small notebook or on a piece of paper or file card that fits into your pocket, wallet, or purse. On the piece of paper make three headings: **purchase**, **amount**, and **feeling**. As you spend money, jot down the purchase, for example, *cup of coffee and donut*. Next to the purchase on the list put the amount paid. In the final column, write a brief note, even one word will do, about how you feel when you spend the money. If you are hungry when you buy the coffee and donut, write *hungry*. If you feel good because the coffee shop has your favorite flavor, write *happy*. If you are annoyed when your children want more money to go to the movies, write *annoyed*. Try to be honest with yourself when you keep track of these expenditures. For example, many people eat when they're not hungry. You may find food comforting when you're anxious, or reach for a snack when you are bored. Remember, this is not an exercise about dieting. Just jot down what you are really feeling when you spend money. There are no right or wrong feelings!

At the end of the week or month—whatever time period you have selected—look over your log. Total up the amount you spend each week. Break your expenses down into categories and add up how much you spent on snacks, or children's activities, or household items. Develop categories that work for you. Now take a look at the feelings you have listed. Can you see patterns in your spending and moods? How do you typically feel when you spend money? Is your mood somehow tied to what you are buying or your feelings about the person who is asking for the money? Does buying something improve your mood? Are there particular times of the day or week when you're likely to spend more? Understanding what you spend money on, why and when, will help you develop a plan for your spending and to think about ways to change your spending habits.

Now go back over your log, and after each entry put an "**N**" if the expense was a **need,** and "**W**" if it was a **want**. A "need" is a necessary expenditure. A "want" is something you would like to have but perhaps can do without. People often get into trouble when their wants become needs, that is, when they convince themselves that something they could get by without is really essential to their well-being. Were your expenditures necessary or optional? Take a look at your "Ns" and "Ws." Which is more frequent? Are your "Ns" really needs, or have some of your wants crept over into the need column? Consider carefully the money you have spent on your children. Have your children's wants become your needs? Close analysis of your needs and wants may help you think about ways to decrease spending on things that aren't as important to you and, perhaps, increase spending on more important things. Analyzing your needs and wants will help you set priorities and maintain control over your household finances, a strategy that worked for Emily:

> *I've found that getting my priorities in order is the best way for me to save money. When I do a budget, I try to rank budget items in order of importance—what are my needs versus my wants? My needs would include food (not a lot of junk food), medication for my bipolar illness, rent, clothes (not too many designer labels), basic cable, and utilities. My wants include such things as video rentals, eating out, movies, a newer car, and "feel good" shopping (where I actually believe that buying that rotating potato peeler advertised on TV will help me feel better when I'm feeling depressed at 2 A.M.).*
>
> *Ranking my needs is important because I'm less likely to skip my medication in an attempt to save money, which has been disastrous when I've tried it in the past. Prioritizing my needs helps me realize that I can stop having cable TV for a while if I'm short on cash, rather than stopping my medication or having my family go without food.*

It's not uncommon for parents with depression to cut back or stop taking their medication altogether in an effort to decrease spending. While parents do make sacrifices for their children and family, *it is important not to stop or alter your medication schedule as a means to save money.* Your short-term solution will only compromise your well-being and your family's happiness in the long run.

A Budget Is a Management Tool

Once you've given some thought to your values and attitudes about money and have collected some data on what you spend money on and why, the next step is to establish a monthly budget. With a detailed budget you can monitor your routine expenses and plan for unexpected expenses like an emergency hospitalization. An itemized budget should include, but not necessarily be limited to, home expenses, transportation, food, treatment and medication, childcare, clothes, legal expenses, entertainment, and miscellaneous expenses. You can use the information you collected in your spending log to estimate your monthly expenses more accurately. You may also have other periodic or annual expenses (car insurance, property taxes, etc.) that do not appear monthly. Divide these yearly expenses by twelve and add them to your monthly budget.

The following guide will help you, though you have to make the final determination of budget categories to be sure they fit your circumstances and situation. Use the data you collected in your spending log to decide on what categories make sense. Insert your financial information on the lines below. If these categories don't quite work for you, or you need additional categories, modify or add new ones in the space provided. Your partner and even your children, depending on their ages, can be involved in budget plans. If you have difficulty with this worksheet, you may want to ask for help from a trusted relative or friend. As we mentioned before, you should not fill this out when you're feeling depressed.

Budgeting Worksheet

Current Budget

Home/Utilities

Rent or Mortgage: _____

Home Heating (oil/gas/wood) : _____

Water/Sewer: _____

Trash Collection: _____

Taxes (e.g., property taxes): _____

Phone: _____

Future Budget

Home/Utilities

Rent or Mortgage: _____

Home Heating (oil/gas/wood) : _____

Water/Sewer: _____

Trash Collection: _____

Taxes (e.g., property taxes): _____

Phone: _____

Hadn't thought about the importance of this

Cable/Satellite: _____   Cable/Satellite: _____

Electricity: _____   Electricity: _____

Homeowner's Insurance: _____   Homeowner's Insurance: _____

Auto   *Auto*

Car Payment: _____   Car Payment: _____

Car Insurance: _____   Car Insurance: _____

Gas: _____   Gas: _____

Excise Tax/Registration: _____   Excise Tax/Registration: _____

Transportation   *Transportation*

Bus/Subway: _____   Bus/Subway: _____

Van/Taxi: _____   Van/Taxi: _____

Food & Clothing   *Food & Clothing*

Food: _____   Food: _____

Household Items
(e.g., soap, toothpaste): _____   Household Items
(e.g., soap, toothpaste): _____

Clothing for You: _____   Clothing for You: _____

Clothing for Partner: _____   Clothing for Partner: _____

Medical & Professional   *Medical & Professional*

Health Insurance: _____   Health Insurance: _____

Medications: _____   Medications: _____

Doctor: _____   Doctor: _____

Dentist: _____   Dentist: _____

Therapist: _____   Therapist: _____

Psychiatrist: _____   Psychiatrist: _____

Legal fees: _____   Legal fees: _____

Child-Related

Clothing for Child(ren): _____

Childcare: _____

Baby-sitting: _____

School Expenses: _____

Pre-School: _____

After School Programs: _____

Child Support: _____

Allowance or Spending Money: ____
Entertainment

Eating Out: _____

Movies: _____

Video Rentals: _____

Newspaper: _____

Lottery: _____
Other

_____

_____

_____

Total Monthly Income

(After Taxes): _____

Total Monthly Expenses: _____

Amount Over/Under Budget

(Income minus Expenses): _____

Child-Related

Clothing for Child(ren): _____

Childcare: _____

Baby-sitting: _____

School Expenses: _____

Pre-School: _____

After School Programs: _____

Child Support: _____

Allowance or Spending Money: ____
Entertainment

Eating Out: _____

Movies: _____

Video Rentals: _____

Newspaper: _____

Lottery: _____
Other

_____

_____

_____

Total Monthly Income

(After Taxes): _____

Total Monthly Expenses: _____

Amount Over/Under Budget

(Income minus Expenses): _____

When you have completed your current monthly budget, you may want to use the same guide to write in revisions based on your analysis of your values and spending patterns, and your needs and wants. You can then establish a future monthly budget based on changes in priorities and new goals you would like to set. You may not achieve your future monthly goals next month, particularly if it requires setting limits on spending with your children. Give yourself a few months to make changes in your spending and your children's expectations. Remember, a budget is a tool to help you, not another standard against which to judge yourself harshly.

One additional thing you should consider as part of your budgeting process is the actual paying of bills. Paying bills makes some people feel great—particularly if there is enough money to cover expenses and they are living a lifestyle they enjoy. For others, paying bills is a source of stress—especially if there is not enough money to cover necessities. If you are in tight financial circumstances, you may want to pick a time to sit down and tackle this task when you are feeling well and are less inclined to spiral downward. Some parents find themselves particularly prone to negative thinking and self-doubts in the evening, after they put the children to bed and are exhausted. This would not be a good time to sit down and agonize over your money problems. Perhaps you have more energy after lunch, when the children are in school, and you can sit at the kitchen table with a fresh cup of tea. Pick a time when you're less likely to feel distracted or overwhelmed. And if you tend to become distressed when paying the bills, choose a time and setting when your children are not likely to be exposed to your distress.

Make a plan, too, for how your bills will be paid if you are not feeling well enough to handle your money, or you are in the hospital. It is important to make arrangements ahead of time for someone to assist you during these times—your partner, a friend or family member, or an advocate. This person should be someone you trust and feel comfortable with, to allow them access to your financial records and your money. This is an important decision and not one that should be hurried or decided when you are experiencing major depressive symptoms.

There are many guides and resources, like computer software programs, to help you set up a budget and manage your finances. Check out the resources at your local library or bookstore.

Coping with Emergencies and Preventing Crises

A parent's depression can have a sudden, significant impact on a family's financial situation. There is nothing like a major set back such as an unexpected hospitalization or loss of a job to strain your financial resources. Such setbacks can come without warning.

How can you prepare for such situations so they won't strain your finances? Joseph learned this the hard way.

When I experienced my first hospitalization for depression, I quickly learned about the importance of having disability insurance. I never thought it would happen to me, even though my father had depression (undiagnosed because of his fear of doctors), and one of my brothers has it. It took me a while to get back on my feet. I lost the income from my job and went quickly into debt. My wife had to go from part-time to full-time work, and I found myself home with the children feeling less than adequate.

I was lucky that my wife's family was close by to help out with the kids, so I could make doctor and therapy appointments. I think the shame of having this illness has been more difficult to deal with than the debt we went into. I have been able to return to work on a part-time basis, and we've started to chip away at the debt. I still can't believe how devastating an illness depression is and how quickly it has changed our quality of life.

This story illustrates the sudden, significant impact a bout of depression can have on a family's financial situation. Are you prepared for such a situation? Do you have access to disability insurance through your employer? Contact your employer's human resources manager to learn about what benefits are available to you. If you are self-employed, have you considered purchasing your own coverage? You may be able to purchase disability coverage through your professional group or organization. If not, contact your insurance agent for more details.

An alternative to disability insurance is to set aside money from each paycheck for an emergency savings fund. Financial planners generally suggest having an emergency fund equal to three to six months worth of your salary for situations of illness or unemployment. This may seem like an unrealistic goal for you, especially if you live on a limited or fixed income. Financial planners also always say that every little bit helps, and it is getting into the habit of saving on a regular basis, as much as the amount you put aside each pay check, that's important.

Because depression can be disabling and may interfere with your ability to work, you may be eligible for various types of financial assistance. Such programs and benefits were created to help alleviate financial difficulties, so you can focus on your recovery. Sandra tells how she dealt with her financial situation.

My financial situation became so bleak that I was forced to file for bankruptcy. I never discussed these money problems with my psychiatrist, nor did I realize my finances were having a major impact on my depression. Eventually my doctor became aware of my situation. After discussing my feelings about being unemployed and my financial situation, it was decided that I should apply for disability income. I was not aware that depression is a disability, nor was I aware that you could collect Social Security if you are disabled. At first I was hesitant to apply, but my doctor explained this was part of the Social Security system, and that I had contributed into this account for many years. This was not a free ride. I applied for and was awarded Social Security Disability Income (SSDI).

You may feel too proud to accept these benefits but, in many cases, these are resources you have earned and are now entitled to. Talk to your doctor, psychiatrist, therapist, or advocate about these entitlements. The professionals can help you overcome any concerns you have regarding entitlements and help you determine whether you're eligible. Remember, these resources benefit not only you, but your entire family. This is another one of those times when you may need to set your feelings aside to do what's in the best interest of your children. Your dependence on these entitlements may be time-limited as you progress in your recovery and return to work.

Some of the programs for which you may be eligible are listed in the Resources section at the end of this book. Contact information for these resources can usually be found in the telephone book under the name of your state, or under "United States Government" listings. Your local town hall and private service agencies may have information on other programs and resources in your community.

Planning Ahead to Avoid or Cope with a Financial Crisis

It's always wise to identify support people and create back up plans when you are feeling well, so that you're not making critical decisions at a time when you are not functioning at your best. We recommend working together with your partner and family, if appropriate, to develop plans that work for everyone.

If you have discovered your spending patterns are related to your moods or symptoms of your depression, identify a support person—perhaps your partner, a friend or family members, or even your therapist—you can call when your moods and spending are out of control. You want to avoid building up debts, as the prospect of paying them off may leave you feeling hopeless and desperate. You and your "spend friend" can agree to monitor your spending behavior. You can call your friend when you feel the "need" to buy something to help yourself feel better. Or, if your friend notices you are becoming more manic, excited, and agitated, she can suggest you turn over your credit cards to her for safekeeping for a few days.

It's important to inform your partner about the family's financial situation, engage him or her in establishing a budget and setting goals, and consider his or her input in creating plans for managing household finances if you are unable to function in that role. Be sure he or she knows where you keep financial records, bills to be paid, the checkbook, and credit card information. You may consider engaging your children in this process to the extent they are willing and able, given their ages and maturity levels. While you don't want to burden young children with responsibilities beyond their years or capacities, older children and young adults may be taught how to handle an emergency or short-term situation. These skills may help them feel empowered, alleviate their current anxieties about the family, and serve them well in the future, as they begin to function independently from you.

You can officially designate someone ahead of time, through a power of attorney form, to manage your money in the event you become extremely disabled or are hospitalized for a lengthy period. This should be done with an attorney's help. By signing the power of attorney in advance, you can have an influence over the choice of a person to act on your behalf. Since this document essentially gives your financial decision-making powers to someone else if you become severely disabled, it is critically important that you choose someone whom you really trust. It may be reassuring to your children to know you have made plans for managing the household and providing for them when you are not able.

Many people who are extremely depressed think about death and dying all the time; it is a constant preoccupation. While you may think no one would care if you weren't around anymore, the loss of a parent to a family is devastating. Not only is it an emotional blow to your children, but also, if you are the breadwinner or the primary caregiver, your loss can have tremendous financial implications for your family. Preparing a will allows you, in a better moment, to provide for your family in the event that you are no longer with them. You can designate beneficiaries for your various accounts and assets, and identify a guardian for your children, choosing individuals you feel will best meet your children's needs. Again, your children will be reassured to know that you have planned for their needs.

Complete the checklist below to mark off steps you have taken to ensure your family's well-being when you are not well.

Financial Well-Being Checklist

☐ Identify a "spend friend," someone you feel comfortable with, who can help you monitor your moods and spending and suggest other activities to you when you feel like "going wild" with your credit cards.

☐ Make a list of accounts and credit cards, with account numbers and customer service telephone numbers.

☐ Create a file for financial records. You may need several files if you want to separate your documents by source or type; for example, credit card records, bank account statements, tax returns, etc.

☐ Show your partner or other trusted family member or friend where you keep your records.

☐ Create a budget. Work together with your partner, children (if they are old enough), or another individual you trust to plan for paying your bills when you're not well. Write the name and phone number of the person who will manage that responsibility for you here:

_____

☐ Review your insurance options. Contact your employer or insurance agent to see what choices you have regarding disability coverage and life insurance. Make decisions with the advice of your family, a friend, or another support person if that would help you feel more comfortable.

❑ Sign a power of attorney form to officially designate someone who can legally manage your finances and property if you are severely disabled for a length of time. If you have signed a power of attorney, write the name and phone number of the individual you have chosen here:

_____

❑ Draft a will to protect your children and your resources in the event of your death. Where do you keep it filed? Write that information here:

_____

Dealing Directly with Children

As a parent, you may feel several obligations related to your children and money. Meeting their needs and wants is probably the first, and we have discussed this in the previous sections of this chapter. Teaching them values about work, money, and spending, and guiding the development of healthy, effective behavior around these issues are the second. How you approach the teaching and guidance task will vary with the age and developmental stage of your children.

While young children may understand that money can be used to buy things, they often do not understand where it comes from. Children need to learn that before they can spend money, they first must earn it. This may be difficult to do if your depression limits you to part-time work or prevents you from working entirely. Walter felt this limitation keenly.

How do I explain to my son that I can't work because of my psychiatric disorder? When he's older, will he think any less of me because of my illness? The thought of my son feeling any shame or embarrassment over me is unbearable. Yet, I also realize that right now, at four years of age, my son doesn't care that I'm not working full-time. In fact, he enjoys having me around to spend time with him, even though I don't always have the energy to play with him very much. I worry that there won't be enough money to buy him the things that other kids have, and that I won't be able to help pay for his college education. But maybe I can help him understand that psychiatric disorders are not something to be ashamed of, and that money isn't everything in life. If I can't give him material things, I can at least give him plenty of love and encouragement, which money can't buy.

Regardless of your situation, you can still help your child understand the satisfaction that comes with work and earning money. You may want to start your child off by letting him earn a weekly allowance by doing some chores around the home, even if it's only a dollar or two per week. You can encourage an older child to find part-time work, or to do odd jobs in the neighborhood like cutting grass or shoveling snow. Children can also learn about saving by putting money into a piggy bank or opening a savings account at a bank or credit union. Allow your child to use some of this money for short-term spending, like candy at the corner store, and encourage her to set some aside for longer-term goals, like a bike or special doll. When children work to earn money, they quickly realize that money doesn't grow on trees, and some of those "must have" items may start to lose some of their appeal. Leslie found that giving her daughter an allowance was helpful.

> *One other thing that's worked out pretty well has been giving my daughter a weekly allowance—not much, only a few dollars. She has since started a savings account. I'm really impressed at how quickly she has learned to manage her money. Of course, I would always prefer to have more money than I currently do, but maybe some good has come out of not being well off if it teaches my daughter to be responsible with her own money.*

Although you may feel uncomfortable, many experts agree that including your children in discussions about family finances is usually a good idea. What you say and how you say it depend on your child's age and maturity level. Providing children with information and engaging them in decision making about family issues at an age-appropriate level can help them feel like they have some input and control over things that happen in their family. However, you don't want to scare them or place a burden on them by providing too much information, particularly about family financial difficulties. You must be sure they do not feel blamed for family financial problems. David found his teenager's input helped them both.

> *Initially, I didn't think my teen would be interested in helping me do up our family budget, but she really wanted to know how much things like groceries and utilities cost. She could also see that the cost of my prescription medication for my depression was pretty high. We even looked at areas where we could try to save money. I was surprised at the good suggestions she made, such as turning off the lights when leaving a room to save on electricity and taking shorter showers to save on water. Now, instead of having to tell her that we can't afford this or that, she already understands what our financial situation is and why we can't afford certain things.*

Before talking with your child, think again about your own values and attitudes toward money. Children develop their values and attitudes about money in large part by watching you. A child becomes aware of money at as young as three years of age. Your child sees you and others use money every day and quickly begins to understand that it has value. As children grow, they are constantly bombarded by television and magazine advertisements, all of which are designed to make your child believe they need certain products—toys, games, clothing, sports drinks—to be happy and popular. By involving your child in your budget planning, you can help her understand the difference between needs and wants and that having an advertised product is not the key to happiness and success in life.

Providing Your Children with Opportunities for Practice

Children benefit from opportunities to practice new skills and a safe environment in which to make mistakes and learn from them. You can give your children a chance to learn about their values, their needs and wants, and how to manage their money to achieve their goals. One possibility is to give them an allowance or spending money and walk them through the process of identifying goals and setting up a budget or plan for meeting their goals. A young child might be given an allowance equal to her grade in school, for example, one dollar a week for a first-grader. You can have conversations with her about how she might spend or save her money, setting short- and long-term goals. This lays the groundwork for her to develop an understanding of the choices to be made about money.

A school-age child who purchases snacks or lunch at school might be given a week's worth of money to budget. A teenager might be given a monthly clothing allowance and allowed to decide how to spend it, as long as expectations are laid out clearly ahead of time. For instance, do you expect your teen to buy the "big ticket" items like a winter coat with his clothing allowance money? Or is it only to cover more routine expenditures like T-shirts or blue jeans?

The activity below will give you a framework for teaching your child about spending money, saving, and budgeting. Take advantage of a time when your child asks for money to buy something, like a doll or bike. Talk with her about planning to save her own money as a way of purchasing the desired item. Create a document or contract like the one below so she has a plan in hand for achieving her goal.

My Savings Plan

What I want: _____

How much it costs (plus tax): $_____
(Be sure to help her look through newspaper or store ads for the best price.)

How much I receive each week (money from chores, other work): $ _____
(She may want to include money she receives from birthday gifts or the tooth fairy.)

How much money I want to save each week toward my goal: $_____
(Encourage your child to budget for short- and long-term goals. Short-term goals might be two candy bars per week at the corner store. Long-term goals usually are more costly items that require saving for a period of time. People need to learn to balance "immediate

gratification," which we all need sometimes, with the achievement of long-term goals. Pleasure can be derived from each type of spending.)

Based on the amount to be saved each week, calculate how many weeks it will take to save enough money to purchase the item (the cost of the item divided by the amount to be saved per week): $ _____

So imagine the bike costs $80, and your child earns a $5 allowance plus $20 in tips from a paper route per week. If she decides to save $10 per week, she will be able to purchase the bike in eight weeks. By that time, your child may decide she no longer wants the requested item! In any event, this activity allows your child to manage or budget a fixed amount of money, as well as to develop an appreciation of how much effort and discipline it takes to save money.

A Better Understanding of Moods and Money

Moods and money are closely intertwined for many people, especially those with depression. Managing a household, balancing a budget, and meeting the needs of children can feel like overwhelming challenges. However, acknowledging your values and attitudes about money, understanding how they affect your behavior, and developing skills to manage your moods and your finances can help you feel better as a person and as a parent. Taking advantage of opportunities to explore these issues with your children and helping them develop money-management skills allows them to feel a sense of control and mastery when you might not be feeling well and gives them a head start on achieving their own goals.

Chapter 4

Feeding Your Family and Yourself

Your mood and food go hand in hand. Depression is, by definition, related to diminished interest in daily activities, like fixing meals or eating; significant changes in your weight, either loss or gain; and the loss of energy or inability to concentrate that can make planning meals, shopping for groceries, and fixing dinner the last things you feel like doing. Nausea, vomiting, anorexia, or weight gain can be side effects of taking antidepressant medication (Kaplan, Sadock, and Grebb 1994). Your diet may be limited because certain foods interact in a bad way with your medications. If you are disabled by your mental illness, you may be collecting benefits and living on a fixed income. You may have to budget carefully to pay for your groceries and rely on public transportation to get to the store.

As a parent with depression, you are probably responsible for fixing meals for both you and your children. It can be very difficult to find the motivation to prepare meals for your family when your appetite is poor and your energy level is low. You may respond by eating fast foods or whatever is convenient and then overeating later because you are left feeling unsatisfied. Your attitude toward food in general may be an issue, too, especially if you have ever had to deal with an eating disorder. You may overeat to fill the void left by depression, or limit what you eat because you feel you don't deserve to indulge yourself. You may worry about how your habits, values, or attitudes about food affect your children.

While these problems can seem overwhelming, with a little thought and planning you can provide your family with healthy meals even when you are depressed. Involving your children in choosing and preparing foods and keeping meals a comfortable family time will help reduce the feeling of burden that feeding your family can evoke when you're not feeling well. Women with depression considering pregnancy or breast-feeding need to discuss medication, nutrition, weight gain and, perhaps, alternative sources of nourishment for their newborns.

You Are What You Eat—and Maybe More

"You are what you eat" is a familiar cliché that may be only partly true, but one thing is certain: The choices you make about food, what food means to you, and the way you react to it are part of your identity. During infancy, you bond with your parents when you nurse or bottle feed. Throughout your life, you reconnect with your family at mealtimes and receive both physical and emotional nourishment. Family get-togethers almost always revolve around food—trips, outings, picnics, ball games. Food is often what people remember most!

As a child, you may have helped your parents prepare special dishes that reflect your ethnic and cultural heritage. Food is associated with every holiday and major life event, including births, christenings, weddings, and funerals. Small wonder then, when you're ill, depressed, lonely, or homesick, you console yourself with familiar foods from childhood.

Food can be associated with negative feelings, too, depending on the experiences we connect it with. Perhaps you were forced to eat your vegetables as a child, and you promised yourself you would never eat them when you grew up. Maybe family members argued and criticized each other during dinner. You may have weighed more or less than you or your parents hoped. Perhaps you felt guilty each time you took a second helping or angry when they yelled at you for not eating enough.

You are your children's primary role model and greatest source of feedback. You reinforce their earliest habits, values, and attitudes about food. Have you thought about what food means to you? How are your feelings about food communicated to your children? What do they see? What do you say?

Communicating with Your Children About Food

Most of what you do on a daily basis you probably do without paying much attention, especially when it's something as routine as eating or fixing meals. Take some time to listen to your interactions with your children about food. How do you respond when they ask for a snack? How do you call them to the table for dinner? Do you fuss at them for eating too much candy? Is their weight an issue for you? Do you find yourself watching what or how much they eat and commenting on it or them for the selections they make? Many children make terrible food choices, selecting primarily from the "sugar" or "fat" food groups! Do your children make good choices in this area, or could they use some help? Do their eating habits affect how you feel as a parent? Some parents feel guilty if their children are eating too many sweets, as if their children's choices reflect poorly on them.

Keep a list of your interactions with your children about food for several days or a week. Make notes about how you feel about these interactions and your children's responses. Are the majority of your interactions about food positive, neutral, or negative? If they are negative, look at the patterns and identify themes, times, or settings that provoke bad feelings for you or your children. Make a list of comments or habitual interactions you would like to avoid or change. Write down something you might say instead. Work to replace the negative interactions with positive ones.

Improving Family Food Talk

Comments I would like to avoid or change:	Replace them with:
Example: *There you go, stuffing your face with candy.*	*Let me fix you some popcorn.*
_____	_____
_____	_____
_____	_____

A Note About Eating Disorders

If the latest magazine articles and stories about too-thin movie actresses make you anxious, or if you suffered with an eating disorder yourself, you may be concerned about your children's eating habits and weight. Eating disorders are complex illnesses, often the consequence of a variety of factors. Bulimia and compulsive overeating often are characterized by increased food intake. Some of the symptoms of bulimia include binge eating, purging, weight fluctuation, bathroom visits after eating, brittle hair, graying teeth, and secretive eating. People who suffer from bulimia will try to purge themselves of the food they eat by making themselves vomit or overusing laxatives or enemas. Those with an overeating disorder will want to continue to eat despite being full. Symptoms of compulsive overeating include binge eating, depression, fear of not being able to stop eating voluntarily, guilt feelings following binges, and having weight be the focus of your life. In contrast, individuals with anorexia will try to avoid eating food and may exercise excessively. Symptoms of anorexia include significant weight loss, denial of the seriousness of the weight loss, distorted views of how one's body is perceived by others, fear of gaining weight, depression, and mood swings.

These symptoms can indicate some other medical conditions, in addition to an eating disorder, so it's important to seek the advice of a health professional to clarify the diagnosis. Treatment for eating disorders may include individual therapy, group therapy, hospitalization, and the use of antidepressant or anti-anxiety medications (Becker, Grinspoon, Klibanski, and Herzog 1999).

You can play a role in preventing eating disorders in your children. Encourage a healthy lifestyle for your children, one that involves both some exercise and wise eating practices. If you are depressed, you may say negative things about your own weight and body or see only the negative in your children. Take special care not to make negative comments. Don't watch television programs or movies that make fun of people because of their weight. Children need to understand that thinness does not mean happiness. You can create a household in which people are taken seriously because of what they say and who they are and not because of their weight or body shape.

Feeding Your Family: Pleasure or Pain?

Feeding your family involves a variety of tasks—thinking ahead about what to fix, seeing if you have the ingredients, going to the store if you need something, preparing the food, setting the table, and cleaning up afterwards. A great deal of time and effort over the course of a day or week goes into feeding your family. You may take great pleasure in some or all of these tasks, or you may really dislike them. When you're depressed, they can seem especially overwhelming.

Your "Family-Food-Related" Activities

Weight-loss programs often begin with a "self-study," where you make a list of what and how much you eat during the day and, perhaps, how you felt before, during, or after you ate. By keeping a chart or journal, you begin to discover your eating habits, whether your feelings cause you to eat, and how you feel afterward. Then you can set goals for changing your habits, and come up with healthier ways to deal with your feelings.

Keep a log for a day or two (or even a week if you can), not of *what* you eat, but of your "family-food-related" activities. Jot down anything you do that is related to feeding your family and how you feel while you're doing it. Include time you spend thinking about what to fix for dinner, for example, or baking cookies for a birthday party. Are these activities a source of pleasure and pride or an overwhelming burden? Using your log, make a summary list of the tasks you do and don't enjoy and the time you spend on each. By describing how you spend your time and energy and how you feel about it, you can begin to identify what you want or need to change.

Family-Food Activities Log

I enjoy these tasks:	Time spent:	I don't enjoy these tasks:	Time spent:
Example: *grocery shopping*	*3 hours/week*	*putting groceries away*	*1 hour/week*
_____	_____	_____	_____
_____	_____	_____	_____
_____	_____	_____	_____

Your ultimate goal is to decrease the amount of time you spend on activities you don't enjoy or have bad feelings about and increase those you like. Look carefully at the list of tasks you don't enjoy and think about whether you can streamline them, assign responsibility to someone else, or eliminate them. For example, if you really don't enjoy making cupcakes for the school bake sale, go to the bakery and buy them. This does not make you a bad parent. There may be activities you can't eliminate, like grocery shopping, but that are less annoying at a different time of the day or week, when the store is less crowded. You may be able to simplify tasks or share responsibility with other family members, including your children.

Streamlining Family-Food-Activities

Some days it may feel like putting food on the table, meal after meal, is your only accomplishment. Other days, you may not even accomplish this much. Planning ahead and shopping well can help you feel more on top of things and less overwhelmed. Involving the family in meal preparation can offer opportunities for positive interactions and contribute to children's feelings of self-esteem and growing independence as they learn the skills they will need later in life.

Menu Planning

You have probably seen the United States Department of Agriculture/Department of Health and Human Services Food-Guide Pyramid, which serves as a guide or map to reach the goal of good nutrition. See the Resources at the end of this book for information on how to obtain information about the pyramid. The Food-Guide Pyramid comes in two versions, one for adults and children six years of age or older, and one for children under the age of six. The pyramid gives you an idea of what numbers of what size servings you require from each food group—the bread, cereal, rice, and pasta group; fruit group;

vegetable group; milk, yogurt, and cheese group; meat, poultry, fish, dry beans, eggs, and nuts group; and the fats, oils, and sweets group. The pyramid is a guide, *not* a means to punish yourself if your children do not have exactly the right amounts from each food group every day.

Your children may not eat food from each group every day. They may eat extra food one day and a lot less the next. Watch to see what your children eat over the course of a week, and make sure they receive food from each group during that time period. Sometimes a small child will only accept a particular food for several days in a row. Keep serving all the food the rest of the family eats, and eventually that child will most likely want to eat the food they see you eating.

Remember that the purpose of the pyramid is only to suggest guidelines; no one expects you to follow it perfectly. Do not feel guilty because your children do not fit this perfect model. The most important thing you can do for your child is to set a good example by keeping healthy foods available and making the right choices for yourself.

Many people plan a menu and shop for food once a week because they receive a weekly paycheck or salary. You may receive a monthly check or have to rely on public transportation, which makes carrying a week's worth of groceries very difficult. Plan your menu and shopping to fit your own situation. Begin by planning a menu for one day, and repeat the process for however many days you need.

Try using this menu planning form:

Menu Planning

	Breakfast	Lunch	Dinner	Snacks
Day 1				
Day 2				
Day 3				

When you're depressed, or you are feeling tired because of medication side effects, it may be very difficult to meet the nutritional needs of your family. It's a good idea to have a plan in place for times like this. These strategies might help.

- Have a list of simple recipes that require ingredients you usually have on hand.

- Double recipes when you are feeling well and freeze half.

- Keep ready-to-eat foods on hand.

Janet, a mother with depression, explains,

It's hard when you don't feel well. I try to keep things like yogurt and cheese in the fridge because my son likes that and he can get it himself.

Other examples of ready-to-eat, nutrition-packed foods are peanut butter, baby carrots, and different kinds of fruit. Cold cereals with fruit and milk can also be a quick easy way to provide nutritious food for a child when you're not feeling well.

A staff member who is responsible for meals at Employment Options, Inc., a psychosocial clubhouse in Central Massachusetts, offers the following shopping tips for planning nutritious and economical meals.

- Since meat is the most expensive part of a meal, check the newspapers to see what meat is on sale. Then you can plan the week's meals around the meats.

- Always have pasta, rice, and potatoes on hand.

- Serve meat (including chicken and fish) dishes three times each week, pasta and bean dishes on alternate days. Soups are a good way to use pasta or beans.

- When buying hamburger, buy a large package, break it up into three packages for three meals, and put them in the freezer. This way you can get a more economical price, because many foods are cheaper in larger quantities. You can freeze part of the meat to keep it fresh.

- Always have fresh fruit and vegetables in refrigerator.

Develop your file of low-energy recipes—meals you can fix when you're feeling low. Magazines often have articles on one-pot meals or recipes you can prepare in thirty minutes or less. Check out the cookbook section of your local bookstore or library. Many of these books have been written for working parents, whose time is limited. All of them may be useful to you when your energy is limited.

Food Shopping

You've heard all the rules about food shopping. Don't shop without a list, you might forget something. Don't shop when you're hungry, you might buy things you don't need. Don't take the children and, if you do, don't let them put extra items in the shopping cart. When you are depressed, you may have the opposite experience. You may not have the energy to get a list organized, much less get yourself to the store to shop. It may be extremely difficult to feel motivated to shop when you have no appetite. You may find food totally unappealing.

There are several ways to make a shopping list. When you are well, make a list of all the staples you routinely need on hand—flour, sugar, salt. Add to the list the items you know you need every week—milk, fruit and vegetables, and other perishables. Knowing your children's favorite foods can make grocery shopping much easier. Think of a typical day for each child. Are there foods your children prefer? Can you think of other foods to perhaps provide a little more balance to their daily diets? Don't forget those ready-made snacks and foods the children can fix for themselves.

When you are really feeling energetic, go to the store and make a map of the aisles, with the food in each aisle. Some grocery stores have lists of products already available, organized by location in the store. Organize your items by aisle to reduce the amount of time and energy it takes to make your way through the store.

Another way to make or add to your list is to review the meals you have planned for the next few days or week and write down the ingredients you need. Use the form on the next page to organize your shopping.

In the "Ingredients" column, list all of the ingredients needed to prepare all of the meals in the menu you have made. Then place a checkmark beside the items you already have in the column beside it.

In the "What I Need" column, write down the items you need to purchase. Cut on the dotted line and take this half with you when you go shopping. Bring a pen along and use the last column to check off the items as you buy them.

Shopping List

Ingredients	☑	What I Need	☑

Contrary to popular opinion, you may want to take your children with you to the store. Depending on their ages, you can read down your list and assign them items to bring back to the shopping cart. They may make the shopping go faster and the trip a little more enjoyable. Why not stop for a cookie at the bakery department on your way out of the store as a reward for everyone!

Meal Preparation

You have the opportunity to nurture your children by preparing and serving them nourishing meals and also by involving them in family routines that revolve around mealtimes. When you're feeling depressed, you might find it helpful to shift some of the workload, and even the decisions about what to prepare, to other family members. One way to streamline meal preparation is to involve the rest of the family in all the steps. Once you have taken the time to teach them how, even small children can help quite a bit.

In her book, *Cooking with Kids for Dummies* (Heyhoe 1999), Kate Heyhoe describes what type of tasks are appropriate for children of different ages. We've created our own list by using some of her suggestions and adding a few of our own.

Preschoolers can:

- Stir food (away from the stove of course) and mix ingredients using a spoon;

- Help to measure and add ingredients;

- Drop cookie dough onto cookie sheets;

- Help to shape meatballs;

- Fold napkins and help to set the table;

- Dry plastic dishes;

- Clear off the table.

Children ages six to nine can:

- Do all of the tasks preschoolers can;

- Chop food and tear lettuce into bite-sized pieces for salad;

- Use a can opener, toaster, and microwave oven;

- Scrub vegetables and shred vegetables and cheese;

- Knead dough;

- Crack open raw eggs and peel cooked eggs;

- Sweep the kitchen;
- Put away leftovers

Children nine to twelve can:

- Do all of the above;
- Use the stove, oven, and other appliances with supervision in the beginning;
- Chop food;
- Wash and put away dishes.

Teenagers can:

- Do all of the above;
- Whatever else you can convince them to do!

You can encourage your children to help you by preparing snacks and light meals themselves and by putting ingredients and equipment in the cabinets and drawers they can reach. Store your cereal bowls next to the cereal, for example, and put the milk within their reach on the bottom shelf of the refrigerator. A number of cookbooks for children of all ages are colorful and appealing. Check the resource list at the end of this book for some suggestions. Experiment with new recipes when you're feeling well. Not only will your children feel proud as they help you with their new cooking skills, but you will have fun in the process.

Do you have a friend or relative who lives close by who would prepare a meal for your family in an emergency? If not, try to arrange this. Perhaps you could offer to perform this service for someone with similar needs in exchange for being on call for you and your family.

Some Money-Saving Tips

If you are living on a fixed or low income, you may struggle to provide your family with healthy food. We asked several parents for ideas about how to survive on a limited budget. Here are their suggestions.

Fran is a mother with mental illness who lives on a fixed income. She has learned to save money using both coupons and store cards.

Every Sunday I cut out coupons from the Sunday newspaper. My friends also send me coupons they know I can use. I also use savings cards from the supermarkets. You're allowed to get a number of items with an amount off of each one of them by using the savings cards. Sometimes if you buy one or two of the same item, you can get an additional one or two free. It really adds up when you're allowed to get two free items for each single *item you purchase. I have been able to save between $30 to $50 a month. To receive a store savings card, go to the customer service desk and sign up. I use cards from three different stores because I go to the one that has the best sales on the items I need at the time.*

Most grocery stores publish weekly sales flyers that advertise their current specials. These flyers usually contain coupons for reduced prices for the benefit of their customers. Coupons can also be found in the newspaper, in magazines, and on the packages of many products. Some manufacturers mail out coupons in order to influence you to try their products. Some stores have automated this practice by issuing plastic "store cards." The checkout clerk will swipe the card through a machine that registers the card and automatically reduces the price of any sale item that is purchased.

Of course, the key to saving money with coupons is to use only the ones for food you would normally purchase. A dollar off of a package of $3.00 cookies you wouldn't normally purchase will reduce your available funds for items that you really need and end up *costing* you money instead of saving you money. Sometimes the store brand is still cheaper than a name brand with a coupon. Be careful!

Food banks, shelters, kitchens, and pantries can be valuable resources for a family living on a fixed income. Each of these organizations will usually provide food either for free or at reduced cost. Ray, a father of five with bipolar disorder, takes advantage of a food bank that operates in his area. He describes the process.

I've been going to the food bank since 1995. I learned about it from the clubhouse. When you go to the food bank you have to show an ID, license, Social Security card, or public welfare card. Then the food bank gives you a blue card good for five months. After five months, you can renew it. Next, you put your hand in a box full of numbers and draw a number from one to forty. That tells you where you are in line. If you get a low number, you can get in and out real quick. You do have to bring your own bags to take the groceries home.

You go down an aisle full of shelves that have different groups of foods. For example, one shelf might have three different kinds of macaroni, like shells, noodles, or elbows. A man asks you what kind you want, and you pick one and move on to the next shelf. The next one might have soups and stews. The food is donated to the food bank by local stores. You can end up with about $30 to $40 worth of food. There are also clothes and stuff donated by church members. The last time I went I got books for my kids.

How can you find a food bank in your area? The best place to begin searching for one is among local churches in your area. Churches run more than half of these programs, often serving a wide variety of people with a similarly wide variety of hardships, like unemployment, illness, mental illness, unexpected emergencies, and other disabilities. There are many good reasons to participate in food distribution programs. No one should hesitate to try to seek help. This is especially true of parents trying to provide food for their children.

The next step is to determine if there are requirements that must be fulfilled before you can participate in the program. These requirements may include: a referral from an outside source (such as a social worker); proof of residence (perhaps a phone or electric bill); an income statement; a photocopy of a driver's license; or donating a few hours of service to the agency that runs the food distribution program. The individual volunteers are asked to work in exchange for food from the program. These requirements are not intended to pose big problems for people who wish to participate in the food programs. Agencies do not want to turn people away, but sometimes they need to prove that all of the participants in their program meet a certain criterion or they will lose their funding. Often, the agencies running these programs may be able to suggest simple ways to satisfy their requirements. Many are willing to help homebound people obtain food.

It may be helpful to make a distinction between food banks and pantries, and shelters and kitchens. Shelters, and especially kitchens, usually provide a single, cooked meal. The meal usually is prepared and served, cafeteria-style, for all those who enter the program site. On the other hand, pantries and food banks usually function more as distribution centers of unprepared foods. At food banks and pantries, there is usually a package of unprepared food that has been assembled into a paper bag, box, or basket. These packages vary in size. The food bank or pantry usually determines the size of the package that any one person may take, based on the number of people for whom he or she is retrieving the food. For example, a father with four children and a wife would, out of necessity, be given a larger package than a single person would. Inside these packages, there may be some type of meat, fish, poultry, or bread. However, the packages usually are limited to nonperishable goods such as juice, coffee, canned products, rice, beans, cereal, pasta, or crackers. If the program does offer some perishable items, such as meat, fish, poultry, bread, etc., it usually will keep them on separate tables, where staff will distribute them. In addition to having separate tables for perishable items, food banks or pantries also may have separate tables for diabetic, salt-free, or baby foods. Even if the food bank or pantry does not have these separate tables for different kinds of food, the staff usually can help those individuals with special dietary concerns, for example, diabetes, food restrictions due to medication, or food allergies, to find the food they need. Furthermore, there are some food banks and pantries with registered dieticians or dietary counselors on staff. Some dieticians and counselors may even be willing to help the people who participate in food programs to plan their daily meals.

Food co-ops are an alternative to shopping at grocery stores. A food co-op is a group of people who buy food together in large quantities to save money. Members usually divide or take turns at tasks like ordering, distributing, and record keeping.

A food co-op can be especially useful for people who have food allergies, need specialty foods that are hard to find in regular grocery stores, or for people who are interested in organically grown foods. For example, many people are allergic to milk products and need soybean-based products instead. Vegetarians also use soy products and meat substitutes. In some areas, these foods may not be available in local grocery stores but can be ordered directly from the manufacturer or wholesaler. Specialty and organic foods can be expensive to purchase, but by purchasing in bulk the price is lower. The price range for food from a co-op is usually higher than foods purchased from a regular grocery store but less expensive than a health food store.

On the down side, food co-ops usually require a commitment of time on your part. Typically two or three nights a month are spent meeting with other members of the co-op to decide on what and where to order food and in what quantity, contacting suppliers, distributing the purchases, and organizing the necessary operations. On the other hand, you might find the social interaction with other members rewarding. Another thing to consider is the fact that grocery store chains seem to be offering a greater number of specialty, ethnic, and organically grown foods lately, and you might find these foods at lower prices in these regular stores. It all depends on what you're looking for and what is available in your particular area. Food co-ops can be difficult to find. You can try looking in the Yellow Pages, surfing on the Internet, or by asking friends and acquaintances.

Making Mealtimes Pleasant

Families have all kinds of routines around meals. Some families sit down together at breakfast, and then their busy lives keep them apart for the rest of the day. Others make a point of coming together at suppertime, at least two or three times a week, so family members can check in with each other. Regardless of whether you have prepared a gourmet meal or a macaroni and cheese casserole, mealtimes often have a greater significance than simply being a time to eat. As a parent, you set the tone for the meal, as well as expectations around behavior and how family members treat each other at the table. As a parent with depression, you may have less energy than other parents, combined with a greater need than many to have mealtimes go well.

Providing healthy food for your children is one matter; getting them to eat that food is another. A certain amount of conflict at the dinner table may revolve around behavior or preferences that are actually developmentally appropriate. Each age group has its own set of issues, which are a normal part of childhood that all parents deal with whether they have depression or not. These behaviors are not an "attack" on you personally. Toddlers, for example, often throw their food and also refuse to eat it. They may not eat what you consider to be enough, or they'll choose to eat only one thing over and over. Teenagers food choices are often influenced by their peers and where they spend their leisure time. They might consider a meal without French fries and cola a total nightmare. Keep in mind that making these choices is a normal part of the learning process we all go through as we develop our own food preferences. You are not a "failure" as a parent if your child exhibits behavior you don't agree with.

Here are some tips to make mealtimes pleasurable experiences.

- Encourage family participation in preparing and serving meals and cleaning up afterwards.

- Keep the conversation relaxed. Save confrontations or arguments for another time.

- Turn off the television, so you and your children can focus on what everyone has to say.

- Try turning on soft music.

- Give children a choice in picking one of the menu items or planning a meal. Some families assign each child a day of the week.

- Plan an ethnic meal—from your own cultural heritage or another.

- Have a picnic in the back yard or living room.

Changing Things at Your House

To change people's behavior, you have to come up with something for them to do instead. If you are really desperate to change the tone of mealtimes at your house, plan ahead. Make a quick list of neutral topics that family members won't argue about and keep the list available in your pocket for quick reference. Have each family member talk about one good thing that happened during the day. Adapt some of those travel games you play on car trips, like "I Spy" or an alphabet game, to provide the structure you need to make your family's pattern of interaction more positive.

Special Circumstances: Pregnancy and Breast-feeding

Along with discussing the use of antidepressant medication during pregnancy, you may want to talk with your doctor about weight gain and appetite issues. Some of the medications used in treating depression have been linked with weight gain. However, pregnant mothers should not be afraid to eat or gain weight. If you are concerned about your depression, medication, and weight gain during pregnancy, talk with your doctor. You may also find that symptoms of your depression or medications affect your appetite in the opposite way, causing a lack of interest in food. Perhaps your doctor will prescribe a nutritional supplement.

A mother's eating habits after childbirth still affect her child's nutritional intake if she chooses to breast-feed. Breast-feeding is recommended by the American Academy of Pediatrics as an ideal way to nurture and feed a newborn child.

However, if you are taking medications, be sure to clear this with your pediatrician, because some medications can affect the infant through the mother's milk. Do not worry or feel guilty if you cannot breast-feed your child for any reason. Milk-based and soy-based formulas are available that contain all the nutrients a baby needs. Mothers who have raised healthy children have been relying on these formulas for years. You have not "failed," but are making a choice that is best for both your child and you.

Questions to ask your doctor

- If you are thinking about becoming pregnant, what does your doctor advise about your psychiatric medication? Do you need to stop taking it during part or all of your pregnancy? Can you take a lower dose or try another medication?

- How does your medication interact with food? Are there foods you have been told to avoid that would be important for you to eat during pregnancy? How can you get the nutrition you need given your particular medication and the requirements of pregnancy?

- How will the medication affect your weight gain during pregnancy? How can you adjust what you eat to be sure you are meeting your nutritional requirements and gaining the right amount of weight for your baby's healthy development? What about exercise?

- If you have been depressed before, how likely is it that you will experience a postpartum depression? Will you need to be taking medication to treat or prevent this?

- Will depression affect your ability to breast-feed your newborn? If you are unable to breast-feed, what alternatives does the doctor suggest for making sure your infant is well nourished?

Feeding Your Family Provides Opportunities

Your mood and food *do* go hand in hand. While your depression may affect your interest in or capacity to feed yourself and your family, there are many ways to organize your menu planning, shopping, and meal-preparation activities. As a result, you may feel less overwhelmed by these tasks and more competent and confident about meeting your family's needs. Encouraging children's participation in mealtime activities—food preparation and dinner table conversations—can enhance their development and support family relationships. Feeding your family and yourself can be a positive experience that actually helps you feel less depressed and more engaged in family life.

Chapter 5

Creating a Safe Environment for Your Family

Psychiatric disorders. Violence. Abuse. These words are often linked together by people who assume that being diagnosed with a psychiatric disorder like depression means that a person is likely to lose control, become violent, and abuse those around him or her. Having a psychiatric disorder, however, does not make you more likely than the average person in the community to be violent, except where drugs or alcohol are involved (Steadman et al. 1998). In fact, when you're depressed, you may feel quite powerless. A person with depression may be more vulnerable and more likely to be the victim of violence than to be an abuser. And certainly, being a victim can contribute to depression.

The focus of this chapter is abuse in your current relationships. Some types of abuse you may easily recognize as fitting your definition of abuse. However, you may not have thought of some of the other behaviors or actions described in this chapter as abusive. You may change your definition of abuse or realize you have been a victim in the past, or that you are currently being abused. If thinking about these topics causes you distress, you must find someone you trust to talk with about these experiences and feelings.

What you learned from your own parents (or the people who raised you) about coping with stress, resolving conflicts, and expressing anger affects your current relationships with your partner and children. If your parents were abusive to each other or you, you may not have had good role models for relationships or parenting skills. You may be in a relationship with a partner who is abusive to you or your children. If your parents did not keep you safe, you may not understand the importance of keeping your own children safe. You may not have a good understanding of child development because your parents had unrealistic expectations for you as a child and treated you harshly when you did not meet their expectations.

Abuse is the misuse of power that is likely to occur in situations of stress and conflict when people have no other way to reduce their anxiety or ease their pain. Stress can be the side effect of any event or situation, positive or negative. Your experience of the event is what really matters. For example, planning a wedding, having a baby, or moving to a new home may be viewed as positive events filled with great happiness, but they can generate a great deal of stress. Losing a job, breaking up with a partner, or dealing with a child's illness, more typically thought of as negative events, are also stressful. Your ability to cope with stress affects how you function as a parent and your relationship with your children. If you are "stressed out," you are more likely to become abusive and to hurt someone else or yourself.

Conflict occurs when meeting one person's needs or wishes means those of another go unmet. Disagreements between people come about in simple, everyday situations. Family members argue about what to eat for dinner or which television shows to watch. Children protest when their parents want them to go to bed. When disagreements are not resolved in satisfying ways, people get angry. What distinguishes violent or abusive responses from the normal expression of anger in day-to-day disagreements is the degree to which a person loses control of his feelings and the extent to which he or she harms him- or herself or another person. It's important to develop strategies for yourself and to teach your children strategies for resolving conflicts, feeling angry, and staying safe.

Again, being diagnosed with depression is not directly related to being an abusive partner or parent. You can learn ways of coping with stress and solving problems so you do not lose control or resort to physical fighting to end an argument. You must also believe that you deserve to be treated with respect and dignity. You are responsible for providing an environment for your children that is physically and emotionally safe.

What Is Abuse?

Abuse is defined in Webster's dictionary as "improper use or treatment" (Webster's 1991). Other words in the definition are "damage" and "shame and disgrace." The damage in abuse may be obvious, like bruises or burns you can see. Or the consequences of abuse may be less obvious, like undermining your confidence or self-esteem and contributing to your depression. In either situation, abuse may contribute to feelings of shame and disgrace for the victim and, sometimes, the abuser. People who are treated poorly, whether they are children or adults, begin to believe they deserve poor treatment and come to expect it. It is easy to understand how a cycle of negative thinking can develop.

When a situation or experience is labeled abusive, there is usually someone with more power and someone with less power. Power can be related to a person's size, physical strength, gender, age, financial resources, education, professional position, or status in the family or community. You may be more powerful because you're smarter or a better talker than someone else, or simply because you have something that someone else wants or needs. You may be less powerful if you are vulnerable in some way. You may be smaller, or younger, or disabled by a medical condition or illness. A person who is more dependent or who needs something from someone else may become abusive, particularly if he feels ashamed of his inadequacies or is humiliated by his deficits.

People living in different family or cultural groups may have different definitions of abuse or different values about how to discipline family members and how to teach children rules. The beliefs of people in immigrant groups, for example, may conflict with those of the new culture in which they are living. People from one cultural background may believe in certain types of punishment for children; people in other groups might not agree. Members of some religious groups do not believe in using certain medical procedures and come into conflict with health care professionals who believe that to withhold treatment is abusive or neglectful. What is abusive in one person's mind may not be in another's.

It's important to note that states have definitions and policies about abuse, regardless of an individual's background or beliefs. Some people think the government should not intrude into their family relationships or how they raise their children. They believe "a man's home is his castle," and what happens "behind closed doors" is nobody's business but the family's. Society may disagree. Conflict between families and agencies can occur when their values do not match.

Abuse Takes Many Forms

Physical abuse includes slapping, punching, shoving, biting, kicking, breaking bones, serious injury, withholding food or sleep, threatening with a weapon, breaking or destroying personal possessions, and harming pets. Any unwanted sexual contact is *sexual abuse*, regardless of whether it involves physical force or not, and even if the abuser is a spouse or partner. Any sexual contact or conduct by an older person involving a child is abuse.

Abuse does not just include physical violence or contact. Threats, insults, name-calling, criticism, and mind games and manipulation are examples of *verbal abuse*. Least obvious as verbal abuse are the subtle messages you receive from "well-meaning" family members and friends, for example, putting down your ideas, plans, or dreams, or causing you to doubt yourself or your abilities because you have an illness. Not giving your partner or family member enough money when it is available to pay for necessary clothing, food, or medicine is *economic abuse*. One person in a relationship may dole out the money or withhold it altogether to control the other person. Demeaning another person's financial decisions or keeping a spouse or partner from working when she wants to are forms of economic abuse.

Keeping a person isolated from friends and family, and always checking on where they are and whom they talk to may be *social abuse*. Efforts to control a person's behavior may be disguised as concern. For example, a husband may not allow his wife to leave the house at night, claiming that it's dangerous to be out after dark. Obviously there may be relationships in which this type of control or scrutiny is warranted and even expected. Parents may appropriately exercise some measure of control over their teenagers' social lives, for example, especially if safety is a concern.

Neglect may be equally as traumatizing, but may not have physical harm as its early signs. Neglect occurs when a person's basic needs are not met. A child may not be provided with enough food to eat or without warm clothes to wear in winter. Neglect may occur on purpose, for example, in a situation where a parent may favor one child and dislike another and treat the latter child poorly. Neglect may happen due to a circumstance beyond someone's control, like when a parent loses his job and can't put food on the table. Neglect may be the by-product of a person's bad judgment. A mother who spends her money on alcohol or cocaine may not have enough money to buy her daughter a winter jacket. Neglect may occur unintentionally, for instance, when a parent is ill and unable to meet a child's needs.

Abuse crosses all social and economic classes and all ethnic and racial groups. Family members, friends, or strangers may abuse adults or children, at home or in the community. People may know abuse by different names—domestic violence, battering, and child abuse. Some types of abuse may not be experienced as damaging when they are happening. A child may experience sexual abuse as warm, nurturing cuddling and, only years later, recognize the inappropriateness of an adult expressing affection to a child in that way. A woman whose partner may be loving in one instance and violent in the next may not realize the abusive nature of the relationship until she is able to get some distance from it, perhaps by separating from her partner. Shame and disgrace may actually be triggered not so much by the abuse itself, but by the negative reactions of others when the abuse is publicly recognized or acknowledged.

Knowing Your Own Perspective

To understand your own values and attitudes about power in relationships, consider the stories below and decide whether you feel there is abuse involved. Think about who has power in each situation and why. Then, pick one of you current relationships to consider, for example, with your partner or your children. List ways you are powerful or vulnerable in that relationship on page 91.

- *A family goes to a restaurant with two children, ages four and five. The children misbehave at the table. The father complains loudly to the mother that she never makes the effort to "teach these kids anything." If only she'd "get out of bed in the morning," maybe they would have better manners. The mother is mortified. The father removes the children from the restaurant and leaves them in the car, returning to the table to finish his meal.*

- *A mother is outside talking to her neighbor while her seven-year-old youngster runs into the street after a ball, just missing being hit by a car. The mother runs after her, grabs her arm, smacks her on the bottom, and speaks to her sternly about safety. The neighbor looks disapprovingly at the mother, mumbling something about never hitting children. The mother responds by saying, "That was nothing compared with what my parents did to me."*

- *A thirteen-year-old fails to clean the kitchen after being given three chances. When his mother yells at him, the teenager yells back, swearing and calling his mother a "psycho-loser," and saying, "I don't have to listen to you any-way—you're crazy." The mother was going to send him to his room and ground him but, thinking there was truth in what he said, felt guilty and backed off.*

Pick a current relationship. Consider who has power in the relationship. Are there ways in which you are powerful? Are you vulnerable in any way? Is power being misused? How can you increase your personal power?

_____

_____

_____

_____

Your Childhood Experiences

Your first role models for relationships with partners and family members and for raising children are the people you grew up with—parents, foster parents, grandparents, and other relatives. Often, children's needs are met by several people, at the same time or over the course of growing up. If your parents were unable to care for you or mistreated you, you may have been cared for by others. People outside the family may have affected your life—a friend, a priest or minister, a coach, or a teacher.

You may be proud of your parents and how they raised you, especially if you were encouraged or supported by them. You may feel you're disappointing them if you have difficulties with depression. On the other hand, sometimes people blame their parents for their problems. It's much easier to say, "I drink because my mother didn't love me" or "I hit my kids because that's what my mother did to me," than it is to identify problems within yourself and try to fix them. You cannot change who your parents are or what they did to you—good or bad. You can only change how you think and act today.

Being mistreated as a child doesn't automatically mean you will be abusive as a parent. Many parents with depression who were abused as children talk about not wanting their children to go through the same types of experiences. You can learn both negative and positive things from your past. You may be motivated to be a better parent and to keep your children safe. Carol Ann's story is a good example.

> *I was a young teen when I was abused. I tried to hide it from everyone, and it just built up inside. I was afraid to get married and have children. But it happened. Well, when the children came, I swore to myself that I would be open and truthful to them. I was afraid to punish or hit them. I used "time-outs" and talking, and they worked well. I always thought I would take my anger out on them. It was scary. Each day I told myself that I could handle disciplining the kids without abuse. Now the children are young adults, and they trust me, talk to me, and are proud of how I raised them.*

If you were abused as a child or had a disrupted family life, you may find yourself being "overprotective" and afraid to allow your children to participate in normal childhood activities, making them stay inside even on nice days to keep them safe. Sometimes parents with active depression may keep children indoors, not because they are being overprotective, but because the children are needed to help out around the house—to fix meals or watch younger brothers and sisters. You may live in a neighborhood where danger is very real. If so, you may have to make decisions about your children's activities based on concerns about safety. If you are confused or question your ability to make reasonable decisions about these issues, consult with a friend, neighbor, or relative whose judgment you do trust.

If you grew up with parents who had unrealistic expectations for you, you may have unrealistic expectations for your own children. For example, your parents might have believed that "children should be seen and not heard" and now, as a parent, you find yourself becoming upset when your young children express their views. If you lived in a stressful family environment, you may have responded in ways children typically respond to stress at certain ages, for example, wetting your pants or wetting the bed at night. You may have been punished for wetting the bed, when what you really needed was someone to help you learn better ways of coping or expressing yourself. As an adolescent you may have "acted out" your feelings rather than expressing them with words. Perhaps you were punished for skipping school or running away. Consequently, you may have no idea what "normal" behavior is for a child of a particular age, and you may not know how to help your children cope with stress or express their feelings in age-appropriate, healthy ways.

Thinking Back

Take a few minutes to think back on your childhood and how your experiences affect your feelings about yourself, your expectations for yourself as a parent and your relationship with your children, your ideas about "normal" behavior in children, and your approach to parenting. People often associate feelings with childhood events. If you find yourself becoming too upset, sad, angry, please take a break from the activity that is prompting these extreme feelings. You may need to find someone to talk with about your feelings, like a friend you trust or a helping professional.

1. Pick a childhood experience when your parents thought your behavior was "bad" and write it down for yourself or describe it to a friend, relative, or helping professional. *Hints:* What were the rules in your family, and how were they made? Who did the punishing? What were common punishments? Were you rewarded for doing something "good"? If there was more than one child in your family, was one child always "good" and one child always "bad"? Which one were you?

2. Play your memory "tape" back in your own mind, remembering the event from your perspective as a child. If possible, have your friend, relative, or helping professional act out the event with you, playing the part of your parent or parent-figure. *Hints:* You may have to coach your friend to act the way your parent would have acted. Give him or her some suggestions. When you have role-played the story, take a few minutes to talk about how it felt to be you. Is there anything you wish you could have said to your parent when you were a child in a situation like this? How did your friend feel about acting the way your parents acted?

3. Now switch perspectives or roles. Write about your parent's perspective as you understand it. If you are role-playing, take the part of your parent and have your friend play your part as a child. *Hints:* How does it feel to behave like your parents? Is it similar in any way to how you interact with your own children? Ask your friend how he or she feels playing your part. What do they think it must have been like for you as a child? How do you wish your parents had handled the situation?

4. Think of a recent incident with your own children. Write about the incident in your journal or describe the incident to your friend and choose parts to role-play. Then switch parts so you each have a chance to be the parent and the child. *Hints:* When you play the parent role, are there ways you are reminded of your own parents? How does it feel when you are the child? Ask your friend what it's like to play each part. Does he or she have any advice for you?

5. On your own or with your friend's help, compare yourself as a parent with your own parents. What are the similarities? The differences? What have you learned from the way you were raised? How would you like to respond to your children? Make a list of things you're satisfied with and want to keep the same and the things you would like to change about your parenting style.

Stress

Stress can be the response to an event or the anticipation of an event, an experience or series of experiences, or even a conversation you have with someone. When you are "stressed out," you may feel very tense, agitated, upset, or even frightened. Sometimes people who are really tense feel they must relieve the pressure by hurting themselves, perhaps by cutting or some other self-destructive behavior, or hurting someone else, verbally or physically.

There are better and worse ways to cope with stress. Better ways allow us to survive a stress without hurting ourselves or someone else. Worse ways are those that are harmful. How you cope is also important because, while children may bring considerable pleasure into your life, they can contribute to stress. They can stress you either directly through the things they do, or indirectly, by increasing the pressure you feel to provide for them. As a partner or a parent, the ways you cope take on greater significance, because you can hurt each other or your children in the process.

As a parent with depression you need to think carefully about coping strategies, since stress can make your symptoms worse. You may have problems with thinking or perceiving that lead to an increase in stress. For example, you may always expect bad things to happen or misunderstand a situation or interaction; you may be anxious or worried all the time. You may be more prone to stress if you feel that, because of your depression, others are watching your performance as a parent. This may not reflect paranoia but, rather, the actual situation for a parent with a psychiatric disorder. Family members or agency professionals may be concerned about anticipated or potential risks for your children because of your depression and may be monitoring your functioning quite closely.

The first step in managing stress is to identify sources of stress, both things that occur at one point in time and those that may last a longer time. For example, getting a flat tire on the car on your way to an appointment is a stress that occurs at one point in time. Being out of work for a period of months is a longer-term stressor. It's important to develop skills to manage both single stressful events and longer term daily life stresses. If you have many stresses in your daily life, you may need to prioritize them or break them into smaller issues to tackle, so you're not overwhelmed trying to cope with everything at once.

Some stresses are crises; you have no warning or preparation. For example, your partner's sudden announcement that he is leaving the home may be stressful. In these crises, it may be important to remove your children and yourself from the immediate situation if possible, particularly if there is any risk of danger. You may need to sit still, to calm down, count to ten, or to take deep breaths to regain some feeling of composure. It may be helpful to say positive statements like, "I will get through this," out loud or to yourself, over and over. If you're so overwhelmed with stress you cannot function well enough to get through these first moments or hours of the crisis or to help your children, you may need to seek the support of friends, family members, or helping professionals immediately. Check your telephone directory for emergency mental health hotline numbers.

Some of the more common ways of managing the stresses of daily life may be difficult for parents with depression. Routine exercise is often suggested as a way of dealing with stress. People who have physical exercise in their daily lives seem to have greater ability to manage stress when it comes up. However, if you are a parent with depression, you may have difficulty mustering the energy to get yourself up and out to exercise. You may not be organized enough to find a baby-sitter, or you may feel that you don't deserve to take time and energy away from home to exercise. You may require support to develop an exercise plan, identify an exercise partner, or find an exercise that fits into your lifestyle and doesn't cause you greater stress or feelings of failure when you cannot follow through.

You may be encouraged to "take better care of yourself" to combat stress. This may include taking medication or visiting with a doctor or therapist regularly. Partners or family members who do not "believe" in psychiatry or psychotherapy may not support you in seeking professional help. Your well-being and the well-being of your children can be compromised by the negative attitudes of partners or family members. It may require a great deal of strength to follow through with treatment recommendations. You may feel supported by making connections with other parents in similar situations.

Other common suggestions for stress management are establishing a daily or weekly routine and nourishing spiritual connections. Creating a calendar to document the routine and make notes of special events can help a you feel on top of things—especially when the many events of your children are involved (school concerts, meetings, or other appointments). Participating in a religious community can serve several functions, including nourishing spiritual needs, helping you feel connected to a "higher power," adding meaning to life, and providing connections to other parents and families. Having your children participate in a religious education program may help you feel you are fulfilling your responsibilities as a parent. You may want to check your local telephone listings or newspaper, or talk with friends or neighbors about local churches or religious groups.

Parents are encouraged to take a "time-out" for themselves, which is often hard to do when there are children involved. It may be difficult to find a time during the day to take a bath or have a quiet cup of coffee if the children are demanding or requiring your attention. It may depend on how old your children are and whether they require constant supervision. You may have children with special emotional or behavioral needs, who require even more attention than other children. It may be more difficult for you to find baby-sitters due to your children's special needs, or because your relationships with family members, friends, or neighbors are strained. Identifying informal supports, such as family members, friends, or neighbors, and overcoming conflicts in those relationships may be important investments in your entire family's well-being. You may want to explore and/or develop baby-sitting options at your day treatment or psychosocial rehabilitation program site, if you are participating in programs such as these.

Coping with Stress

Think about times when you are stressed and how you handle your stress. Use your journal to list some things that cause you stress. Are some more "important" than others? Do some cause you more stress than others do? When are you likely to feel stressed? Is it in the morning, when you're having a hard time getting out of bed? Or, do you get more stressed in the evening, when the children are yelling at each other? Under what conditions are you most stressed?

Write about a time when you were really stressed out and "lost it." How do you feel when you think about it now? Do you feel yourself getting tense again? How did you get over it? What happened after that?

What helps you calm down? Remember that there are many books, articles, Web pages, and videotapes about managing stress. Remember that the goal is to manage stress without hurting yourself or someone else in order to provide a safe family environment. *Try to avoid being stressed out over stress.*

Managing Conflict Through Problem Solving

Conflict occurs in all relationships, between parents and partners or children, and even with strangers, like the clerk at the grocery store. People are in conflict when they don't see things the same way, or if they don't agree on how things "should" be. Conflict grows in situations where people feel their differences cannot be overcome. Most conflict is resolved when people find ways to meet half-way, to compromise. Other times, people just walk away. It's important to be able to resolve conflict without becoming so angry, tense, or frustrated that verbal or physical abuse seems to be the only answer.

A Step-by-Step Process

There are some situations of conflict that are simply dangerous and need to be handled right away without any discussion. A child who insists on running into the street to meet a friend on the other side must be kept from running in front of cars. Safety is the bottom line in any family situation and must receive attention first.

Conflicts are not usually resolved successfully in the heat of the moment. Arriving at solutions is a step-by-step process. Try the following steps the next time you find yourself in a conflict situation. You might list the steps on a file card or small piece of paper and carry them with you for use as a quick reference when you come up against conflict.

1. **Take a break.** The first step in resolving a conflict is to step back, if you can, and take a few deep breaths or even leave the room for a while, until you have calmed down enough so that you can think about things more

clearly. At the least, try not to respond to someone's angry demands until you feel you can think and talk things through more calmly. This may be difficult if your conflict is with your two-year-old, who is demanding an ice cream cone "right now!" and embarrassing you in front of friends or relatives (who may doubt your capacity to manage your toddler anyway). You may not be able to deal with your child in that same moment—in the grocery store, the restaurant, or your kitchen. You may have to carry your toddler to a quiet spot, or send your ten-year-old to her room, or go for a walk around the block yourself until things have calmed down a bit. If the conflict involves your child, be sure she is properly supervised before you leave the room or take a walk. How you handle this calming-down time will depend on the age and stage of your child and what works for you.

2. **Identify the problem—talk and listen.** The next step is to identify the conflict or problem. People don't always agree about this, in part because people's perceptions, assumptions, or expectations may be involved. This may be particularly difficult when you are depressed and feeling criticized or belittled, or if your perceptions or judgments are questioned by others. Professionals suggest there should be ground rules for solving problems that include no name-calling and telling the truth. This is especially important in situations involving individuals with psychiatric disorders, who may be called names or be treated disrespectfully by others. It's critical that each person has the opportunity to talk about his or her perceptions and listens carefully to the other person. Each person in a conflict situation, adult or child, needs to feel the other person is hearing her definition of the problem.

3. **Brainstorm potential solutions—seek help if necessary.** This can be a creative process, with all possibilities suggested and none chosen until the process is complete. It may be hard to be creative when you're having trouble thinking clearly or don't have much energy. You may want to engage your partner or another person to assist you in coming up with ideas. In thinking about potential solutions, weigh the pros and cons of each, considering what each person needs to get from this situation.

4. **Decide together on an action plan.** As you identify the steps toward achieving each solution, talk about things that might get in the way of accomplishing the solution and how to overcome them. Talk about what will happen once the problem is solved. You each may be giving in a little, but both of you will be benefiting from the outcome.

Steps like these are possible with children who are capable of talking about their problems and feelings about conflict. For younger or less experienced children, it may be necessary for you to suggest words to use and the feelings they might be feeling, based on how they looked or sounded, as well as suggest potential solutions. A child's or an adult's capacity to resolve conflicts using words will depend on his age and stage of development or level of interpersonal skills, and whether he feels this strategy has worked in the past.

Anger Is Unavoidable

Anger is a normal feeling. Anger may be a healthy response to a difficult situation or a motivator to make changes in times of trouble. When anger takes on extraordinary and unexpected proportions, it can turn into verbal or physical abuse. Managing angry feelings and expressing them appropriately, without harming someone in the process, become goals in family life. Recognizing angry feelings at the beginning of an episode, before they escalate, allows you to manage your feelings, responses, and interactions with other people better. Keeping your angry feelings to yourself may only make you more depressed.

A person's ability to express anger appropriately depends in part on her or his age and stage of development. A two-year-old expresses angry feelings by having a temper tantrum. Because he cannot yet talk about feelings or describe what is causing his stress or displeasure, he simply demonstrates angry feelings physically. Crying, stomping feet, kicking things, biting, and hitting you or a sibling are all signs of a very angry two-year-old. Unless you provide your children opportunities to practice other ways of expressing anger as they grow up, as teenagers or adults they may express anger in the same way.

Helping your children deal with angry feelings is especially difficult when they are angry with you. You may be vulnerable to your children's anger because of your diagnosis of depression and the discomfort it may cause your children. Your children may be angry because you aren't "normal," if your illness keeps them from doing the things they want. They may be angry at the lack of control they have over your illness and their inability to help you feel better. Perhaps they feel their lives are not like other children or youth their ages. A teen who has to take over family responsibilities when her mother or father needs to be in the hospital may be resentful or angry about times when she would rather be at the football game than fixing meals or baby-sitting for her younger brothers and sisters. If you are inclined to think the worst anyway, you may feel your children's anger is deserved and allow them to demonstrate their feelings in ways that are actually harmful to you. Because of your depression, you may feel less than worthy of respect and therefore allow your children to treat you rudely. Others may even encourage your children, in subtle or overt ways, to "make fun of" you because you have been labeled as having a psychiatric disorder.

It's important to try to remember that your job as a parent is to teach your children ways of expressing feelings like anger that are healthy, respectful, and safe, even though it is difficult for you or contradicts how you feel about yourself. It is particularly important for children whose parents are coping with illness or disability to have opportunities to express feelings in ways that allow them to feel they are heard and understood. It may be hard for you to hear your child's angry feelings. However, it is much better for you and your child to be able to talk about feelings than to allow her to act them out in other, potentially harmful ways.

Your child may also benefit from having an "objective" outsider to talk with about feelings—a family friend, relative, or counselor. Seeking outside help is one safe way of coping with stress, conflict, and angry feelings. Seeking help and supporting your child in developing a relationship with another adult are contributions to his current and future well-being.

What to Do About Abuse: Identifying Resources

You may now be the victim of abuse at the hands of your partner or other family members. Or you may be abusive to your partner or your children. In each of these situations, *safety* is the bottom line. You must do what you can to stay safe yourself and provide a safe environment for your children. If you are not living with your children on a twenty-four-hour-a-day basis, your visits with them need to be as safe and stress-free as possible.

If You Are the Victim

Women or men who are battered by partners or spouses may believe they are responsible for their abusers' actions. You may be reluctant to leave a situation, even though you are being abused, because you feel your children should be with their "well" parent. It may be difficult for you to make a decision about what to do if you are depressed and feel you have no options. Batterers may threaten their partners with violence or loss of custody of the children if they should leave, particularly if they have a psychiatric disorder.

Abuse may occur in homosexual relationships as well as heterosexual relationships, between men or women. If you are a gay man or a lesbian, you may feel even more vulnerable disclosing abuse and asking for help, particularly if you are a parent with a diagnosed psychiatric disorder. You may be afraid that society will view you negatively, seeing you as unfit to parent your children either because of your sexual orientation or your depression. It's important for gay or lesbian adults to seek help from providers or agencies knowledgeable about their situations and sympathetic to their issues.

What About Your Children?

As a parent, it is your role to keep your children safe, to teach them how to protect themselves from potentially dangerous situations and people, and to establish patterns of communication so that they will feel comfortable talking with you or another person if they feel threatened or are harmed in any way. If you are the person harming your children, you must seek help to learn safe, healthy ways of parenting. Children who are being abused may have no means of escape or no alternative living situations.

Your children may witness abuse in your home. Perhaps you and your partner have physical fights or loud arguments that frighten them. Researchers have discovered that the effects on children of witnessing violence can be as strong as having been abused themselves.

You may suspect someone else is abusing your children. Perhaps you observed a family member spanking them or slapping them when they misbehaved. Your partner or baby-sitter may have shaken the baby in frustration when she wouldn't go to sleep.

What to Do About Current Abuse

People need to be "ready" to deal with abuse. This depends on whether you recognize you or your children are being abused, what you think will happen if you disclose the abuse—whether you have more to lose or gain, whether you have been threatened, and whether you feel you will be believed. Unfortunately, if you are a parent with mental illness, you may fear you have much to lose or that your disclosure will be disbelieved by those who think you are "making things up." You may fear being blamed for a dangerous situation at home because of your depression. An abusive partner may threaten a parent with mental illness with losing her children if she discloses abuse or battering, knowing that parents may worry about losing custody simply because of having psychiatric diagnoses.

If you're being abused by anyone, either in a domestic violence situation or in a relationship with a helping professional or another person outside the family, you have important decisions to make. No one has the right to harm another person physically or emotionally. No one truly deserves that kind of punishment regardless of what they think they did wrong or how undeserving of love and kindness they feel themselves to be. You may find yourself in a pattern with someone—a cycle of abuse—that is difficult to break. You may be dependent on the person who abuses you for financial or emotional support, even though the price you actually pay is quite high. The partner who abuses you may be the person who drives you to weekly visits with your children. To confront that partner may be dangerous. To leave that partner may cut off your relationship with your children.

If you or your children are in immediate danger from an abuser, you must take steps to remove or protect yourself and your family from this danger. At some point, you may have to leave your apartment or home and go to stay with a supportive relative or to a shelter. You may fear the consequences if your partner is angered by your actions. You may need additional support in moving from a dangerous to a safe environment for yourself and your children.

You may need to seek the help of a professional counselor to develop the strength and courage to leave an abusive situation. You could choose to file a restraining order for police protection in situations where risk has been established. You can decide to contact the child welfare officials—the Department of Social Services or Children and Youth Services as it is known in some states—to obtain assistance in keeping your children safe and to access services that can help you and your family cope with abuse and its consequences. It may be necessary to break up your family to keep yourself and your children safe. While this may seem like a lot to give up, the long-term consequences of living with abuse take an extremely high toll.

If you are abusive, you must take the necessary steps to protect your children and to learn effective ways of parenting that do not involve abuse. Confide in someone you trust who can support you in getting help. There are many parent groups available through local community mental-health centers, clinics, and child protective services. Your pediatrician probably knows of resources in the community and may raise the issue with you if he or she sees that you are stressed by parenting responsibilities. Schools often know of parent support services and may sponsor parent education programs.

There are many resources available to people living with abuse. You can check the Yellow Pages of your telephone book under "Counselors" or under "Social and Human Services," which may have a subheading of "Crisis Intervention Services." You may want to check the government section of the telephone book under your state's listing (for example, "New Hampshire State of") and look for "Human Services Division" or "Social Services" or even "Help Line." A great deal of information is available, using a computer, on the World Wide Web. Many states have Web pages with information about abuse (for example, the Massachusetts Web page http://www.magnet.state.ma.us/dss/info-packet/ profile-abuse.htm). Other organizations have Web pages, too (for example, the National Committee to Prevent Child Abuse, http://www.childabuse.org. fs20.html).

Taking the Healthy Route

As a parent living with depression it is doubly important for you to learn healthy ways of coping with stress, managing conflict, and expressing feelings—to create a physically and emotionally safe environment for your children. It's essential to understand the impact of your past experiences on your current attitudes and behavior. If you grew up feeling bad about yourself because of the things your parents did or said to you, it may make you feel twice as bad to do or hear yourself saying the same things to your own children. If you have poor self-esteem to begin with, feeling that you are "failing" as a parent can only make you feel worse, and quite possibly even more depressed. Creating a safe environment for your family will contribute to your children's well-being as well as your own.

Chapter 6

Communicating with Children About Depression

As a parent with depression, you have choices to make about whether and how to communicate with your children about your depression. Some parents feel that "honesty is the best policy," and want to be as open as possible. Others feel ashamed or worry that their children will be burdened by knowing their parent is depressed and has an illness. Your children may ask questions about how you're feeling whether you are prepared to discuss it with them or not. Whether and how you answer them is up to you.

The purpose of this chapter is to help you make these choices, giving you suggestions for communicating with your children about depression. Communication can happen in many different ways. You may feel comfortable talking in person with your children, or maybe you would rather write them a letter. Children may prefer to listen to a tape rather than talk in person. Later in the chapter, examples are provided of typical worries children have about depression and questions they ask, with strategies for answers. Children may have strong feelings that are tough to deal with.

It helps to know yourself well enough to be able to describe your symptoms and their management to your children and other support people. You may want to explain your medications, psychotherapy, or recovery goals. We recommend identifying supportive family members or friends and making plans with them for your children's comfort and safety when you are not feeling well. Children may benefit from identifying resources and support people with you. It is helpful to plan ahead of time with your children for periods of relapse so that resources for coping are available to them.

An important goal for communicating with your children is to let them know they are important to you and that you care about their needs. You can talk with them about ways to meet their needs when you're not feeling well. You can be a role model for them, so they can communicate effectively with others.

The Pros and Cons of Communicating About Your Depression

You can decide how you wish to communicate about your depression. You may want to talk with your children, but you may not know how. Or you may be "hiding," trying to cope with the guilt, shame, and blame that people with depression often feel. You may want to talk but be worn down by your depression and not have the energy. You may think your children do not want to hear about how you feel, because they are afraid or "don't seem to care." You may not want to burden children or other family members further.

Do You Have a Choice?

In the best situation, you alone have the choice of communicating with your children about your depression. The people you tell and what you say are your decision. However, it may be quite apparent to your children when you are not feeling well. Depending on your family situation and the circumstances surrounding your treatment, information may be shared with your family members and children by doctors, social workers, or other professionals. In the worst case scenario, your children may hear stories from family members, neighbors, or even other children at school.

You may welcome your doctor's efforts to help your family understand your depression. You may regret what the neighbors or playmates say to your children. Rather than having the choice about talking to your children, discussing your illness with them may become a necessity—to help them understand the technical language of professionals, to correct misinformation provided by family members and friends, or to address any misperceptions about how you are feeling. You may not really have a choice at all.

Stigma

The stigma and negative attitudes that go along with a diagnosis of a psychiatric disorder are very powerful and may keep you from talking about your depression. Stereotypes about psychiatric disorders—images that come to many people's minds—may be quite frightening. However, it is communicating about depression that will eventually break down these stereotypes. Talking requires you to work through the stigma and stereotypes, accepting yourself as you are and planning for how you want to be. This is the point Judy makes in her story.

> *The words "mentally ill" always meant someone crazy or violent to me prior to 1970. They were just other people. In 1970, at the age of thirty, I was diagnosed with bipolar disorder, sometimes known as manic depressive illness. I felt an overwhelming shame and despair because I was now mentally ill. I knew I wasn't crazy or violent, yet the stigma stayed with me for many years. Between 1970 and 1975, I tried suicide three times. The strain on my husband and children was terrible.*
>
> *With appropriate treatment and good care, our self-esteem increases and we become more self-confident to face our family, friends, and the general public. It took me about five years to look a friend in the eye and state, "I have bipolar disorder" with absolutely no shame. In time and with help, I learned to take better care of myself. I have become a much stronger person. To those who judge me harshly I say, "Walk a mile in my shoes."*

Many people do not talk about their depression as an illness because of the shame they feel. Not talking can lead to other problems, though. Keeping a secret can take its toll. One parent we know felt that the lack of discussion about her illness caused her to develop feelings of shame and become unusually shy. This affected how she interacted with people her entire life. She wished people had been open in talking about her illness, saving her an enormous amount of worry and self-blame.

Communicating About Your Depression Can Be Risky

When you decide to communicate about your depression with your children you become vulnerable. You open yourself up to a variety of responses, which may vary greatly depending on your children's ages and how they have been treated as a result of your depression. There is, of course, the possibility of positive responses, where everyone is compassionate and totally understanding. Your children may be very supportive of you and view you as a positive role model of strength when times are tough.

However, some children may have negative responses. They may feel shame, guilt, anger, or frustration, or have concerns about inheriting or "catching" the illness. They may feel awkward in social situations or have concerns about family stability. Larry provides an example of how his depression affects his family and how difficult communication about the illness can be.

Having been diagnosed with major depression in 1989, I have had to deal with communication about my psychiatric disorder with my wife, my children, and now my grandchildren. Over this time I have had hallucinations, felt things crawling on me, heard voices, pulled my hair out, and been on medications that made me dizzy and fall down due to lowered blood pressure. So, all of my family have seen me in these various states.

I think, from the beginning, my wife never understood my illness. Since my wife was the main communicator with my children, they knew even less. Since I was diagnosed, no one has realized that I am chronically suicidal. Much of my time is spent planning and organizing for my death. Although I have been hospitalized several times, and in 1995 attempted suicide, no one was aware of my thought process.

My children, in their teen years, knew there was something abnormal with the way I acted and looked. They avoided having friends over to our house. When I attended school or social functions, I would sit by myself and stare as if I was in a trance and never got involved with the activities. My wife would tell them I was okay and these behaviors were the side effects of my medication. When I was hospitalized for being a danger to myself, my wife and children thought I was in the hospital to get my medication adjusted.

My children have grown up and are now young adults. My oldest daughter is married and has three children. My younger daughter still lives at home and my son has moved out. We all live in the same town, so they are in contact with my wife and me on a regular basis. We get together on Sunday for dinner and conversation, most of which I don't get actively involved in. Communicating even today is a difficult task.

My grandchildren are more difficult to communicate with about my illness since they are younger. When I am hospitalized, my daughter tells them I am sick and will be home shortly. They don't know I have a psychiatric disorder. On Sunday, when they come to visit, they laugh and joke about my physical symptoms. When I pull on my hair, they say I look like a "troll doll." And when I isolate myself and go into a trance, they yell "grandpa, grandpa" until they get my attention back. They are old enough now to realize that my actions are not normal, but I'm not really sure what they have been told about my depression.

Larry's situation is quite complex. He is fortunate to have a wife who supports him and helps explain things to his children. On the other hand, because he has depended on her to communicate, he is not really sure what his children have been told about his depression. Now he has grandchildren and is concerned about how they understand his behavior and appearance. Larry feels his adult children, who are now parents themselves, have the right to decide what their children, his grandchildren, are told. He is facing the challenge of opening lines of communication with children and grandchildren of many different ages.

Pros and Cons for You

Below you will find a list of pros and cons to communicating with your children and others about your depression. These are just a few. Some may describe how you feel and some may not. Additional space is provided for you to enter your own ideas. Once you have made your own list, consider the questions below. This exercise should help you to answer these questions about communicating with your children about your depression

Communicating About Your Depression

Pros

1. I might feel less blamed.

2. If people understand me better, they might have more compassion.

3. It would give people the opportunity to help me.

4. Providing accurate information breaks down stereotypes and negative attitudes about psychiatric disorders.

5. I could increase my safety by planning with family members about how to handle the times when I'm not doing well.

6. It would reduce my children's fear or guilt.

Cons

1. I might feel more shame or guilt.

2. Others may show compassion without truly understanding. I don't want pity.

3. My children may feel burdened by knowing I have an illness.

4. Hiding my depression leaves me less vulnerable to stereotypes.

5. People will be afraid of me, or for me, if they think I'm "crazy."

6. My children might feel responsible.

Add your own pros and cons:

_____   _____

_____   _____

_____   _____

_____   _____

1. What have I decided to do? _____

2. What kind of help do I need with this? _____

3. Who can help me? _____

How to Communicate with Children—Your Preferences and Theirs

You have decided to talk with your children about your depression. Or perhaps they have asked you or another family member questions like, "Why does Daddy go to the doctor all the time?" or "Why did Mommy have to go to the hospital?" Most parents find that children ask important questions at what seem to be the most inconvenient times, like on their way out the door to school, or in public places. If you are lucky and think ahead, you might have answers ready for your children. If you are like most parents, you will probably be caught off guard and sputter your way through an answer you will wish afterwards had been better. Sometimes good moments for talking just happen, like when you're going for a long drive in the car, or sitting together waiting for a television show to begin. You will want to be ready to take advantage of these moments, too.

Your Preferred Style of Communication

Families may have very different communication styles. Some families have open lines of communication—they talk all the time. Others have unspoken rules about who talks when. For example, some of us grew up in the "olden days" when the rule was, "Children are to be seen and not heard." Those of us who grew up back then may find it hard to understand that children today are encouraged in many ways to talk and ask questions by teachers at school and even by television personalities like Mr. Rogers or Barney. Some of us may not have much training from the families of our childhood about how to have open lines of communication. It's important to examine your preferred ways of communicating, particularly as they relate to the ages and stages and the abilities of your children to communicate with you.

If you want to answer your children's questions, you may have to practice communicating in new ways. Remember that communication does not only mean talking, but also communicating through our actions and any other ways that seem to work, like drawing pictures, writing notes or letters, or even making audiocassette tapes.

Children's Ages and Stages

Children vary in their ability to identify and express their feelings depending on their age and stage of development and their personality style. For example, as children's language skills develop, they are able to express themselves with words rather than by "acting out" their feelings. Some children, however, seem to have the kind of personality where they just don't ever like to talk. Even as teens or adults, they may prefer to cope with their feelings through physical activity, like exercise or sports. Often, whether children communicate depends on their relationships with people. While a preschooler might cuddle on your lap and share secrets with you, your teenager would probably prefer to confide in friends at school.

Very young children, infants, and preschoolers communicate mostly through action. You can tell when your two-year-old is angry because he'll throw a temper tantrum; he may actually throw himself down on the floor, kicking and screaming. Your three-year-old may refuse to put her coat on when it's time to leave grandma's house. Your four- or five-year-old may return to wetting his pants when his new baby sister comes home from the hospital.

Your young child learns through your actions, too. That is why it's important to try to remain calm and quiet during your toddler's tantrum, keeping him safe while he is angry, soothing him and talking with him when it's over. You can begin to help your youngster identify and express feelings with words by talking with her after the tantrum or stubborn behavior. If your child cannot tell you what or how he was feeling, it's okay to suggest the feeling he most likely had. For example, in the situation where your daughter did not want to put her coat on you might say, "You looked pretty angry to me. I bet you were angry because you didn't want to leave grandma's house." Your guess may be wrong or right but at least you have opened the door to talking about feelings.

Young children learn that they can depend on people if their lives are predictable. Children are most likely to feel secure if their days are organized with routine and structure. The more you can do to provide daily routine children can depend on, the more comfortable they will be. The more information you can give your child about what will happen next, the better he will be able to cope.

The young child hasn't developed a sense of time yet. This makes it more difficult to answer questions like, "How long will Mommy be gone? When is Mommy coming back?" if you need to be hospitalized. With the youngest children, it is important to be as clear and concrete as possible. If you have to be away for a time, to go into the hospital, for instance, you or another family member or friend might use a calendar and mark the days you'll be gone on the calendar with stickers, marking the day you will return with a star. It may be hard to answer questions about where Daddy is, because young children have little notion of what the "hospital" is. It will help them to know that you are safe and comfortable in a place where people are taking good care of you.

If your child is in elementary school, he or she may be much more talkative, though not always about what you want to hear. For example, it may seem like "nothing" is ever going on at your child's school because the only response you ever get to your questions about what he or she learned in school today is "Nothing." On the other hand, your child may have a great deal to tell you about his friend's new toy or video game. The school-age child may be most willing to talk about things that interest him or her.

Your teenager probably not only routinely says he or she is doing "nothing," but also probably goes "nowhere" with "nobody you know." While this might not be true, it's certainly the case that teens often keep their own company or talk only with their friends. A parent may be an inconvenient nuisance or a teenager's best friend, depending on how relationships have developed. Communicating with teenagers requires consistent effort. You might have to spend time just "being there" near the refrigerator when they come in to eat, so that you're available in case they want to talk. You may not be knowledgeable about the new music groups or clothing styles, but simply being available to listen, and nonjudgmental when they bring up topics of conversation, can go a long way toward real communication. If you and your teen develop some form of casual communication, even on an occasional basis, you will be better able to talk about more difficult topics or situations, like your depression.

Ways to Communicate

Communicating with children differs greatly depending on their ages and stages and your skills and preferences. Here are some suggestions we have for communicating with your children. Space is provided to check off your preferences and add others we haven't thought of.

My Communication Preferences

Age

Ways my child and I communicate

0–2 years

__ Showing love and affection

__ Holding her

__ Talking to him

__ Gentle touching

__ Rocking

__ Cuddling

__ Singing

__ Imitating sounds she makes

__ Being there when I can

__ _____

2–5 years

__ Beginning to label feelings

__ Drawing pictures

__ Going for walks

__ Providing reassurance

__ Singing songs

__ Telling stories

__ Explaining things in simple words

__ _____

5–12 years

__ Being concrete

__ Using her words

__ Getting down to his level

__ Talking about feelings

__ Singing songs

__ Telling stories

__ Reading books

__ Playing games

__ Going for rides in the car

__ Eating meals together

__ _____

13–18 Years __ Talking about feelings
__ Discussing things honestly
__ Keeping door to communication open
__ Providing literature
__ Being available
__ Talking on her timetable, when she is ready
__ Respecting his growing independence

__ _____

Adult __ Treating her like an adult
__ Discussing my illness openly and working together on communication with next generation
__ Answering questions
__ Talking about feelings
__ Meeting together with my doctor, therapist, or case manager

__ _____

Styles—The Way Your Child Communicates Best

It's very important with children of any age that you try to figure out the things that interest your child, and his preferred style of communication. Some children are quite talkative. Others prefer to be moving around all the time. Others seem to be able to talk for hours on the telephone but not quite so well in person. More introspective, quieter children might like keeping a diary or listening to tapes in their rooms. The more you know about your child, the better able you will be to match his style of communicating with your attempts. You will be most successful if you determine the best match, which will probably change when your child enters the next developmental stage.

Your child may have signals that let you know when she is ready to talk. Total silence may be a clear signal that your child needs to talk but is unable or unwilling to, for some reason. You might find that letting your child be silent for a while gives him the necessary time to figure things out in his own mind. A child who is quiet for too long, however, may need to be prodded into talking, perhaps by a best friend or a trusted adult or family member, if she is unwilling to talk with you.

Your child may feel more comfortable talking with another person for several reasons. The first is that it's normal for children of certain ages to distance themselves from their parents. The youngster who feels confident starting preschool or kindergarten may appear to go through an "I don't need my mommy" phase and not want you to greet his teacher or enter the classroom. Likewise, the teenager who is trying to separate from parents and family may actively confide in a favorite teacher, baseball coach, or relative. Second, your child may feel that you are vulnerable or overwhelmed with your own problems and not want to trouble you or add to your burden. This is not uncommon for children whose parents have any type of illness or chronic condition. While you may feel jealous of the attention your children give to these other adults, your children may simply be acting in an age-appropriate manner or just trying to help by not worrying you. Psychologists who study the children of parents with psychiatric disorders have found that having another adult available to talk with helps children cope.

It might help to start by thinking about a typical day in your child's life. Is your child physically active from the moment she gets out of bed in the morning? Or is he slow to wake up and quieter, perhaps always reading a book? Does she have favorite toys or television characters, like Barney or Big Bird? If they are teenagers, are they constantly on the telephone with their friends or asking for rides to the shopping mall? What are the signals you notice when your children want to talk? How can you tell what mood your children are in? Are there times when it's better or worse to try to talk with them? If there are others who know your children well, you might ask them about their perceptions of your children or their experiences communicating with them. You can use the next activity to develop a list of your child's interests and activities. From this list, you will be able to develop ideas about the best ways to communicate with your child.

What Does My Child Enjoy?

On the blank lines provided, describe your child's interests and activities. What are the things he likes to do and talk about each day? If she is not old enough to tell you or does not talk much, how do you know what she is thinking and feeling? How is your child most comfortable communicating? If you have more than one child, describe the others on another piece of paper.

_____

_____

_____

_____

_____

You may want to try:

1. Writing a letter to your child. Read it over and make sure you are saying what you want to say. You may mail the letter or use it as a guide when you talk with your child.

2. Making an audio tape. Listen to the tape and check your voice tones. Make sure that what you say makes sense. Will your child understand you? Use the tape as a communication link or as a practice tape for eventual face-to-face talking.

3. Making a video tape. In today's world, children are attentive to video tapes. Make sure you are somewhat relaxed and feel comfortable when you make your video. Review the video to be sure you are communicating at the right level for those who will watch it. Use the video as a practice tool or let your children view it and ask questions later.

There are many books available for children whose parents have depression. You may want to have books available for your child or teenager to read. You may want to read these books together. Check your local public library or book-store. You will find our list and reviews of the selection of children's books we've read at the end of this book in the Resources section.

Children's Common Worries and Questions

As children grow and develop, their activities, interests, needs, and worries change. So, too, do their questions about your depression. There are common themes, however, to questions asked by children of any age whose parents have an illness.

"What Did I Do Wrong?"

It is quite common for children to blame themselves or take responsibility if things are going wrong at home: "Mom is sick; it must be my fault." The benefit for children in thinking they are responsible for your depression is that it helps them believe they have some control over a situation in which they are probably feeling quite helpless. This belief may lead them to think they have the power to keep bad things from happening or to make everything better again, if only they could figure out what to do. This often leads to questions like, "What could I have done to prevent Dad from freaking out?" It's important to reassure your children that your depression is not the consequence of anything they have done wrong.

"What Can I Do to Make Things Better?"

Children may speculate that if only they were better behaved or ate all the food on their plates or made their beds everyday, they would solve all your prob-lems. They may try very hard to be perfect students, getting straight As on their report cards so that you will feel better. While good behavior or great grades cer-tainly may briefly make you happy, your children are simply unable to cure your depression. When they discover that getting straight As does not make you feel better, they may become more angry and frustrated. It's important to remind your children many times, at every age and stage of development, that they are not the cause of your depression and do not bear responsibility for your recovery.

"Why Do You Act That Way in Front of My Friends?"

Your children are as vulnerable as you are to the stigma and negative attitudes surrounding mental illness. Because you have a mood disorder they may feel ashamed, in the same way you do. It's important to remember that, depending on their ages, it may be age-appropriate for them to be embarrassed about you anyway. Parents of fifth- and sixth-graders may find they no longer get kisses when they drop their children off at school in the morning. Junior high youngsters may want you to park down the street when you pick them up from the school dance. It is quite normal, though oftentimes annoying, for teenagers to avoid acknowledging the existence of their parents, particularly in public situations.

Having a parent with depression may increase children's anxiety in these circumstances, because your illness or medications may make you act or look different from other parents. Children may be reluctant to bring their friends home because they don't know how you will be feeling. Children and adolescents may have questions about whether you will be coming to a school event. They may be concerned about whether it will be a good or bad day for you and how you will look to their friends. If you are sensitive to these issues and avoid attending school events to protect your children from embarrassment, they may wonder why you don't go. They may ask why Mom or Dad never joins in family events. They may ask if they will ever have a "normal" family life together.

It is important to remember the ages and stages of your children or teenagers when you are thinking about whether you embarrass them and what to do about it. You may just have to guess whether they want you to go to the school event or not and see what their responses are. You may have to compromise on where you pick them up after the dance or an afternoon at the mall, keeping their safety in mind, of course. They will appreciate your respect and sensitivity to these issues, whether or not you are ill or well.

"Will I Get Sick, Too?"

Another common worry that children may ask about is whether your depression is hereditary or contagious: "Will I be like Mom when I get older?" "Can I catch her disease?" Your teenager may be reluctant to disclose feelings or fears, out of concern that they are the beginning signs of illness. One parent told us her son did not want to talk about his symptoms of depression because he was afraid that "I'll discover I have your illness, and I don't think I can live with it." You may share these worries, and find yourself interpreting their every misbehavior as a sign of developing illness. It may help to obtain information from your doctor or other professional sources about whether your mood disorder does have a hereditary component. Your doctor might be able to meet with you and your children to talk about what researchers have concluded about these issues.

If you would like to obtain more information about your mood disorder and whether there is a hereditary component, your physician or therapist may be able to tell you. The public library may have reading materials, but they may be older and not reflect the latest in research findings. The community mental health center near you may have pamphlets available. Other sources of up-to-date information are organizations like the National Mental Health Association (1-800-969-NMHA), the National Alliance for the Mentally Ill (1-800-950-6264), or the National Alliance for Research on Schizophrenia and Depression (1-800-829-8289). Researchers are finding that the environment in which children grow up may be just as important as genetics in determining how they function as adults and whether they develop problems. This is important, because it means there is much you can do to increase the likelihood that your children will do well.

You may want to think ahead about questions your children might have about your depression. Here are some examples of common questions. Fill in others your children might ask or have already asked. Take time to prepare your answers.

Questions and Answers

List your child's questions   **Think about your answers**

Example: What's wrong with Mommy? _____

Example: Is Daddy mad at me? _____

Example: Will I get sick, too? _____

Example: What did I do wrong? _____

_____   _____

_____   _____

_____   _____

_____   _____

_____   _____

To aid you in answering your child's questions, it may be useful to practice ahead of time. You can be yourself or try taking the point of view of your child. This can be accomplished by the following:

1. Find a friend or relative you feel comfortable talking with.

2. Set up a situation where your friend or family member asks questions your child might ask, or try asking questions as if you were your child.

3. Answer these questions so you feel confident with the way you answer.

4. You may want to audio or video tape these role playing sessions so you can analyze how you responded and whether you are communicating at the correct level.

Describing How You Feel

You must really understand your depression or mood swings to explain them to your children. This means being able to identify when you're feeling well and when you are not feeling well and learning about things that help you feel better or make you less able to cope. Remember that you are not just your illness or the diagnostic label someone has assigned to you. You are a complex human being with many strengths and interests that have nothing to do with having an illness. When you think about the things you would like to say to your children about yourself, remember to tell them about all of you and not just your depression. This is as important to your children as it is to you, because they look to you as a role model, someone to be like when they grow up. Their image of you is shaped, in significant ways, by what you believe and communicate about yourself. They incorporate their image of you into their own identity.

Many people are very much aware of the impact of their moods on their daily lives. You probably know your better days and worse days. On those bad days, you may notice that you're sleeping more than usual or that your appetite has disappeared. You may constantly feel "down." If you are completely drained of energy, you may stop taking care of yourself or getting out of bed in the morning. You may be preoccupied with certain thoughts or compelled to perform certain actions for no apparent reason. You may lose track of who you are, where you are, or why you're even alive.

Some people with mood disorders always feel one certain way. They may notice very little change in how they feel, appear, or behave from day to day. Others are more changeable, with moods or thoughts that fade in and out. Some people have one episode of depression that is time-limited. Others struggle with mood instability for a lifetime. Those individuals with episodic illnesses may have periods of relative wellness that alternate with periods of illness. Sometimes the periods last hours, sometimes days, months, or even years. For people who are trauma survivors, certain things—events, places, types of interactions—may trigger times of great emotional difficulty and negative feeling.

Knowing Yourself

The first step in being able to describe your depression is to identify when you're feeling better and when you're feeling worse and to make a list of the signs of each. Use the checklist below to organize your thoughts. Are you the only one who recognizes these signs, or are they apparent to family members or friends? Talking together about good times and bad times may help you think about signs of feeling good or feeling bad that you might not have considered on your own.

When I'm Feeling Well, I:	**When I'm Not Feeling Well, I:**
__ *feel like getting up in the morning*	__ *don't have any energy*
__ *can focus on my job*	__ *feel overwhelmed by everyday tasks*
__ *like to spend time with family*	__ *avoid everybody and stay in my room*

__ _____   __ _____

__ _____   __ _____

__ _____   __ _____

__ _____

The second step is to make a list of things that help you feel better. Different strategies work for different people. Some people find keeping to a schedule each day helps them stay stable. Others find regular exercise or eating healthy food helpful. Making time for practicing relaxation techniques helps some people manage anxiety.

Things That Make Me Feel Better:

__ *getting some exercise*   __ _____

__ *making quiet time to relax*   __ _____

__ *talking with friends*   __ _____

__ _____   __ _____

Now make a list of the things that contribute to feeling worse. Can you tell when you're getting over-tired? Do you need to avoid crowded, noisy, group activities because they are overstimulating? Does drinking alcohol help you cope in the short run but contribute to feeling worse in the long run?

Things That Make Me Feel Worse:

__ *not getting enough sleep*   __ _____

__ *running from activity to activity*   __ _____

__ *not taking my medication*   __ _____

__ _____   __ _____

It is helpful to look for patterns in how you feel. If you can see the patterns in either direction—shifting from feeling better to worse or worse to better—you can begin to identify what contributes to feeling bad or what helps you feel better. Can you tell when you are starting to go downhill? Think of these as "early warning signs." You might want to ask family members or friends who know you well for their input. They may notice changes in how you act or appear before you do. By involving relatives or friends in this activity, you can begin to develop ways of supporting each other and your children in coping with your depression.

"Early warning signs" that I'm not feeling well:

__ *staying up too late*

__ *feeling lost or disoriented while driving*

__ *feeling overwhelmingly confident*

__ *not recognizing myself in the mirror*

__ *worrying that I am being watched*

__ *anxiety around sharp objects*

__ _____

__ _____

__ _____

__ _____

__ _____

__ _____

Making an Action Plan

Once you have organized your thoughts and described your depression, you can begin to think about planning ahead with your children for their comfort and safety when you are not feeling well. It's important to communicate with your children about the indicators of feeling well and feeling unwell you identified. You can talk about your symptoms with your children. Julia provided this example.

> *Your nose runs when you have a cold. I cry when I have depression. Crying is a symptom caused by chemicals in my brain. It does not mean that I hurt the way you hurt when you cry. It does not mean that life is too hard.*

Your children should be aware of the early warning signs that indicate a relapse of your illness. Many children are taught to dial 911 in emergency situations. Your child can learn to call a relative or trusted friend when he or she recognizes your early warning signs.

You should also take advantage of this opportunity to talk about any medications you take or treatment you're participating in. Children may have questions about medication, particularly if they have had health education lectures in school about drugs and substance abuse. Explain the difference between street drugs and medications prescribed by doctors. Talk about the use and misuse of medications and how you guard against misusing yours. Your children may need to know what symptoms you have when you have a reaction to your medication and what steps to take.

If you are in psychotherapy or group therapy, you may describe these sessions to your children, without going into specific details. You may want to bring your children if there are family activities at your agency, so they become familiar with the setting and the friends you have made there. It will reassure your child to know that you are taking steps to manage your depression.

The next step in making an action plan is to build a list of resources or supports with your children. Resources can be people, places, or activities that are supportive and that help you cope. You may have resources you rely on: a friend or neighbor, community mental-health center or psychosocial rehabilitation clubhouse, or regular participation in a religious group or parent group. Resources that are places or activities should be routinely accessible, and a significant few should be available on a twenty-four-hour basis, for example, the emergency hotline at your community mental-health center. Make an up-to-date list of phone numbers; be sure to list area codes if some are long distance.

Talk with your children about who, what, or where helps them feel comfortable. Your children will have their own list of supportive people, places, and activities: a favorite aunt or grandmother, school or after-school program, active participation in team sports or Girl Scouts. These resources may be different from yours, and you may actually feel uncomfortable with these people knowing about your illness. However, the resource people your children identify probably should be informed about your depression, for your children's sake. Again, put together current phone numbers for these resources, so that your child can reach them when he or she needs to.

After you have discussed your early warning signs and identified resources, it is essential to talk about when it's okay for your child to ask for help. Your child should understand that it is important to take action if you can no longer help yourself. You may find that your judgment is impaired when you're not feeling well. These are times when your child must be empowered to contact resources and take the necessary action, even if it means dialing 911 when a situation has reached crisis proportions. If you make a plan ahead of time, it is likely that you will minimize crises because you will have identified and informed your children about resources that can be accessed before a situation gets out of control.

Complete the action plan below with your children. It will help them understand your psychiatric disorder and know there are resources to help when you are not feeling well.

Feeling Well Action Plan

Feeling Well: List ways you know when Mom/Dad is feeling well.
Example: *Mom/Dad has plenty of energy to fix your breakfast.*

_____

_____

_____

_____

Not So Well: List ways you know when Mom/Dad is not feeling well.
Example: *Mom/Dad is sleeping too much or too little.*

_____

_____

_____

_____

Help Themselves: List things that help Mom/Dad feel better.
Example: *Get some exercise, talk with friends, take medication*

_____

_____

_____

_____

Who Can Help? Name some people who can help.
Example: *Relatives, friends, school counselor*

_____

_____

_____

_____

Take Action: What should I do if things are not going well?

    Example: *Call grandma.*

_____

_____

_____

_____

Some parents worry that going through steps like these and talking with children in this way may make them feel more responsible and burdened by their parent's illness. The goal of this type of planning is to let children know that you are doing what you can to manage your depression, that you are taking steps toward recovery, and to give them alternatives when you are not coping well. A plan can help prevent crises and increase children's comfort and control in a situation, because they know when to seek help and whom to contact. Rather than foster feelings of responsibility or burden, developing a plan with your children will foster self-reliance and independence. Your children are not alone in coping with your depression and neither are you.

The Most Important Message

The most important message you can communicate to your children, regardless of their ages or stages, is how important they are to you. Whether they are with you twenty-four hours a day, or you visit with them occasionally, or they are adults and living on their own, they will have worries and questions about your depression. Talking with them about your depression in person, on the telephone, or in tapes or letters will help them to know you better and allay their fears. If you are caring for them twenty-four hours a day, having an action plan in place will reassure them that you are supporting them and helping yourself cope with your depression.

Chapter 7

Emphasizing the Positive in Relationships with Children

No one gives you an owner's manual when you have a baby. Instead, most people feel like they are parenting by the seat of their pants. Each new day with children brings a new set of challenges and demands. If you are living with depression, you may be inclined to feel indecisive or overwhelmed anyway. Children or teenagers can leave you feeling less than confident about yourself or as a parent. Your partner, other family members, or helping professionals may further undermine your confidence by questioning your judgment or ability to be a good parent. It's easy to fall into the trap of negative thinking about yourself and your children.

Parents living with depression may be more likely to interpret children's behavior negatively or to take it personally. You may find yourself thinking that your toddler is throwing food from the high chair on purpose, to make a mess for you to clean up. If your preteen doesn't use a napkin at dinnertime, you might feel responsible and judge yourself harshly. Understanding "normal" child development and typical behavior-management issues by reading books or talking with your pediatrician or other parents can help you function better as a parent and not blame yourself too much for your shortfalls. Parenting is a humbling experience for us all!

Relationships are a two-way street. How you feel and act affects your children, and they affect you. It is important to "accentuate the positive" and "eliminate the negative," to quote the old song. Focusing on your strengths will help you feel better and do better as a parent. Focusing on your children's strengths will help you invest in your relationship with them.

This chapter is not a complete course in child development or child behavior management. You can obtain information about these topics from the many books and pamphlets, videotapes, and other resources available at the public library, local bookstore, your pediatrician's office, or on the Internet. There are many guides to helping your child achieve developmental milestones and negotiate typical childhood dilemmas, like beginning preschool or adjusting to the birth of a new sibling. Take the time to browse through the shelves on parenting at the library or bookstore. Talk with your pediatrician. Search the Web for information on individual topics. Educate yourself about the broad range of what is considered "normal."

How Your Children "Make" You Feel

Professionals will tell you no one *makes* you feel anything. Theoretically, you are in charge of your feelings and can choose to feel one way or another. Technically speaking, you may have a specific feeling about what another person does or says; what this feeling turns out to be is up to you. You have the opportunity to turn any situation into a positive and the responsibility for making this happen as much as possible. Attitude is everything! But why do great opportunities sometimes feel like tremendous burdens?

Parents living with depression are inclined to misinterpret their children's behavior, as the behavior is so often seen through the lens of low self-esteem, feelings of helplessness, or disorganized thinking. You may have unrealistic expectations or wishes for your children's behavior that suit your needs for peace and quiet, match your low energy level, or lighten your feelings of being burdened. You may judge either yourself or your children harshly when they don't meet these expectations. You may worry that your children's misbehavior is a sign of a developing depression or other psychiatric disorder that you have passed on to them.

The Role of "Normal" in Behavior and Feelings

Being aware of the wide range of what is normal in children's development can help you determine whether your children's behavior is intentional and meant to hurt you, reflects "failure" on your part, is the symptom of a developing psychiatric disorder, or is simply an age-appropriate expression of "where they're at." Let's consider some fairly normal or age-appropriate scenarios across age groups and how you might feel in these situations. Remind yourself that all parents have these feelings—the negative and positive—whether or not they are living with depression. Your feelings may differ in nature or degree from those of other parents depending on how well you are feeling or how depressed you are. But, more than likely, you're not alone in feeling the way you do.

Infants

It's natural for infants to cry—a lot. This is their only way to communicate what they need, whether it's a clean diaper, food, drink, sleep, or relief from teething pain. Unfortunately, you have to figure out why they are crying and provide a solution. For example, a baby who is crying may require a certain amount of soothing to help her feel safe and secure. This may involve giving your infant a soft blanket or stuffed toy to sleep with, humming, singing, playing a tape of lullaby music, and so on. This kind of nurturing may be required at any time—day or night. You may not identify your infant's need right away, especially when you're first getting to know each other. It may be hard to think of creative ways to solve the crying problem in the middle of the night or when you're feeling down. You may feel frustrated and upset with yourself, or you may become exhausted, without the energy or the inclination to soothe or comfort anyone! It's really important to remind yourself that your baby is not crying to frustrate you or to remind you of how helpless you feel or what a failure you are as a parent, even though these are feelings you might have.

Resist the urge to shake your baby. If your stress level is high, place your baby in her crib or another safe place and go to another part of your home to calm down. Call a friend, a relative, or even a helping professional for advice. Finding support can help you when you need suggestions for calming your infant, someone to vent to, or if your feelings of frustration are skyrocketing.

Playing with infants is important. Babies enjoy toys that rattle or squeak or have interesting patterns and colors. Infants explore much of the world by grabbing things and putting them into their mouths. Be sure that toys are not so small that your infant could accidentally swallow or choke on them and that medications or harmful products are not within their grasp. Infants need stimulation from you when they are awake. This can be accomplished through talking, smiling, singing and holding your infant, as well as interesting them in toys or household objects.

Toddlers

Toddlers are starting to crawl, climb, walk, and talk, though they are mostly parroting words and phrases they hear from you or the television. Keep your expectations in check—they will still have trouble putting their needs into words. Toddlers have temper tantrums, in part because they are not yet able to communicate, and they are frustrated. Their temper tantrums may be frustrating for you, too, because it's not always easy to tell what is triggering them, and figuring out how to stop them is often difficult. Tantrums are guaranteed to happen in inconvenient or embarrassing places, like in the car or grocery store, adding to your discomfort. You may be angry because the people in the grocery store line behind you looked at you disapprovingly. You may be frightened by what would seem to be unmitigated rage in your toddler; she may remind you of how angry you feel sometimes. This may add to your worry that she is going to grow up to be as depressed as you are.

Don't consider discipline as the only response to a tantrum, because your child is probably not intentionally misbehaving. Keep your toddler safe by containing her until the tantrum is finished. Help her put her feelings into words by suggesting how she might feel. Wait until the tantrum has subsided to talk about the incident.

Toddlers also challenge limits, in part because they are beginning to understand what limits are. That's why your toddler will say "okay" to your request, then turn around and do the opposite, usually with a smile on his face. If you find yourself saying, "Don't you get it?" to your toddler, you most likely have your expectations set too high. Your toddler will eventually understand, but expect to have to repeat these rules often. This can be difficult when you're feeling angry, frustrated, or tired. In your blackest moment, you may feel hopeless about your toddler ever learning anything. All parents feel this way. Don't let your depression drag you down into an escalating cycle of negative thoughts about yourself or your toddler.

Preschoolers

Along with frequently saying "No!" to requests you make, your preschooler will start to question nearly everything during this stage of development. "Why?" may be a common response to your requests. Preschoolers are still learning to communicate their needs and feelings with words. They may whine, fuss, and grab things from their friends, pushing and hitting in the process. They knock things down, like block towers, just to see what happens next. Your preschooler is learning about behavior and its consequences and discovering her ability to influence the behavior of others. She may insist on doing everything herself, like brushing her teeth or pouring her juice, even if she doesn't do these tasks well.

Consequently, your preschooler may begin to be a lot more work and require a great deal more of your energy than he did as a baby or toddler. His continual questions can annoy you. He may routinely get into trouble with his siblings and friends as he experiments with his behavior and in relationships. You may be constantly breaking up battles. Your life may feel even more chaotic and disorganized, as you have trouble keeping up with him.

If your medications have the side effect of making you lethargic, this is the time when you will really begin to feel stressed by having no energy, as his demands for attention and management increases. If you feel like you want to be alone or need relaxation time to stay healthy, you will need to address this to preserve your well-being. Many people find babies enjoyable, while more independent, mobile toddlers and preschoolers pose a different challenge altogether. You are not alone if you feel this way. This may be the time to join a parent group. You may need additional support to function well at this stage!

School-Aged Children

School-aged children continue to express a natural desire to be independent and show their parents they can do things by themselves. Children at this age may act "grown up," but don't expect them to behave like adults. Limit testing, whining, and occasional temper tantrums are still considered normal behaviors.

The biggest risk parents with depression run at this age is depending on their children too much to behave themselves and not cause trouble or to perform tasks around the house, like baby-sitting younger siblings or cooking dinner. While these are expectations that school-aged children can fulfill over time as they mature, your need for support or lack of resources may result in them taking on too much, too soon. Your school-aged child will still misbehave every once in a while and needs time to play, as well as manage school work, sports, and other activities. If you are concerned about how much or even how little you expect of your school-aged child, talk with a trusted friend, relative, another parent, or a helping professional to get another perspective.

Teenagers

Adolescence is a difficult stage for teenagers and parents alike. Teens are usually dealing with powerful hormonal changes that can bring physical and emotional consequences. Teens may express a strong need to be accepted by their peers and a stronger need to be independent, questioning family values as well as your rules. While it's important to recognize the normal turmoil that occurs during adolescence, it is important to continue to set and enforce limits. You can also expect your teenager to shun public displays of affection. He may ask you not to call him "Jimmy" anymore, but prefer "James."

It is critical that you *do not take adolescence personally.* Your teenager has to work hard to separate successfully from you, to live an independent adult life. If he refuses to follow your rules, it's not because he sees you as weak or vulnerable because of your illness. He is probably not trying to hurt you intentionally, though your feelings of guilt about how your depression may have affected his life might make you think so. Teenagers rebel because they are trying to assert their independence. They think they can make their own rules. If she seems embarrassed by you, it's not because you have depression. All teenagers are embarrassed by their parents. Try to separate your own feelings about and interpretations of your teenager's behavior from what is normal adolescence.

Think It Over

Think about situations in the past week when you noticed your were reacting to your children's behavior. Select a specific incident and write a few sentences about it on a piece of paper or in your journal. It might help to split the page into two columns—one for describing your child's behavior and one to write down your reactions. What was your child doing? Was it within the range of normal for her age and stage? If you're not sure, check with some reliable sources—a book on child development, another parent whose judgment you trust, or your pediatrician or nurse practitioner. What was your reaction? Was your reaction justifiable? Or were you overreacting or misinterpreting your child's behavior? Again, check your reactions with another parent, a friend or relative, or a helping professional. Try this for several weeks in a row to look for patterns in your reactions. For example, are you inclined to feel your child is doing things on purpose to annoy you? Do you consistently take things too personally? Draw a clear line in your journal between your child's behavior and your own feelings. This will help you separate the two. Seeing the circumstances in black and white will also help you consider whether they fall within the range of normal, decide whether to obtain outside consultation, and begin to make changes.

How Your Behavior Affects Your Children

The most obvious, direct way your behavior affects your children is the way you respond to them and, especially, discipline them. Your parents may have used punishment to manage your behavior. As a result, it may seem like second nature for you to use similar methods with your own children. This was the case for Bob, who recalled how he was disciplined, how it affected his feelings of self-worth, and how it influenced the way he dealt with and related to his own children.

> *Physical discipline, or should I say punishment, like spankings by hand or being hit with a wooden ruler, was what I was raised with. I was abused by my parents and other authority figures who shared the same "spare the rod, spoil the child" approach toward discipline. The spankings I received when I was growing up made me fearful of my parents and teachers. It definitely lowered my self-worth, my self-confidence, and my ability to be socially comfortable.*
>
> *In my own family, discipline of the children was left to me. I disciplined my kids in the same way I was disciplined. I was never aware of other ways to discipline, such as "time-outs." Looking back, I feel I was abusive with my children, and I deeply regret the way I disciplined my own kids. Now that they are grown, I have apologized to them for how I treated them. The physical discipline approaches that I used definitely damaged my relationship with my kids.*

No matter what methods were used when you were growing up or what methods you have used with your children up to this point, you can choose how to approach your relationship with your child from this moment on. You can decide whether you want your child to fear you or respect you, depending on what strategies you use. Focusing on strengths and good behavior is more effective than punishment, and this focus contributes to children feeling good about themselves and feeling good about their relationship with you.

Your behavior and attitudes affect your children in less obvious, even passive ways, too. Not paying enough attention can affect children's sense of self-esteem and personal value. If you are irritable and grumpy all the time, your children learn to steer clear of you. You may miss out on valuable opportunities to build your relationship with them because they expect that you won't feel like talking, or that you'll be too tired to play. If you focus only on the negative and are obsessed with past mistakes, your children learn to expect the worst and to try to be perfect, which only adds stress to their lives. If you set goals that are too high for yourself or for them, they learn that people usually fail. You have significant influence over your children's perception of the world, teaching them to see it as a positive, welcoming, friendly place, or as a place where bad things happen all the time and people can't be trusted.

How you feel about yourself, therefore, and whether you take care of yourself affect your children a great deal. If you feel better, you're more likely to be more available to your children and interact positively with them. In addition, you can be an important role model of healthy behavior and a balanced lifestyle. You can focus on the positive in yourself and work on your self-esteem. You can "give yourself a break" and not judge yourself too harshly when you don't achieve what you hoped, or make a mistake. You can apologize. You can eat healthy foods when you're hungry and go to sleep when you are tired. You can call the doctor when you're sick. You can make time to exercise regularly and devote energy to dressing carefully and fixing your hair. You can nurture your relationship with your adult partner. All these activities, while they seem to be focused on you, actually demonstrate to your children on a daily basis that you care enough about them to take care of yourself, to be there for them. Allowing your children to see you care for yourself teaches them the importance of taking care of themselves, too.

Investing in Yourself

Purchase a daily or weekly planner. It's a great way to take a load off your mind, literally. A planner can help you stay better organized, allow you to see how much time you spend with your children, meeting their needs, and keep track of how much time you allow for your own needs. Schedule in time for yourself and your daily tasks as well as time for your children and their activities. Make an appointment with yourself to exercise or practice meditation or attend yoga class. Maintaining a positive relationship with your children requires you to maintain a balance between meeting their needs and meeting your own.

Accentuate the Positive

The most effective strategies you can use for building relationships with your children and managing their behavior, to teach them life skills and keep them safe, are strategies that "accentuate the positive." Two ways to do this are to focus on working with children's strengths and by providing opportunities for personal growth.

Working with Children's Strengths

It can be very difficult, particularly if you are in a depressive episode, to focus on strengths—your children's or your own. Negative thoughts and attitudes give rise to negative cycles of behavior and interactions. You may find yourself constantly nagging your child about one thing or another. It may become more and more difficult to think of punishments for your child, because you may have already taken everything away.

Unless you can identify and begin to work with your children's strengths, there can be no hope for changing their behavior or improving your relationship with them. If you have become focused on negatives, this shift to positives might be difficult. You must identify strengths and acknowledge any positive events or moments during the day. Begin to look closely. Start by finding one thing. It doesn't matter what it is, as long as it is positive. It can be as simple as the way he brushes his teeth. Begin to praise your child. "You did a great job brushing your teeth before you went to bed." We know it sounds silly, but you can't turn around a negative behavior or relationship cycle unless you begin to identify strengths.

You may have to strategize to maximize opportunities for success. Punishing your toddler for behaviors typical of children his age, like spilling his juice or not using a fork, will only result in lowering his self-esteem. Prepare ahead of time for the mess by spreading newspapers under the high chair so clean-up is easier, and enjoy mealtime with your toddler. Focus on his success getting those beans into his mouth and not on all the vegetables he drops on the floor!

Increase the level of praise as you identify more things your child does well. Perhaps she brought in the newspaper that morning. Let her know she did a good job, and that you appreciate it. Maybe he tucked his shirt into his pants before he went to school. Tell him he looked nice. Find anything positive and talk about it. You will find that the frequency of positive behavior increases. If it's a relationship issue, begin to acknowledge positive interactions, too. "I really enjoyed riding in the car to the video store with you yesterday," or "I love it when we watch television together."

You can encourage positive behavior by using concrete rewards as well. Children enjoy earning privileges. Make these contingencies "do-able." The likelihood of success should be high. For example, perhaps your school-aged child could stay up later on Friday evening to watch a favorite television show if he brushes his teeth before he goes to bed five nights out of the preceding seven.

Evidence of the Positives

Try keeping a list of positive behaviors that your child exhibited each day for a week. It will help you focus your attention on strengths. Remember, strengths can be more than good behavior. Your child may have attributes or characteristics that you value. Perhaps she has a good sense of humor or is especially kind to her grandparents. Praise these attributes, too, and jot down evidence of all her good attributes whenever you see it. Use the chart below or make your own chart to post on the refrigerator. This can be a joint project between you and your child. Looking together at all the positive things your child did can be a nice way to end the day and will encourage more of the same behavior.

My Child's Positives

Week Of:	*Positive* Behaviors Observed Today
Monday	
Tuesday	
Wednesday	
Thursday	
Friday	
Saturday	
Sunday	

Opportunities for Personal Growth

It's your job as a parent to help your child learn self-control and responsibility and, at the same time, help him feel good about himself. It's a tall order, and even the most loving, even-tempered parents find themselves pulling their hair out from time to time. You may think your child will never learn how to take care of herself or to function well in the world. One way you can provide opportunities to build life skills is by providing choices and helping your child practice making decisions. For example, even a toddler can choose a bedtime snack if you specify the choices. You can give your child the power to make a choice that will be acceptable to you. This is a "win-win" situation for you both.

You can ask your older child for input in setting limits and rules and review the consequences of various courses of behavior with her. Again, offer your child or teenager some control and responsibility by providing them with choices that are acceptable to you. Then encourage her to figure out what will happen as the result of each choice and what your response will be.

This kind of active parenting may be challenging to parents living with depression. It requires a certain level of energy, the ability to think clearly, and enough organizational skill to follow through with consequences for better or worse choices. You may want to jot down potential choices ahead of time, before you discuss these with your child. It may help you to confer with other parents about the level of responsibility they give their children of various ages or strategies for setting limits they have found useful.

Another important life skill you can help your children develop is the capacity to cope with changes and transitions in life. Changes are hard for most people and can be especially taxing if you are low on energy or are having trouble focusing on the positive aspects of change. Changes can have significant impact on your child's behavior—the arrival of a new baby, a parent losing her job or returning to work, a hospitalization, or a move to a new house or neighborhood may all lead to problems. Your child's ability to adjust to change will depend in large part on how well you prepare yourself and your child for that change and how comfortable your child feels talking with you about it. Preparations could include explaining the reasons for the change, thinking about how you feel about the change yourself, asking your child how she feels, and sharing your feelings about the change with your child. You may want to identify resources or supports to help you and your child negotiate the change successfully.

Take a moment to think about an upcoming change. Respond to the following questions, involving your children if they are old enough. Coping with planned changes also provides children opportunities to practice skills that will be essential in coping with sudden losses or emergencies, such as the death of a grandparent or an emergency psychiatric hospitalization.

Planning for Change

What is the upcoming change?

Why is the change happening?

How do you feel about the change?

What does your child think about the change? (What does he think caused it? What does he imagine will happen?)

What does your child think will help her adjust to the change?

Who can help you and your child make sense of and prepare for the change?

Eliminate the Negative

Nothing reinforces behavior—both desirable and undesirable—more than your attention. Ignoring behavior is a powerful strategy for "eliminating the negative." Your child will usually get bored and stop doing whatever he was doing, because the reward, your attention, isn't there. This approach can require a lot of patience and self-control on your part, but it can be very effective for children of all ages.

Distracting or redirecting a child can interrupt a potentially negative cycle or prevent a bad outcome. Encourage your child to move away from that expensive crystal vase at your mother-in-law's house by showing her a toy in another room. Interest your child in listening to music or reading a book. If you're feeling low on energy, books on tape are a good alternative. Redirecting involves offering a positive option to the activity at hand, like building a tower with blocks rather than throwing them across the room. This may require some creative thinking but can also teach a child appropriate behavior in addition to stopping the misbehavior. Again, you may want to think ahead to anticipate what the challenges will be.

"Time-outs" involve removing your child from the situation in which she is behaving poorly. Try to choose a safe, nonstimulating spot in your house where your child can "cool down" and regain self-control. The typical rule of thumb is one minute in time-out for each year of the child's age. The theory is that your child will take the time to reflect on the consequences of her behavior. Time-outs should be given as calmly as possible and never with anger or harsh physical force. Again, time-outs are a relatively active intervention, requiring you to designate a spot and perhaps physically take the child to that spot. Think about engaging supportive others—your partner or a family member—to assist you in implementing this strategy.

Privileges such as watching television, playing video games, or driving the family car usually are earned as the result of good behavior. It follows that misbehavior or irresponsible behavior results in a loss of such privileges for a reasonable period of time. It's a good idea to warn your child or teenager first that, if a certain behavior continues, he will lose a privilege. You and your child can try choosing three to five privileges ahead of time, ranking them in order of importance. When misbehavior occurs, you can start by removing the least important privilege first.

A note of caution: The act of sitting down with your child and identifying privileges may be an eye-opener. Start by independently drafting separate lists and then compare your notes with your child. You may be surprised to learn your child considers access to cable television a right, rather than a privilege. It is important to discuss your opinions of rights and privileges together. If you don't have this discussion and "mistakenly" take away something your child considers a right rather than a privilege, your child may respond with inordinate rage and indignation. This is not pleasant and can be lessened by having this discussion ahead of time.

These strategies for eliminating negative behavior require increasing levels of organization and planning. You may find yourself varying your use of them, depending on your level of energy and ability to concentrate. They will not be effective if your relationship with your child is more negative than positive. Your child will feel he has nothing to lose by misbehaving, and you will have no power in the relationship.

Investing in Your Children

Your relationship with your children must be more positive than negative for you to have any influence in their lives as they grow. Investing in the relationship does not mean "buying" your children's love with expensive gifts or fancy vacation trips. You can invest in the relationship by employing the strategies described above—emphasizing strengths and providing opportunities for personal growth. You can spend time together doing things that don't cost any money, like playing games or walking the dog around the block. Appear interested in your children's lives. Ask questions about school or sports. Find out who their friends are. Make an effort to get to know their friends' parents.

These investments can be costly to a parent with depression, particularly the ones involving contact with the "outside" world. You may be concerned that your daughter's friends will find out about your depression or that you've been hospitalized, and that they will tease your daughter. You may be worried that their parents won't let them sleep over at your house if they know you have been diagnosed with a psychiatric disorder. You may run into dilemmas regarding disclosure of your depression, for instance, if the teacher asks why you can't chaperone the school field trip.

The typical investment opportunities open to most parents may not be open to you, but you can make accommodations that still have an impact on your relationship with your children. Determine the level to which you can be involved in activities like these without causing yourself more stress. Volunteer to bake cookies for the bake sale, but don't volunteer to be the chairman of the event. Pass on the opportunity to coach the baseball team, but attend home games. Take a nap in the afternoon so you can attend Open House at school in the evening. Manage your illness well to invest in your relationship with your children. These are the investments that last several lifetimes.

Chapter 8

Playing and Recreation

We maintain and strengthen our relationships with important people in our lives by playing, relaxing, and laughing together. Playing together is a vital family activity. When you're depressed, playing with your children may be the last thing you feel like doing. There may be other reasons why play is hard for you. If you had few opportunities to play during your own childhood, it might not come naturally to you now. Leisure and recreational activities can cost money, so if money is scarce, you may feel the options for your family are limited.

You create lifelong bonds with your children when you play with them. Betty, a mother with depression, remembers the following from her childhood.

"Once my dad built a wooden slide for me to play on. It was a wonderful slide with stairs up the back for me to climb on. The whole time he was building it, he sang or hummed the song, "You Are My Sunshine." After it was built, he would often come outside and catch me at the bottom of the slide. I think fondly of my dad every time I hear "You Are My Sunshine."

Betty doesn't always feel like playing with her own children, especially when her depression is at its worst. But she is motivated and tries because she wants her children to have fond memories like hers. One of Betty's daughters plays soccer, and Betty takes her to every game and stays to watch her play.

The Importance of Play

Play is one of the few things humans do from earliest infancy to the end of life. People of all ages need to play. Play is an essential activity for children and, most of the time, learning and playing cannot be separated. Play gives children the opportunities they need to develop their physical abilities, their language and thinking skills, their social and emotional abilities, and their ability to cope with and understand the world around them (Barnett 1990; Coleman and Iso-Ahola 1993; DeMarco and Sidney 1989; Van de Kooij 1989). Throughout childhood, play helps children prepare for the roles they will take on later in life, including student, family member, friend, worker, and, eventually, parent. Play is not only important because it enhances development; play is also important for its own sake. Children play for the pleasure of it, to relieve stress, and to exercise. Ask any child why he is playing and the answer is likely to be, "Because it's fun!"

Play continues to be essential during the teenage years. Teens develop friendships on the basis of shared leisure interests. Leisure activities often provide teenagers their first opportunities to structure their own time and, thus, develop a sense of independence (Larson and Kleiber 1993). Teenagers involved in positive leisure activities tend to have greater life satisfaction and self-esteem and are less likely to engage in negative activities such as drug and alcohol abuse than teens who are not involved in positive leisure activities (Brennan 1985; Feldman and Gaier 1980; Vicary, Smith, Caldwell, and Swisher 1998; Williams and McGee 1991).

Play and leisure are just as important for adults as they are for children. Our leisure activities provide a source of life satisfaction, they allow us a break from work, and they enhance our physical and emotional well-being. Play and recreation provide the foundation for shared experiences, which are essential to build friendships and intimate relationships. Throughout life, play and leisure activities help people cope with stress by providing direct stress relief and by facilitating the development of friendships (Coleman and Iso-Ahola 1993).

Do You Know How to Play?

One of the hallmarks of depression is a lack of enjoyment or pleasure in activities you usually find enjoyable. If you're not enjoying things, it's really hard to do them. When you are depressed, play is usually one of the first things you give up. You may feel like you don't have the energy to play. It may be hard for you to find something funny or to laugh. It might be difficult for you to deal with the noise children naturally make when they play. And sometimes you can misperceive your child's normal play behavior as misbehavior. The guilt you feel when you're not up to playing with your children can make you feel worse. Finally, if you have struggled with depression for a long time, you may not even remember how to have fun.

Your child can teach you how to play. T. Barry Brazelton, the noted pediatrician, makes the point that babies and children teach us as much as we teach them (Brazelton 1998). Even in infancy, a baby has fun simply by exploring the world around her. Watch for cues she gives you: What does she pay attention to or look at? What makes her smile and laugh? When she can move on her own, what does she reach for or get into? Does your toddler enjoy playing in the bath? Set up a small tub of water on the porch so he can splash and play with plastic spoons and bowls under your watchful eye. Children are great at using their imaginations. Your four-year-old might make a space ship from an empty appliance carton or a trumpet from an empty paper towel roll.

The most important thing to remember about play is that it should be enjoyable. Other than that, there are few rights or wrongs. Play is not serious—it's make-believe, silly, and fun. You do it for as long as you like, and you stop when you want to stop. If you can't remember how to play or it feels uncomfortable, follow your children's lead. They can teach you a great deal about playing.

In chapter 2 we wrote about the value of leisure and recreation as a lifestyle "tool" you could use to keep yourself healthy. If you didn't do the exercise in chapter 1 about your leisure interests, you might do it now. Knowing what you enjoy yourself can help you think about playing with your children.

Play at Different Ages

Play can be spontaneous and natural; most children are born with the potential for learning how to play. Children vary quite a bit, however, over time and among each other. Your child will develop her interests and abilities at her own pace, enjoying different activities at different ages. She may engage in playful interactions with objects or people sooner or later than other children. What one child thinks is fun may be totally uninteresting to another child. Your child may never enjoy the activities we describe below, preferring different activities altogether. These paragraphs provide simple guidelines for children of different ages, so you know what to look for.

You can recognize what your child enjoys by observing her response in particular situations. An infant may make eye contact and smile, if he is old enough, or make cooing noises, or reach for something or someone. A toddler is able to communicate pleasure in more ways through his words and actions, smiling, laughing, and demanding, "Do it again" or "More!" A teenager can appear "bored," but you may see their disappointment when an activity ends or a friend leaves. Learn to recognize your child's cues.

Infants

Infants enjoy interacting with their parents and love to be held and rocked (Chandler 1997; Leach 1986 and 1997). They like the sound of your voice and enjoy being read to, even though they cannot understand what you're reading.

They also like to listen to music and especially like to hear their parents sing to them. Remember, you can't "spoil" a baby at this age by holding or carrying her too much. Hearing the beat of your heart and smelling you gives an infant a sense of security. When your baby is awake, you might carry her in a front pack that lets you have your hands free to do things around the house. It's fairly easy to make the daily activities of caring for an infant playful. When you change your baby's diaper or feed him, you can kiss his belly, head, or toes, tell nursery rhymes, or sing baby songs.

Infants enjoy looking at faces, pictures of people, and bright, colorful objects. You can take advantage of this by placing mobiles above the crib and putting up pictures and posters where the baby can stare at them. As babies mature beyond six months, they are fascinated by games of peek-a-boo and simple toys that squeak or rattle. They begin to crawl and enjoy toys they can use for teething. At this age, babies are excited to see the effect they have on the world—that is why your baby might drop that block from her high chair twenty times and not be bored.

Toddlers

Toddlers, between eighteen months and three years old, also love you to talk and read to them. They enjoy music and nursery rhymes, and take an interest in toys that can be opened and shut or pushed and pulled. Toddlers like to build things with blocks and then knock them down. They also begin "imitative play"; they might "feed" a doll or push a toy shopping cart. Toddlers are naturally curious and like to explore the world around them, so this is the age when you should "baby-proof" your home. You can encourage your child's curiosity and language by teaching him the names of objects and actions.

Preschoolers

Preschoolers, children between three and six years old, do a tremendous amount of changing and growing. At three, talking is usually a high priority. Children at this age like to count, enjoy learning rhymes, and singing simple songs. At four years old, children love to use their developing muscles by running, skipping, jumping, bouncing, and hopping. They like to dance and play on playground equipment. Four-year-olds also like to draw, cut out paper, fasten buttons, and open and close zippers. They begin to learn the alphabet and numbers. Five-year-old children love pretend and dramatic play. They like to sing, try to read, and participate in games that provide movement, such as tag and hop scotch.

School-Age Children

Children between the ages of six and ten years old are in elementary school. They begin to take an increased interest in friends and classmates. They enjoy real-life tasks, cooking, craft projects, music, dancing, reading, and writing. They enjoy being physically active. Children in elementary school like noncompetitive sports with rules, although they sometimes consider rules they did not make up unfair. This is also the age when kids begin to get involved in organized activities like Scouts, Little League, or soccer teams.

Preteens

For preteens, ages ten through twelve, friends become increasingly important and they are almost always of the same sex. Children at this age like time alone to daydream. They love to talk on the phone and enjoy keeping secrets. They may prefer to exclude you from some of their recreational activities at this stage, but you might engage them in strategy games such as checkers and Monopoly or a family night with a movie.

Adolescents

Young teenagers twelve and thirteen years old are in junior high school and are going through a very unstable and confusing period as they begin to establish themselves as individuals. Don't be surprised if your young teen begins to lose interest in previously enjoyed activities. Young teens also begin to become less involved with family. They tend to anger easily and act out. It's normal for children to pull away at this time, but remember that they are still dependent on you and need your love, support, and guidance. Teens need you to be available, so they can approach *you* with suggestions, rather than you setting the agenda for the family all the time. At this age, it may begin to feel like you and your children have few leisure interests in common. Shopping, fishing, going to the movies, or watching television might be activities you can enjoy together, as they provide few demands for communication but many opportunities to talk about things as they come up. Other naturally occurring activities during the day, like eating breakfast or fixing dinner, offer opportunities for spontaneous conversation and fun. Take advantage of your adolescent's many trips to the refrigerator; hang out in the kitchen where you might catch him in the mood for a playful interaction. Keep communication open so you know what's going on with your child.

Teens who are fourteen through seventeen are in the midst of their high school years. They are unsure of themselves and critical of others. They are still interested in their friends but also begin to take a stronger interest in particular friends and may begin to date. At this age, activities like "hanging out" with friends can be very important, although you might wonder exactly what they are doing. Music and sports are also often important at this age. At age eighteen and beyond they begin to take on the adult roles of college, work, and intimate relationships. Young adults of this age may seem closer to you than they have been in years because they have gained a significant amount of maturity. You might find they want to spend more time with you than they did before (Savin-Williams and Berndt 1990).

Keep In Mind

There are many reasons why a child may seem bored or unhappy, ranging from being hungry, tired, or sick, to having a developmental delay or emotional difficulty. You will want to rule out or respond to problems your child may be having. If nothing seems to interest or please your child, or if your child seems bored or unhappy for longer than usual, be sure to check with your pediatrician or another childcare professional for advice.

Play Should Be Fun

Play should be fun, and it should be easy! Children need and want time with you, but they also need time with others. Many parents today feel they need to be "entertainment directors," scheduling their children's every waking moment. This can be too much for you *and* for your child. Just like you, children need "downtime" to relax and do nothing, and to learn to entertain themselves.

Opportunities at Home

You can create the circumstances and environment for your children to engage in play with you, on their own, or with others. Have some regular play routines. For instance, make Friday night a family night with pizza and a rented movie. Make a tent with blankets and camp out on the living room floor. Create a "busy box" or "fun drawer," in which you collect old jewelry, bottle caps, colorful magazine pictures, rubber bands, or whatever else might be put to use as part of an art project or creative building activity.

You can make daily activities around the house playful for your children. Set aside a drawer or cabinet in the kitchen that your toddler or young child can reach filled with plastic containers, wooden spoons, and other nonbreakable items your youngster can play with while you're fixing dinner. Let your kindergarten child help you fold laundry and match socks. Turn a chore like setting the table into a creative endeavor by encouraging your child to make place mats. Make a game of putting toys or laundry away by having a race. Your child will feel proud to have taken on an important family job.

Many families focus on television in the evening or on weekends. Lots of people—professionals and parents alike—have opinions about how much television is okay and that too much television is bad for children. But it's the rare child or adult who doesn't some watch television. Everyone needs time to relax, and sometimes television serves this purpose. Some children watch television as a way to make the transition from school to home or from one parent's house to another's. You and your children can watch shows together, and your child can watch television when you need to do something else. However, if you think you are using television as a "baby-sitter," or if you worry about the amount or types of shows your child is watching, then maybe it is becoming a problem. When presented with the option of an interesting, fun activity, many children will choose to turn off the television.

Planning a Play Space

Set aside a safe space for playing in your home. It may be your child's bedroom, or the family room, or a corner of the kitchen. Try to make it a space where you don't mind the mess of toys, where the furniture is sturdy, and where you don't keep fragile objects. Keep play materials and toys in boxes or drawers that your child can easily reach. If you have created a safe place for your child to play, fixing dinner while she splashes in the kitchen sink or relaxing next to her while she builds block towers on the living room floor might satisfy you both. Remember that it takes children a long time to be responsible for picking toys up and putting them away.

Use this worksheet to plan a play area for your child.

My Child's Play Area

Activity Level:	My Child Likes To:	Necessary Materials or Resources:	Examples:
Active Play			*Jump rope* *Hula hoop*
Moderate Play			*Jacks* *Yo-yo*
Quiet Play			*Books* *Paper and crayons*

Neighborhood and Community Resources

Children need and want time with you, but they also need time with others. Get to know what resources are available in your community. Many communities have recreation departments or committees; check your local phone book under the name of the city or town. Organized activities can be great for parents. Town recreation departments may sponsor soccer or softball teams, craft classes, summer camps, activity programs during school vacations, and music classes. Your child's school may have information about local Boy and Girl Scout troops or other community activities. YMCAs or Boys and Girls Clubs offer basketball and swim classes, often at a low cost. Libraries and community centers often sponsor play groups for toddlers and their parents.

These community activities can be wonderful opportunities for both you and your children to make friends and get involved in your neighborhood. Children need to socialize with others. Yet, you might feel stressed by the demands some of their activities put on you. You might be asked to coach your daughter's soccer team, raise funds for your son's Boy Scout troop, or drive the car pool for your daughter's dance class. Make sure you consider your own needs, energy level, and what you can handle. Don't put your physical or emotional health on the line. Your daughter can probably still play soccer, even if you don't coach.

While these activities give your child a chance to be with other children, they can also give you an opportunity for adult company and to connect with other parents. It can be really helpful to hear from other parents about the child rearing challenges everyone shares. Through these relationships you can also develop the support every parent needs. But pay attention to how you feel about spending time with other parents in these situations. A play group for you and your toddler can be great, but if you can't relate to the other adults, or if you are comparing yourself to others and feeling you don't measure up, then it may not be the place for either of you. If you feel others are judging you negatively, remind yourself that this may be a feeling coming from your depression and not really from the other parents.

Recreation Safety

Remember that play needs to be safe as well as fun. Make sure your children are dressed appropriately for the weather and the activity. Use sunblock, except with infants, who should be kept out of the sun. After six months of age, use a "baby approved" sunblock. Ask your pediatrician or pharmacist to recommend one. Insist that your child wear safety gear, like a helmet for bike riding and wrist and knee pads for skating or skateboarding. If you ride a bike, you should wear a helmet, too. On day trips, make sure you and your children wear seat belts in the car and have everyone stick together when you reach the destination. Remember, you are the parent, and what you say goes! Encourage your children to memorize your address and phone number, in case they do get separated from the group.

Young children need to be supervised on playground equipment and near water. A bucket of water is enough for a child to drown in. A child who does not know how to swim should wear a flotation device. Enroll your child in swimming lessons at the local Boys and Girls Club, YMCA, or community pool. Even if your child knows how to swim, don't let your child swim in a pool or lake without adult supervision. If you've promised your child a day at the lake, and you wake up in the morning worried that you won't be able to pay attention to him, pick a spot on the beach where the lifeguard is able to see your child, ask your spouse or partner to take over, invite a friend to come along, or decide to go another day. Only skate on ponds that are fully frozen—or better yet, only skate at indoor ice rinks.

Low-Cost Recreational Activities

Recreation and leisure activities can be expensive. Planning for your family can be difficult if your finances are limited. A movie ticket may be $8.00 for an adult and $5.00 for a child, not to mention the cost of the popcorn! Even taking your children to a fast-food restaurant or an arcade can drain you of money. Summertime and school vacation weeks can leave you struggling to think of inexpensive activities. Whether your children are with you full-time or you have them for weekend or vacation visits, it may seem like you can never find enough inexpensive activities to keep them busy.

Inexpensive Play Activities

Remember that having fun and spending time together are more important than what you do or how much you spend. Inexpensive, fun activities can include arts and crafts, cooking and baking, hiking and biking, dressing up in old clothes, dancing in your living room, playing tag at the local playground, making and flying paper airplanes, playing catch, gardening, singing and making your own homemade instruments, and reading, just to name a few. You will find some useful books and Web sites with lots of great ideas for play in the Resources section at the end of the book.

In warmer months, you can go swimming at a nearby lake, beach, or community pool. You and you children could take a bike ride on a bike path or on a street with little traffic. A trip to the local park can be a fun day. Younger children can play on the swings, slide, and jungle-gym equipment. Older children might enjoy a game of catch, basketball, or one-on-one soccer with you. Both young and old may like flying a kite on a windy day. A park is also a great place to have a picnic or point out the stars to your children after dark.

In the fall you might want to take your children on a short hike to see the changing leaves. They may also enjoy a day at a local farm picking apples, using them later to make homemade apple pie. Perhaps there is a petting zoo or animal farm nearby. During the Halloween season, picking pumpkins and letting your children decorate them with markers and paints can be a fun and inexpensive afternoon.

There are plenty of activities to do when rain threatens to ruin the day. You could rent a movie and make some popcorn. This is a lot cheaper than going to the theater. You and your children can play board games, put a jigsaw puzzle together, do arts and crafts, or play charades. An indoor picnic can be the perfect activity for a rainy afternoon. Just spread a blanket on the floor, make some sandwiches, and enjoy your living room.

As the colder months approach and it begins to snow, you can plan to go sledding or ice-skating. Make sure, if you go skating outdoors, the pond you choose is completely frozen. You should not be able to see the water through any portion of the ice. Your children may also like building a snowman, an igloo, or making snow angels. Tinting the snow colors can be fun for children. All you need is a spray bottle, food coloring, and water. Fill a spray bottle with water, add a few drops of food coloring to it, and put the top on tight. Your children can try to write their names, draw pictures, or color their snowman or snow angel. When the snow melts away, the color will, too. After a day outside in the cold, make your children a warm mug of hot chocolate with marshmallows to chase away the chill. Swimming in the winter can be a special treat for children. Check with your local Boys and Girls Club or YMCA to see if they offer free or low-cost swimming hours for children.

Hidden Treasures for Parents

Some play and recreational activities require materials and equipment. Children outgrow their possessions so fast that buying used equipment is usually smarter than spending a lot of money on something new. If you are on a limited budget or just enjoy bargain hunting, there are many options for saving money. Yard or "tag" sales or flea markets are the perfect place for parents to find play and recreation materials for their children. Toys, games, books, puzzles, and outdoor clothes are just some of the items that can be found at yard sales. People hold yard sales from the spring through the fall, generally advertising them in local newspapers. Usually, the person hosting the sale is trying to get rid of things they no longer use or need. Because of this, prices can be dramatically reduced. You can find things that are practically brand new or sometimes have never been used. Sporting and recreational equipment such as bikes, basketballs and soccer balls, tennis rackets, hockey or ski equipment, fishing equipment, rollerblades, and cameras can also be found at yard sales or at flea markets, Salvation Army stores, used sporting-goods shops, or pawn shops.

Libraries

Public libraries are a fantastic resource for families. Contrary to popular belief, books are not the only items found in libraries. Many libraries lend magazines, videos, music on CD and tape, toys, story kits, puppets, and books on tape, along with the traditional books. A library card allows you to borrow anything a library lends. Most public libraries also have computers and connections to the Internet. You and your children can use the computers to look up information for school or to explore child-friendly Web sites. (See the Resources list at the end of the book.)

Typically, libraries offer programs and services geared to children and families. These can include story hours, puppet shows, or playgroups for young children and parents, craft classes for older children, and baby-sitting classes for pre-teenagers and teenagers. Libraries may also offer homework assistance for school-age children, summer reading programs, and Internet and computer classes for children and adults. Some libraries show family movies for free or a small fee, or sponsor programs for teens such as special movies, dances, theater groups, and volunteer programs. This may be the perfect way for your teenager to stay busy and out of trouble. Occasionally, libraries offer parenting classes or support groups, or lectures on relevant topics such as managing your child's behavior or dealing with homework.

In addition, many libraries have passes to museums and other family-friendly places in your area. You may need to reserve the pass ahead of time and return it promptly. Check with your local library to find out about services, programs, and passes.

Special Occasions

Special occasions, like holidays or birthdays, offer the possibility of happy family times. The hours and minutes spent in pleasant anticipation and your expectations about how wonderful everything will be certainly add to the excitement. Unfortunately, your fantasies may be better than the event itself. Planning and preparing together with your children can be fun. Worries and disappointment can be managed ahead of time and minimized during the event.

Make a Calendar

The anticipation of major holidays or birthdays can be difficult to manage, particularly for younger children who do not yet understand time and waiting. Even older children get "burnt out" if they become too excited too early. Make a calendar with your children to help them keep time in perspective. This calendar will work for any special event, like a holiday, birthday, vacation, or even the return to school in the fall. Draw a calendar of the month that includes the day of the celebration on a piece of poster board or heavy cardboard, like the back of a note pad. Tape a wrapped piece of candy or small trinket or toy to each date. As each day comes, let your child have the prize for that date, marking it off on the calendar until the anticipated event arrives. Remember to have a candy or prize for each of your children. As you mark off each date, talk about the event to come. Ask your child what she thinks will happen on that day or how she would like it to be. Gently correct any misperceptions or mistakes in your child's understanding of what will happen, for example, who will be at her party or how many gifts she will receive. It may be hard to hear her fantasies or even her memories about the "best ever" birthday or Christmas, particularly if you can't afford this time to take everyone to an amusement park or you can't guarantee that a particular relative will show up. However, gently leading her to a more realistic picture of the anticipated event will help you both avoid disappointment and anger later on.

Holidays

Holidays can be difficult for anyone, but having depression can add to the burden. Holidays may bring up unpleasant memories or may fuel family conflicts. They may leave you feeling sad, lonely, or just completely stressed. If family holiday gatherings are stressful for you, make choices about the extent of your involvement. Know your own energy level, your family's needs, and your ability to tolerate family get-togethers. If your extended-family party on Christmas Eve feels like too much, decide to only go for an hour or two. Or, remember that you can always decline with regrets, spending a quiet Christmas Eve with your immediate family. It's always appropriate to take the necessary action to take care of yourself and your children.

If your holiday memories are not the happiest, remember that you can make things different now. Think about traditions you can build for yourself and your family. Create happy memories of important holidays by making favorite foods, playing special music, or decorating your home together. You might make holidays a time when you do something special for others, like volunteering together at a nursing home, serving dinner at a shelter, or visiting a neighbor who is lonely. Include your children in the planning as much as you can. If your finances are limited, make simple Halloween costumes or Christmas or Hanukah decorations with your children. Your children can draw pumpkins and ghosts for Halloween. They can color pictures of pilgrims for Thanksgiving. Make a New Year's Eve hat by folding a piece of paper or cardboard into a cone shape and stapling the sides together. Then let your children decorate the hat with markers, paints, and glitter.

Keep in mind that holidays can be stressful for young children as well as for you. They may be expected to interact with relatives and others they don't see often, to "dress up" in clothes that they don't wear every day, to perform in school holiday concerts, and to otherwise be on their best behavior. While some children may enjoy the festivities, holiday activities can tire them out and leave them cranky. Children may also sense changes in your mood or energy level, and their behavior may reflect this. To decrease your children's and your own stress, keep to your routine as much as possible. Try to keep daily activities such as bathing, mealtimes, and bedtimes close to routine times. Limit television viewing during the holiday season. Your children will be bombarded with hundreds of advertisements for toys and holiday programs that may be overstimulating. And try to spend the same amount of time with your children as you normally do. Give them permission to relax and enjoy themselves.

Birthday Parties

Birthday's can be fun for you and your children. However, you may feel inadequate when you compare your party plans with the birthday parties other parents give their children. Some rent magicians and ponies when their children are three and entire movie theaters when their children are nine. This is not necessary. Birthday parties need not be expensive or elaborate to be fun for your child and her guests, and for you.

Birthday parties should be age appropriate. Children's first birthday parties are more for the parents than for the children. Have a small party with close family. For children who are two to four years of age, simple parties are the way to go. All you need is cake, birthday hats, and simple games such as "Simon says" or the "hokey pokey." One rule of thumb is to only invite the number of children equal to your child's age, plus one. So, if your child is three, invite four children. Keep parties for young children no longer than an hour or two. More time than that can be overwhelming for the guests and for you. Many parents of the children you've invited will be happy to stay and help, so take advantage of this.

Children five through ten enjoy theme parties. Involve your child in planning the party. At this age, children like craft activities, parties with games, and parties with videos to watch. Many bowling alleys, skating rinks, gymnastic centers, and arcades host children's birthday parties. Typically, the facility charges for each child invited, and the time is limited to two or three hours. While parties at these facilities will cost more than a party at home, they can be easier than hosting a party in your house. There is less to prepare and no clean up afterwards. Such parties can be a fun option, if it is affordable, and might reduce your stress.

Preteens and young teens love slumber parties. Usually two to five friends are plenty for an overnight. Sleepovers can be inexpensive and easy, but can also be nerve-racking. Provide teens with inexpensive nighttime entertainment, such as movies or card games, and snacks like popcorn and soda or juice. Set some simple, clear rules about which rooms they can play and sleep in and whether they are restricted to staying in the house. Let them sleep on the living room floor, and monitor them periodically until they fall asleep. Don't plan a large breakfast. Cold cereal, donuts, or frozen waffles for the toaster are fine. Set a time for the party to end in the morning. Slumber parties are probably easiest to manage if there are two adults in the house. If you are a single parent and are worried that a slumber party will be a bit overwhelming, you might ask a close friend to help host. Your children do not need a party every year. Older children might appreciate a special day or evening out with you.

The best thing you can do when planning a birthday party is to keep it simple, give yourself time to get organized, and enlist the help of at least one other trusted adult. Most of all remember that it's easy to feel overwhelmed. But you can combat this feeling by taking a different perspective on things and turning your thoughts around. Eve, a mother who has struggled with depression for many years, remembers one especially difficult birthday party.

> *"My daughter had her second birthday just two months after I got out of the hospital for the first time. I had planned a party for her and had invited lots of family and friends to help us celebrate the occasion. I had worked hard preparing, sending out handmade invitations, cooking, and cleaning the house. On the evening of the party, just as the guests were beginning to arrive, I suddenly felt overwhelmed by the prospect of playing host and ended up sobbing in my room. I called my doctor and told him that I had all these guests arriving and was holed up in my room, a total basket case. He said to me, "What do you want to get out of this night?" I told him I wanted people to have a nice time, and I just wanted to get through it. He asked whether I had help, which I did, and whether my guests were aware of my illness, which they were. Then he suggested that I just keep my thoughts on enjoying the company and forget about trying to make everything perfect. I was able to go downstairs and join the party and everything worked out. It doesn't seem like a huge revelation, but I have often since then asked myself that question, "What do I want to get out of this day?" It really helps to keep me focused on the task in front of me and reminds me that it's okay to ask for help and that things don't have to be perfect.*

Play Is a Positive Priority

Play is important for everyone in your family. Play helps to cement relationships, relieve stress, and provide relaxation whether it's done alone or together. It doesn't have to be elaborate or last a long time to be meaningful. Planning ahead when you're feeling better and exploring and creating options at home and in the community will allow you to respond even when you are not feeling as well. If you're having a bad day, if you feel tired or unable to concentrate, recognize that you need support and call on a relative or friend. Depending on your child's age and ability to understand, it's okay to let her know you are having a difficult time. If you feel overwhelmed when your child says, "Play with me," remind yourself that what he is really asking for is a chance to be with you and have fun. To be considered a desirable playmate is a compliment for any parent. So be prepared, and enjoy the moment.

Chapter 9

Advocating for Yourself and Your Children

As a parent you are, by definition, an advocate for your children. It's your job to protect your children from difficulties that may come their way and to secure the resources necessary to their continued survival and developmental success. As an adult with depression, you may also be in the position of advocating for yourself—for the respect and treatment you deserve and need.

Parents often have trouble acknowledging their own needs and communicating them to others. How many times have you needed something and been unwilling, reluctant, or even afraid to ask your partner or children for help? You may not have even thought to ask!

Situations requiring advocacy range from simple, informal interactions with family members or friends to complex interactions with large, formal, public institutions, like the school system or the court. Situations requiring advocacy at home may involve common family squabbles, like one child always picking on the other, or one child in three always being blamed for starting trouble. As a parent, you may intercede in the family to advocate for the child who is the victim or underdog.

Likewise, if your child has unmet needs or is being treated unfairly outside the home, you may intercede in the larger system to advocate for his needs to be met. The only difference between advocating in the home and outside the home is that at home, as the parent, you set the rules. Larger institutions have rules and regulations regarding people's rights and the resources that must be made available to them to meet their needs. Oftentimes these are complex, and you may need to enlist the services of an attorney or another specialist to advocate for you.

Successful advocacy requires a set of attitudes and skills that many parents do not have, unless they happen to be professional advocates like lawyers or social workers. These attributes include the willingness to face an issue and acknowledge a need and the know-how to advocate—to communicate your needs, identify resources, document your efforts, overcome obstacles, and follow through to a successful outcome. The key to successful advocacy, which is particularly difficult for individuals with depression and other kinds of mental illness, is the belief that you deserve to have your needs met. This is related to your own attitudes about depression and the attitudes of others, which can present the most significant barriers to successful advocacy.

If you are living with depression, your efforts to advocate for yourself or your children may be compromised. You may feel guilty asking for help because others have let you know that they think you should just "pull yourself together" and "get moving." You may feel vulnerable and reluctant to disclose your needs, which you perceive to be signs of weakness or failure. You may be distractible and not able to focus clearly on your children's particular issues. You may not always have the energy to follow through, to be sure your needs or those of your children are met.

However, parents who feel undeserving of help or who are unwilling to ask for things for themselves often can be powerful advocates for their children. Somehow they muster the courage and strength to take action, ensuring their children's needs are met. You may even be concerned that your depression has somehow caused your children's problems and, therefore, contributed to their needs. Yet, you may be able to overcome your feelings of embarrassment or guilt to actively advocate for your children. In many ways, parents living with depression may be stronger and more courageous advocates than other parents, simply because they have to overcome "self-stigma" to try harder on behalf of their children.

Facing Issues and Acknowledging Needs

Problems are funny. Sometimes they creep up slowly. Small concerns can pile up until it occurs to you that there's a real problem. For example, you may notice on a daily basis that your son has trouble getting along with siblings and friends. You may even discuss this in the evening with your partner, after the children have gone to bed. You may not define this behavior as an issue requiring active intervention until your son is kicked off the playground at school for fighting. You may be confronted with other problems without warning, like accidents or emergencies. All of a sudden, you slip on the ice and break your wrist, or your daughter spills a jar of hot caramel sauce and burns her hand.

It's easy to acknowledge the need for help when the issues are immediate, obvious, and accidental. Unfortunately, people with depression are inclined to view problems as their fault, whether or not they had any responsibility for or control over them. In fact, people with depression may go to great lengths to develop rationales for why they are to blame. If you feel this way, it may be harder to acknowledge legitimate needs and seek the help you deserve.

Sorting Out Your Own Issues

Your success as an advocate depends in large part on your attitudes about yourself in particular, and the world in general. People with depression often have negative thoughts about themselves and negative views about life and the world. Low self-esteem and feelings of worthlessness, guilt, shame, and blame are common barriers to facing issues and acknowledging needs. If you believe you don't deserve something, you will not advocate for it. If you think you are causing your children's problems, you may not see yourself as part of the solution. If you see the world as a dark and punishing place, you will not expect to be successful in your advocacy efforts.

Where do you get these beliefs? They come from your interpretation of your experiences up to this point in your life and your own perceptions of how the world treats you. Negative attitudes influence the choices you make in life by limiting your perceived options and taking away hope for positive solutions. Thus, your chances to improve things may seem slim. However, many people throughout history have suffered with depression, like Abraham Lincoln, Winston Churchill, and Ernest Hemingway, and they all managed to overcome their depression to do great things. You can choose, like they did, not to believe the negative messages.

Face the Facts

Recognizing the good in yourself is crucial to believing you and your family deserve support. Each of us has strengths, talents, and abilities. If you are like many people, it's hard to remember what these are. When you're feeling depressed, it's easy to forget anything positive. It is important to recognize the things you do well, no matter how insignificant they seem to you. Make a list of each strength, talent, or ability you can think of or that others have pointed out to you. It may help to focus on your strengths as a parent. Write them on the lines below. These may be things like "I'm a good listener," or "I love my children," or "I'm good at fixing broken toys." You may need the help of a friend, relative, or counselor to do this task, particularly if your thoughts are not coming freely.

My Strengths, Talents, and Abilities

_____   _____

_____   _____

_____   _____

_____   _____

Refer to this list often, especially when you are not feeling your best. Read it out loud, if you can. You may want to copy the list onto a file card and laminate it, carrying it in your wallet or keeping it in your desk drawer for easy, frequent access. Add to it when you notice something you have done well or when others have complimented you. At the end of each day, as you are preparing for bed, remind yourself of three things you did well that day. Your personal power and your ability to advocate for yourself and your children will increase with every item you add to your list and the more you believe in them. You must first accept the notion that you are a worthwhile person in order to believe that you have rights—the right to have your needs met and to be treated well in the process.

You Have Rights

There are certain common rules or guidelines—basic human rights—that should be guaranteed in all settings, whether you're advocating for yourself at home with your partner or for your children at school with the teacher. If you are depressed and have spent most of your life believing negative thoughts about yourself, you may not have a clear understanding of basic human rights. It's important to become aware of these and to begin to understand the consequences of denying yourself these rights—for yourself and your children. Children learn from their parents' examples. You are their primary role model. If you do not embrace these basic rights in how you treat others or how you allow others to treat you, your children will not expect to be treated well, either. The list below is adapted from work done by Bourne (1990).

You have the right to

- Say no

- Expect people to be truthful with you

- Be angry with people you care about

- Follow your own values and standards

- Be as healthy as you can be

- Change your mind

- Make friends

- Be yourself

- Make mistakes

- Express your feelings

- Live in a safe environment

- Have your needs and wants respected

- Be treated with dignity and respect

- Set your own priorities

- Change and grow

- Have fun

- Say "I don't know"

- Feel scared

Being aware of these rights can help decrease the likelihood of people taking advantage of you or your children and increase the likelihood that you will be an effective advocate. in the spaces below, write down the personal rights from the list above that are difficult for you to "buy into" or believe. Use additional paper, if you need to. Below each right, list the reasons why it is so difficult to embrace. Then, list the possible consequences for yourself and your children of *denying* yourself this right. This exercise will help you become more aware of how denying yourself a basic human right can contribute to a cycle of disempowerment and ineffectiveness. Here's an example.

Example: I have a hard time believing I have a right to: *Be treated with dignity and respect.*

Because: *I am depressed and therefore feel useless and undeserving.*

The consequences of denying myself this right are: *I allow my children to treat me rudely at home and in public, and consequently they haven't learned any manners.*

Rights I Struggle With

1. I have a hard time believing I have a right to:

   Because:

   The consequences of denying myself this right are:

2. I have a hard time believing I have a right to:

   Because:

   The consequences of denying myself this right are:

3. I have a hard time believing I have a right to:

   Because:

   The consequences of denying myself this right are:

Complex organizations or systems have rules and regulations, and clients or consumers have rights. You will need to determine what these are for each setting in which you find yourself advocating, like the school system or at work. Not only do you and your children have rights in these settings, but you may also have rights, as a person whose mental illness is considered a disability, to be treated fairly and not to be discriminated against. Contact a lawyer or your state's agency for protection and advocacy, or your state's disability rights center, to find out what additional mental health and consumer rights you are entitled to when dealing with service, treatment, or legal issues. You can call the National Association of Protection and Advocacy Systems at 202-408-9514 to get the telephone number of the protection and advocacy agency and client assistance program in your state, or visit their Web site at www.protectionandadvocacy.com.

Essential Components of Advocacy

Advocacy requires skills that come naturally to some people, but not to most. If you're not one of the "naturals," you will need to learn and practice these skills. You may learn most effectively by reading, studying, and then trying things out, or you may benefit from meeting and talking with people who can serve as role models to you. There are many wonderful organizations for adults and children with all types of needs. These organizations offer advocacy, training, and support services (like parent groups) as well as written educational materials. Many are listed in the Resources section at the end of this book. You may find others on the

Internet. Consider how you learn best and obtain the information you need, in the format that works for you, to master essential advocacy skills.

Develop Your Communication Skills

Advocating for yourself and your children requires good communication skills to explain your perception of a problem or need and to seek a satisfactory solution. Remember that communication can be verbal or nonverbal. Your body language communicates a great deal about how you feel about yourself and your children and whether you feel you deserve what you're asking for. The communication tips below have been compiled from several sources, including David Burns' work on depression (1989) and the National Mental Health Consumers' Self-Help Clearinghouse's *Self-Advocacy Technical Assistance Guide* (April 2000 Pilot Version).

- Insist on being treated with respect and dignity. You are a person with depression and many other strengths and virtues, *not* just a depressed person.

- Be firm and persistent when saying "No" to what you feel are unreasonable requests or anything that goes against your personal rights or values.

- Ask questions when you don't understand something or if you're having difficulty concentrating. There is no such thing as a silly or dumb question when it involves your well-being or that of your children.

- Decide ahead of time what you want to communicate. Write down the points you wish to make. It's okay to use and take notes when you speak with someone, especially if you are anxious about losing your train of thought.

- Listen well. You may not always agree with what other people say, but try to understand their points, and think about how you might help them see yours.

- Match your tone of voice with the other person's. If she is quiet, try speaking quietly. To prevent a conversation from becoming an argument, remain calm and don't raise your voice.

- Check your posture. People who don't feel good about themselves tend to slump. Position yourself so you are face to face with the other person, about three to four feet apart.

- Focus on the other person's eyes to show them you are interested in what they have to say.

Picture Yourself in These Situations—and Practice!

Take a moment to read over the situations described below. Visualize yourself in each situation. Practice what you might say in front of a mirror or in the car while you're driving by yourself, using some of the tips mentioned above. You might want to try out your communication strategies with a trusted friend, relative, or counselor, or even your children.

1. Your pediatrician seems to be rushing through your child's physical examination. You tell her you have several questions you would like to ask, and she seems irritated by your request.

2. During a special school meeting about your child, several school personnel start using terms you don't understand.

3. At a child custody hearing, your ex-partner expresses concern about your depression and its effects on your child.

4. The principal denies your request for an evaluation of your child for special education services, even though you have expressed your concerns.

Review the communication tips again. Practice them often in front of a mirror or with your partner, trusted friend, or counselor. Stay calm and cool when things don't seem to be going your way. Wait for your turn to speak, stick to the facts, and try not to get too emotional.

Identify Resources and Document Your Efforts

Clarify your thoughts about your child's need and the potential solutions you are willing to accept. The more clearly and accurately you can define the issue or need, the more likely you will succeed. Whether you're advocating for entitlements, treatment, or school services for yourself or for your children, it helps to gather as much information on the topic as you can. Once you have all the facts, start to develop an outline of what you will need to do to be successful in your advocacy efforts. The Advocacy Agenda below can help you organize your thinking and document your efforts. Review this with someone you trust for feedback to improve your agenda and, ultimately, your chances for success.

The Advocacy Agenda

What needs of my child are not being met? How do I know? _____

_____

_____

What do I hope to accomplish? _____

_____

What information do I need to help me advocate better (old report cards, evaluation reports, medical records, support letters, etc.)? _____

_____

_____

_____

What questions do I want answered? _____

_____

_____

_____

Who can help me advocate, including people, agencies, and organizations? Do I need a professional advocate or advice from a specialist? _____

_____

_____

_____

_____

Who can support me in my advocacy efforts (my partner, a relative, or a friend)?

_____

_____

How will I follow up? Have I set dates for follow-up phone calls to check on my request? _____

_____

_____

Keep a detailed log of the steps you take, including names of people you call or meet with, their titles, phone numbers, what they said, as well as the dates and times of any telephone messages you leave. Keep copies of *all* documents and letters in a file for reference or to bring to meetings.

Overcoming Obstacles

Some of the biggest obstacles to effective advocacy are our own attitudes about depression and the attitudes of others. You may consider yourself unworthy of respect or support. You may have experienced the pervasive influence of stigma and been a victim of the notion that people with mental illness are second-class citizens. Perhaps professionals, family members, or friends ignored your requests or denied your concerns because of their ignorance, false expectations, or even fears about mental illness. Their beliefs and actions have much less to do with you as a person than they do with their lack of understanding of depression as an illness.

Advocating can be frustrating. You may feel angry when your goals aren't met. If your first efforts are unsuccessful, rather than think of these experiences as opportunities to learn, you may be inclined to dwell on them as "failures" or "mistakes." When you're depressed, you may view any setback as proof positive that you are worthless and undeserving. The end result of such unrealistic thinking is that you feel powerless. Instead of dwelling on what you should have done or could have done, take note of what you might do differently the next time you're faced with a similar situation.

In the space below, describe a recent situation in which you feel you were not successful in achieving your goals. For example, perhaps you felt ignored at a recent meeting with school officials when you tried to explain your concerns about your child and her learning difficulties. After you describe the situation, think about what you might do differently next time. Ask someone you trust for feedback.

Planning for the Future

The situation in which I was not able to have my children's needs met was:

_____

_____

If a similar situation arises in the future, I could: _____

_____

_____

The goal of this exercise is to shift you from dwelling on your "failure" to thinking about alternative ways to advocate. It's very unusual to experience success the very first time you advocate for something. It is far more typical to experience frustration and anger as you try to advocate for what you or your children need.

You may want to exercise caution in your relationships with providers and other professionals with whom you are negotiating to meet your children's needs. Fostering and maintaining appropriate boundaries is important. One mother advised us that it is important to be careful not to give out more information about yourself or your child than is absolutely necessary. For example, it may not be necessary to divulge to the school principal that you have a mental illness and have recently been hospitalized for suicidal thinking when you are only trying to get extra tutoring for your child in math. This was Molly's experience as she advocated for special needs help for her son.

> *I still can't believe how differently the principal of my son's high school now treats me. She had been so supportive in arranging special help for my son and keeping me informed of his progress. After one of the progress report meetings at the school, I spoke with the principal and briefly mentioned that I had bipolar disorder. I told her I was worried that my son might have to deal with this illness when he gets older. Now, whenever I see the principal, she talks to me like she's walking on eggshells or something. Whenever I try to talk with her now, she suddenly doesn't have the time of day for me. I really feel like confronting her about the whole situation, but I don't want to mess up the services my son is receiving.*

The situation described above demonstrates that stigma and fear of mental illness may be all too real. While this mother has every right to be upset with the way the principal acts around her, she realizes that the more important issue is making sure her son continues to get the school support he needs. Although you may grow to respect and trust the various professionals and providers you deal with, this mother advises against treating them in the same manner you treat a trusted friend or relative in whom you can confide.

Persistence and Follow-through: Case Examples

Advocating for your children can be a lengthy, time- and energy-consuming process, requiring persistence and follow-through. The following are examples of parents' advocacy efforts and experiences in a setting where children often need help—the school system. If you suspect your child is having difficulty in school, you have the right to request that your child be evaluated for special education services. Special education services are available to all children with disabilities. Yet, insuring they receive these services can be challenging. This was Bill's experience when he and his wife tried to convince school officials his son needed help.

> *When my son started school, the teachers, my wife, and I realized quickly that he could not keep up with the normal class level. It was determined that he should be in a slower-learning class level. Through his years in school, the teachers continued to attempt to raise him to the standard class level. This approach meant that he would start the year in one class and, in short order, be moved to the slower class.*
>
> *This pattern continued until he reached the eighth grade. At the beginning of the school year, he started with the normal-learning class and*

was having difficulty keeping up. My wife and I had yet another meeting with his teachers and counselor. We tried to explain that for years he had been in a slower-learning level, but the teacher and counselor insisted that he remain in the normal class and that all he had to do was to try harder. Unfortunately, toward the end of the school year, the teacher and counselor agreed that he should have been in a slower level class. At that point he was failing the eighth grade.

It was extremely difficult to advocate for our son. The school system had the final say, and all of our concerns were ignored. It was easy to be intimidated by the teacher, counselor, or principal because of their training. It was more difficult to advocate when my self-esteem was low due to my depression. You just don't know when to take control of a situation and when to rely on the system.

This situation demonstrates how advocacy efforts can sometimes stretch over a long period as your children develop and their needs grow or change. Bill's depression undermined his confidence in his knowledge of his son and his judgment of his son's needs. He concluded, "Advocating for your child takes much effort. You may feel discouraged, but don't give up. The results of your efforts can be very rewarding." His son is a successful adult today because of his parents' efforts.

Irene offers these tips.

The challenge is to find the right support for yourself and for your child so that it is in place and operating before any crisis occurs. In order to do this, you need to meet and form a relationship with the people at school who come into contact with your child on a regular basis. Your child also needs to identify people at school whom he likes and who he believes support him. These can include your child's teachers, guidance counselor, school nurse, coach, principal, vice-principal, special-education teachers, administrators, librarian, advisors, or even the school secretaries.

Be visible. Attend parent-teacher conferences and get-acquainted nights. Do whatever you can to include yourself in a positive way. Pick up your child at school or drop him off occasionally, and meet the office staff. Write notes to the teacher when there are times your child may need additional support. Be only as specific as you need to be. Disclose only what you will not later regret saying.

Be aware of your rights as a parent and your child's rights. Know the school policies about attendance, classroom behavior, homework policy, grading, and so on. Make sure your child understands these policies, too.

Your success will depend on your willingness to make yourself available, to expend the energy necessary, and to follow up on open issues. It's a difficult task for any parent. But for one with depression, it often means that the times requiring the most vigilance and attention are those when the parent's energy and attention are at their lowest point. Furthermore, parents with a mental illness fear disclosing anything about their home life that will expose them to stigma or misunderstanding or that will cast them in an unfavorable light. Many parents with mental illness are exposed to scrutiny in every aspect of their lives; most fear having their children taken away. They fear their attempts to support their child may lead to misunderstanding or overreaction by school personnel.

These examples point to the importance of overcoming your own feelings of inadequacy or lack of energy to advocate for your children, even when you're intimidated by professionals. Advocating involves identifying resources and supports. Supportive relationships develop over time and in many ways. Become familiar with rules, regulations, policies, and your children's rights. Persistence and follow-through are key to overcoming obstacles and achieving your advocacy goals.

Get the Help You Need and Deserve

Many parents have a hard time asking for help. As a parent living with depression, you and your children may have greater needs than other families, making advocacy skills key to your children's optimal growth and developmental success. Set aside your negative believes and attitudes to overcome obstacles in your path. You and your children deserve to be treated with dignity and respect and to have your needs met.

Chapter 10

Negotiating the Legal System

because often this system stands in the way of getting help (in my opinion)

Legal cases involving divorce, custody, visitation, or the termination of parental rights are often scary, costly, and emotionally charged. Dealing with any of these issues can be incredibly stressful for any parent and even more so for the children involved. Such cases often require the court to scrutinize every aspect of a parent's life to determine what is best for the children. If you have been diagnosed with depression, you can expect your mental-health history to be closely examined. Events of the past, such as prior suicide attempts or psychiatric hospitalizations, can become key factors in disputes over child custody and visitation.

Judges and attorneys vary greatly in their attitudes toward and knowledge about mental illness. Court decisions may be made on the basis of the fact that you have been labeled with a psychiatric diagnosis, how you appear to be doing on the day your case is heard, and the court's possibly inaccurate or out-of-date knowledge regarding parenting and depression. You and your lawyer will need to provide the court with a comprehensive picture of your mental health and information about whether or how your depression affects your day-to-day functioning as a parent. This makes your choice of an attorney critical, as she must be educated about mental health and willing and able to represent your strengths as well as your weaknesses to your advantage.

Understanding your children's needs and your own will help you cope and will also help you prepare for evaluations you request or that the court requires. The court may order an evaluation to be conducted by a mental-health professional or a guardian ad litem (GAL) who may or may not be a mental-health professional, if your depression is at issue. You may want to know about your legal rights and options. You may be able to use the legal system to protect and provide for your children. Whether you're satisfied with the outcome of your case or not, you may find yourself dealing with some pretty strong emotions.

Choosing an Attorney

Choose an attorney who has handled many cases like yours. A qualified, experienced attorney can have a positive impact on how your situation is resolved. People often start by asking friends or relatives to recommend someone. It's also a good idea to ask professionals you respect, like your counselor, caseworker, minister, or doctor. When you get a referral, take the time to find out if the individual has handled cases similar to yours and whether he has a reputation for representing individuals with histories of mental illness in a knowledgeable, fair, and balanced way. Be sure the lawyer you choose understands your perspective and is willing to advocate actively for your interests.

Custody cases often require careful preparation and the legal fees, which are based on the amount of time an attorney spends on your case, can add up. You may be able to find an attorney willing to negotiate a flat rate, a reduced fee, or even to provide free legal assistance. Depending on the issue, you may qualify for a court-appointed and court-paid lawyer. However, your ability to influence the court's choice of attorney may be very limited. The court will usually provide an attorney if you can't afford one in cases involving criminal matters or when a child is removed from the custody of his parent, as in the case of the termination of parental rights.

Requests for modifications or changes to the amount of child support you pay, the amount of visitation time you have, or your children's custody arrangement typically require finding an attorney yourself and paying out of pocket. Yet, even in these cases, it is still possible to receive reduced-fee or free legal assistance if you cannot afford a lawyer. Contact your state attorney bar association or check your local Yellow Pages under "Legal Assistance," "Legal Advocacy," or "Legal Aid." Many family courts also have "proof of indigency" (low income) forms available at the clerk's office at your local courthouse. Ask whether low-cost or free legal representation is available for your particular case, whether or not you appear to meet the low-income criteria.

Questions to Ask

Consider asking the following questions when you are hiring an attorney.

1. Do you have prior experience with mental-health and legal issues in cases where a person's depression is at issue?

2. How do you feel about the ability of a person with depression to parent?

3. How far are you willing to go with my case? What would be the terms and conditions of our contract? Would you be willing/available to appeal if my initial case is not successful?

4. What will it cost to have you represent me? How are your fees determined? Do you offer a sliding scale fee or a payment plan option? What will it cost to appeal my case if I need to?

5. Do you think that an alternative solution to a court battle with the other parent or party is possible? Can my issue be resolved without going to court? Can you help negotiate a compromise?

If you decide to represent yourself in court, make sure you clearly understand what is at stake. Talk it over with your counselor, trusted friend, or supportive relative. Even though an attorney's fees can be high, there is no substitute for experienced, well-regarded representation, especially when your mental health and parenting abilities are in question and maintaining custody or contact with your children is at issue. The emotional costs to you and your children of a poor outcome may far outweigh your monetary savings.

Coping with the Custody Determination Process

There are several situations in which your ability to parent may be questioned because you have depression. These include divorces in which parents are in conflict about the custody of children and situations in which abuse or neglect has been alleged, with the state child welfare agency considering your children to be "at risk." In both instances, the issues before the court are your children's "best interests," and your rights as a parent. It is in your children's best interests for you to meet their physical and emotional needs in a safe, stable home environment where they are at minimal risk. Their well-being typically outweighs your rights as a parent in the eyes of the court.

Research indicates that parents diagnosed with mental illness often lose custody of their children (Mowbray, Oyserman, Zemencuk, and Ross 1995). This question weighs heavily in the minds of many parents. You may wonder, "Will I automatically lose my children if somebody finds out I have been diagnosed with or treated for depression?" A psychiatric diagnosis is a red flag to many judges, attorneys, and social workers, who may be concerned with the risks to children of having parents with mental illness. In some states having a diagnosis of mental illness alone is reason enough for the courts to decide against you (Burton 1990).

There are two important things you can do to prepare yourself for negotiating this process: 1. Know your children; and 2. Know yourself. Custody proceedings are stressful in the best of circumstances. Having a contingency plan in place for times when you are depressed and not feeling well can contribute to a favorable outcome in a custody case. Knowing your children's needs and your own and being thoughtful about how to meet these needs will also help you cope during the custody determination process.

Knowing Your Children's Best Interests

Parents need to know their children—their strengths, weaknesses, habits, and routines—to meet both their physical and emotional needs. Children's physical needs are simple: they require food, adequate clothing, a safe home. This translates into being able to support and maintain a daily routine that meets these needs. Are you able to provide your children three healthy meals a day? Are they clean and dressed appropriately for the weather? Is the crib safe, or do they have their own beds? If you live on the upper floor of a building, are the windows and screens secure? Can you meet their requirements for healthy development; for example, have they had their routine pediatric check-ups and immunizations?

It's in your children's best interests and yours to think more carefully about their emotional needs, too. These are often less clearly defined. This will help you function better as a parent during a custody proceeding and will help you prepare your case with your attorney. Your attorney will most likely be the person in court who will explain your situation and concerns, so she must thoroughly understand your perspective. Use this outline to organize your thoughts. Take a few minutes to jot down your responses.

- **Rules and guidelines** are important for keeping your children feeling safe and secure. What important household rules do you have in place for your children? What are your expectations for their behavior? Do they know the rules? Do they understand your expectations? Are your rules and expectations appropriate for your children's ages and stages of development?

- **Companionship and emotional support** are essential to healthy development. Who is in your children's support system? You? Their other parent? Relatives? Peers? Can this support system be expanded or improved?

- **Healthy role models** are not just people without physical or mental health issues. A healthy role model is someone who provides an example of sound judgment, good hygiene, healthy eating habits, and a drug-free lifestyle. Are you a good role model for your children? Who are your children's role models? Do you consider them to be healthy? Can you think of some new or alternative role models for your children?

- **Good communication** in relationships with both parents is a tremendous help. Do your children come to you when they have something on their mind? Can they talk it over with you? How do you support good communication between you and your children, as well as with their other parent? Are there ways you might improve it?

- Your children may have **other specific emotional needs**, depending on their ages and developmental stages or special needs that we have not included in this list. Write them down. How are they being met now? Can you provide more support? How will your children's needs change as they enter new developmental stages?

A Back-up Plan

Now that you have considered your children's needs, construct a back-up plan for their care when you're not well. This may be an agreement with a family member or friend (Ward and Shaw 1995). Think of this plan as an insurance policy for when you are unable to care for them. It's very important to do this before your situation requires it. For example, you'd certainly want a plan in place if you had to go in the hospital. Make sure you have several people in your back-up plan in case one person is not available. If you want to make a more formal, legally binding back-up arrangement, see the section in this chapter on standby guardianships.

Consider the following questions when creating your back-up plan. Work on your own or with your support person to develop more specific arrangements. For example, your plan should include arrangements for day care for times when your children's alternative caregiver is at work, and transportation for your children to attend activities and treatment appointments.

- Who will care for my children in the event that I'm unable to? In the short term? Over the long term?

- What additional resources or supports, beyond immediate relatives or friends, can I contact if I'm having difficulty caring for my children (school guidance counselor, pediatrician, babysitter)?

- What would my children prefer? Have I talked with them about alternatives? Are they aware of my back-up plan? Does my plan minimize disruption to their lives and ease their worries?

Your Self-Care Plan

A self-care plan can be persuasive in court. (See chapter 1, "Managing Your Mood and the Demands of Parenting," for information on how to prepare one.) Such a plan is evidence of your understanding of your depression, the factors that trigger times of illness or contribute to wellness, and your active efforts to manage your illness, working in collaboration with professionals. Showing that you recognize your limits, address your needs, and seek support when you feel you need a break are all signs of your good judgment. Asking for help is not a sign of weakness, even though you may think it is perceived that way. Trying to hide or deny your depression, ignoring your limits and needs, and withdrawing from others when you really would benefit from support can all be viewed by the court as examples of poor judgment. Having a self-care plan will help you educate the court about how stable you are, and how you live with and manage your depression. It will also help you take care of yourself during the custody process, when the additional stress may make you depressed or anxious.

The Role and Process of Evaluations

Parents, the judge, attorneys, or the representatives of the child-welfare agency in family-court matters may request evaluations to provide additional information for two main purposes: 1. To inform the court about "the best interests of the child"—parents' abilities, children's needs, and potential resolutions to custody conflicts; and 2. To inform the court about your depression, its "treatability," your compliance with treatment recommendations, and the likely prognosis or outcome. A GAL is appointed by the court to represent your child's best interests and to evaluate your ability to parent and whether you are capable of meeting your children's needs. A GAL may be a lawyer or a mental-health professional. The GAL's specific role is outlined in the court order. The court may require you to have a psychiatric or psychological evaluation by a mental-health professional if you have a diagnosis of mental illness. Sometimes the mental-health professional will also be asked to evaluate the effects of your illness on your ability to parent and on your children. Either type of evaluation may focus on whether you have a good understanding of your children's physical and emotional needs and whether you put these needs ahead of your own (Ward and Shaw 1995). It's common for a GAL or mental-health professional to be involved in cases where parents have mental-health issues.

There is wide variability in what constitutes an evaluation for the court, depending in part on what state law requires. There is no official definition of "good parenting." Specific language in the law about parenting varies from state to state. It's probably fair to say that most judges rely on the notion of what a reasonable person would say as to what constitutes a good parent. However, because there is no formal definition, it is often left to the GAL or the evaluator to decide what questions to ask and what information to present to the court.

Likewise, there is wide variability in the training, quality, and integrity of evaluators. Some GALs or evaluators, attorneys, or mental-health professionals do this type of work because they care about children. They may not necessarily have formal training or extensive experience in mental health or family relationships. Others may be experts in a particular area, like psychiatric diagnosis, and be encouraged to comment on aspects of the case outside their expertise. For example, a psychiatrist or psychologist may know a great deal about adult mental illness but know nothing about parenting and children, or vice versa.

The most comprehensive evaluations are conducted by a multidisciplinary group of professionals who use a team approach to collect information, and who check their findings and conclusions with each other (Jacobsen, Miller, and Kirkwood 1997). These teams are costly, however. Many evaluations are conducted by attorneys or mental-health professionals working alone, who may be strongly influenced by their own values and attitudes about parenting, children, and mental illness.

The evaluator, whether serving as a GAL or conducting a mental-health evaluation, should begin by explaining the process to you. You have the right to ask what the evaluator's qualifications are. You also have the right to ask the evaluator questions about who will have access to the final report. In evaluations required by the court, any information you provide to the evaluator can be used in the report and potentially shared with everyone involved. The court order will indicate whom the report may be shared with. It may be that only the attorneys are allowed to read the report, at the courthouse, and that no copies of the report can be made. Your attorney may have to seek the court's permission to allow you to review the report.

The Guardian Ad Litem (GAL)

A GAL may be a lawyer or a mental-health professional. The best GAL for a parent with depression has specialized training in family law, and is familiar with the current clinical literature on mental health and parenting. We interviewed an experienced GAL in Massachusetts who is a licensed psychologist provider. The following is taken from our interview with this GAL and her responses pertain to Massachusetts. Practice may vary greatly in other states.

Question: What is the purpose and process of having a guardian ad litem assigned?

Answer: GALs provide information to advise the court. They are usually assigned by a judge, and their evaluation is one piece of evidence in the overall determination of someone's ability to parent and of the best interests of their children. GALs can be either attorneys or mental-health professionals, such as psychologists or social workers. Either parent can request a GAL, but it's ultimately up to the judge to decide if a GAL evaluation is a useful addition to the court case. The judge also decides whether one or both parents can pay for the services of a GAL, and the proportion that each parent must pay. If both parents have the ability to pay, then the cost is split between them. If only one parent has the ability to pay and the other parent does not, then the parent with financial resources pays. In cases where both parents are poor, there may be state funds available to cover the cost. Custody and visitation decisions may be heavily influenced by the GAL report.

Question: Should a parent assume the GAL has experience with and knowledge of mental illness? What can a parent do if the GAL seems to have limited mental-health background?

Answer: No, the GAL may be a lawyer not specifically trained in mental-health issues. The parent should ask her lawyer, the court, or the GAL about the GAL's background and experience. Keep in mind that the GAL needs to be qualified or the GAL report is no good to the court.

Question: What questions can a parent ask of the GAL?

Answer: Parents should feel comfortable asking the GAL any questions they may have. The GAL will tell parents when they've posed a question the GAL is not allowed to answer.

Question: What does a GAL evaluation usually consist of?

Answer: Every GAL differs in the way she conducts an evaluation. The American Psychological Association has guidelines for custody evaluations that a GAL can choose to follow. GALs are interested in multiple sources of information. Each piece of information is gathered for a dual purpose: to determine each child's needs and each parent's ability to meet those needs.

An evaluation can include meeting with the parents at the GAL's office two or three times to gather information on their marital history, the history of the relationship from which the children come, the developmental history of the children, how the children are doing at the present time, what the parents' concerns are, and what they hope the court will order. At least two office interviews are conducted where each parent brings the children in, and the GAL observes how each parent and the children respond to one another. If the GAL is a psychologist, psychological testing may be administered to screen for any psychological problems. Children are sometimes interviewed individually at home and observed with each parent, in each parent's home. The GAL prefers to see each home as it would look if a friend was coming over for coffee. She wants to know how the children live day-to-day. The weight given to the child's preferences about custody is usually determined by the age and maturity of the child and the context in which the statement is made.

After these interviews take place, a GAL may talk to school personnel, the pediatrician, therapists, some neutral friends, a neighbor, or a grandparent. A GAL might call a parent's boss to find out if the parent is reliable and comes to work on time, which shows the GAL whether the parent is organized enough to meet the demands of day-to-day life. While this information is considered "hearsay" because it comes from a third party, a GAL can include it in her report, noting the source.

GALs use research data to strengthen and support conclusions and recommendations they give to the court. GALs advise the judge on relevant research findings related to the case and the limits of the research. They will tell the judge if they believe a parent is a risk to the child.

Question: What suggestions do you have for a parent with depression preparing for a GAL evaluation?

Answer: Be organized and work cooperatively with the GAL. Be open and honest. In and of itself, mental illness is not a reason to deny custody or access to children. If you refuse to sign a release for the GAL to be able to speak with your therapist, the GAL is likely to imagine the information you're withholding is much worse than it actually is. Remember, it's okay to need and use supports. This shows the GAL that you have good judgment. The GAL will worry about the parent who denies problems.

Make a list of providers you're working with. Have your medical history, psychiatric history, history of hospitalizations, and a list of any medications you are taking. Gathering this information for the GAL demonstrates that you are responsible and organized, two important qualities in being a parent and in being able to meet your child's needs.

(Note from the authors: We encourage you to discuss disclosure of your illness and treatment records with your attorney and your providers, determining what information from your past records must be released and what your providers or records will say. The determination of your ability to parent may not require review of all records [for example, your juvenile records may not be relevant]. It may be in your interest for the GAL to talk with your provider, rather than review records, or vice versa.)

Question: Is it possible to change a GAL?

Answer: A parent's lawyer can petition to have the GAL removed from the case, but you need to have very good reasons for such a petition.

Question: What suggestions do you have for a parent with depression dealing with an unsympathetic GAL?

Answer: GALs are supposed to be objective, and they may appear to be unsympathetic because they are staying neutral. Parents need to show good judgment as well as good boundaries with the GAL.

Typically, GALs review their evaluation with each parent before the report is presented in court. The GAL should explain his perception of the parent's strengths and weaknesses, and his conclusions about the children's needs and the parent's ability to meet them. This can be a difficult and painful process for both the parent and the GAL, because the GAL may be saying things the parent does not want to hear.

The cost of a GAL evaluation typically depends upon how many hours the GAL spends collecting materials, interviewing family members and other contacts, putting the information together, and writing a report. Some states limit the total cost of court-ordered GAL evaluations. If you are paying, however, the cost of the evaluation may only be limited by two things: 1. the amount of time the GAL spends to complete the job; and 2. the amount of money you have. You can reduce the GAL's time investment by organizing information, providing required reports and records, and preparing for interview sessions.

GAL Investigation Preparation Checklist

When you first meet with or speak to the GAL, find out what information you can provide to help complete the evaluation. Remember to consult with your attorney about what information to share. The following checklist of items typically requested can help you prepare for a GAL evaluation. Put a check mark in each box as you prepare the item.

❑ A list of immediate family members and background information: ages, dates of birth, current occupation or school placement, educational history, employment record

❑ Copies of evaluations or reports about your children: developmental or educational assessments, report cards, specialists' evaluations, medical records, consultations, etc., particularly if your children have any special education or medical needs

❑ Copies of evaluations or reports about yourself: medical history, psychiatric or psychological evaluations, treatment and hospitalization records, particularly as these may document your commitment to actively managing and treating your depression

❑ An outline of your current treatment plan, including any medications you are taking, dosage, timing, etc.

❑ A copy of your back-up plan for your children for when you're not feeling well and your self-care plan, if you have written them

❑ A list of supportive people the GAL can contact for more information about your family, including names and phone numbers of: school teachers, pediatrician, close relatives, neighbors or friends, psychiatrist or psychotherapist, etc.

❑ An outline of the dates and key events in your family's history, including dates of marital separation, any previous custody or visitation orders, restraining orders, date of divorce, etc., and copies of these court decisions

Collecting this information will help you organize your thoughts for the evaluation. It will also demonstrate your capacity to organize and report information. You should do this even if the GAL asks you to sign release of information forms to obtain copies of records and reports directly from their sources.

Psychiatric or Psychological Evaluations

Judges aren't necessarily mental-health professionals. Most want to make informed decisions when parents have psychiatric diagnoses and will order psychiatric or psychological evaluations to obtain the information they need. The judge may want to know how you are managing your depression, how well you are responding to treatment, and if your ability to parent is affected. If your parental functioning is compromised, the judge may want to know about your prognosis, that is, whether and when you might be expected to feel better. A well-done evaluation by a psychiatrist or psychologist can answer these questions and address these concerns.

If you are being treated for depression, you have probably met with a psychiatrist or psychologist before and are familiar with the evaluation process. The psychiatrist or psychologist will begin by reviewing the purpose of the evaluation and confidentiality issues with you. A thorough psychiatric interview will include questions about your personal history, psychosexual history, family history, present illness, and previous illnesses (Kaplan and Sadock 1998). The mental-health professional will also be looking at your general appearance, including: posture and grooming; behavior and activity level; your mood; your speech; any signs of hallucinations or other strange sensations; your thought processes; alertness, memory, and ability to concentrate; ability to control your impulses; judgment and insight; and your ability to report facts about your situation accurately. Because the court has made the evaluation request in the context of a custody proceeding, the mental-health professional may also ask you questions about your children, their needs, and your ability to meet their needs.

A psychologist evaluator may also administer formal psychological testing of intelligence and personality (Kaplan and Sadock 1998). Psychologists administer what are called "standardized tests," sets of questions and tasks they ask of everyone, always in the same way. Because the tests have been given the same way every time to thousands of individuals across the country, psychologists can see how your responses compare with those of others and can draw conclusions based on these comparisons. Psychologists then put test results together with interview information to write a final, comprehensive report.

You may have a hard time understanding what an evaluator's questions have to do with parenting and your children. In fact, psychologists have almost no scientifically proven ability to directly predict a person's functioning as a parent from standardized test results (Budd and Holdsworth 1996). However, your interview answers and test responses help the evaluator understand your characteristic strengths and weaknesses and how you make sense of the world. Many of these characteristics contribute to your ability to parent. For example, a test might measure your ability to put things in a logical order—to tell a story about what happens first in a picture and then what happens next. While the test or the picture might not seem to have anything to do with being a parent, the ability to describe the way things *usually* happen would help you predict what was going to happen next. And parenting involves a lot of predicting—of what will help an infant stop crying or what a teenager will do when a limit is set.

The Evaluation Experience

An evaluation can be a very stressful experience. If you were depressed or anxious before the custody proceeding, you can expect your symptoms to flare up. The evaluator has a great deal of power over you and your family in the present and, potentially, for years to come. It makes complete sense that this will feel intimidating and overwhelming and that you might become angry and even more depressed. Be prepared to cope with the stress. Refer to your self-care plan, seek support from friends, relatives, and professionals, and focus on making the experience as easy as possible for your children.

An evaluation can take a long time—sometimes a year or longer. It can be hard waiting for the evaluator's recommendations and your day in court, especially if you're requesting a change in custody or visitation because your access to your children is limited, or if you have concerns about their well-being in the care of the other parent. The evaluation itself may feel intrusive. The evaluator asks many questions, some of them very personal, and you may feel exposed and vulnerable.

You may feel like you are being observed and monitored, which you are. The evaluator's attempts to see your family at home, in their natural environment, may seem phony or even stupid. One woman we know talks about how inappropriate she felt it was for the evaluator to sit on the living room floor while interviewing her about her grandchildren. And it never seems "natural" to have a professional checking out your home furnishings.

It may be hard to know what to say about your desire to parent your children. "While it is natural to communicate to everyone how much you want and need your child, these comments are sometimes viewed as focusing on your (own) needs instead of your child's" (Ward & Shaw 1995). You may be confused about what or how much to say about the other parent and fear that, if you share your concerns, you will be seen as "telling stories."

An evaluation can also be a positive experience, however, providing you with an opportunity to have a voice equal to that of the other parent. Evaluations can work to your advantage by educating the court about depression, treatment, and parenting. The evaluator can document for the court your efforts at managing your depression and steps in recovery from your illness. And, if your children are old enough, the evaluation can provide them a chance to talk about the living situation in which they would be most comfortable. An evaluation can give you hope that things will be resolved or changed for the better. Kim, a mother with bipolar depression, described her evaluation experience and the positive outcome.

> *I had my first psychiatric hospitalization when I turned thirty-eight. I had tried to kill myself. At the time, I was faced with a bitter separation from my verbally abusive husband. I voluntarily gave physical custody of my seven-year-old daughter to my ex due to the instability of my bipolar illness. After two years of trying different psychiatric medications, individual therapy, and group therapy, my illness stabilized and, with support from my therapist, case manager, and lawyer, I began to rebuild my life.*
>
> *During the two years it took to get my illness under control, I was also going through divorce proceedings with my spouse. I sought physical custody of my daughter after noticing signs of neglect when she came to me for visits. As part of the divorce proceedings, my husband and I were investigated by a court-appointed guardian ad litem to help determine which of us should have physical custody of our daughter. I was surprised when the GAL report recommended that I receive physical custody of my daughter. The GAL reported to the court that I was very involved in all my treatments (individual therapy, group therapy, manic-depressive support groups), I had good support from my relatives, and I had a closer and more interactive relationship with my daughter than my ex had.*

Other Situations Involving the Legal System

You may find yourself in other situations that involve contact with the legal system. You may feel the system is working "for" or "against" you, depending on how you got there and what the outcome is. Having some knowledge of the legal system and the way things work will increase the likelihood that you will be satisfied with your experience. The legal system actually offers opportunities for you to protect and provide for your children. Some of these situations and opportunities are described below.

Visitation

After a custody decision has been made in a divorce or care and protection case, a schedule for visitation for the noncustodial parent is decided. A visitation schedule can be left up to the parents to work out or, if the parents cannot agree, a judge will determine one, perhaps based on an evaluator's recommendation. This may not be the schedule either parent hoped for. If the court finds, after a hearing, that visitation would seriously endanger the child physically or emotionally, the court might not allow any visitation. However, a parent has the right to visit with his children unless it would endanger them. Supervised visitation, where the visit is monitored by someone like a relative or social worker, is not uncommon in cases where a parent has a history of severe mental illness with active symptoms or a history of not complying with prescribed medications or treatment.

You can request changes to an existing visitation order. Check with the clerk of court's office at the local courthouse for the forms you'll need to fill out and file. You may be charged a small fee for filing this paperwork. If you have a low income, ask the clerk if the fee can be waived. Before you file the forms, be aware of the following.

- There must be a significant change in the circumstances of the parent asking for a change in visitation. For example, if you were not taking your medication in the past and you are now, you must show that you are seeing a psychiatrist and taking your medications as prescribed. This is best proven by testimony from the psychiatrist or case manager in person, not just in a letter or note (Ward and Shaw 1995).

- If you have abused substances in the past and you are asking for changes, you must show that you're getting help and must have a witness to testify on your behalf, like a doctor, case manager, or therapist.

- *You need to be flexible.* Do not walk into court *demanding* anything. Be prepared for things to change in small steps so you can show the court successes.

There are other situations in which you have a right to contact or visit with your child. If your child is placed in foster care by your state's child-welfare agency pending an investigation of your parenting ability, you still have a right to maintain contact with your child if such contact does not put the child at further risk of harm. It may also be possible to maintain contact with your child through a legal guardianship or an "open" adoption.

Foster Care

Foster care provides a child with a temporary home. If you require psychiatric hospitalization and don't have a partner, relative, or friend to care for your children, you may voluntarily ask the state child-welfare agency to provide foster care. When child abuse and neglect allegations against a parent are found to be true, a child may be placed in foster care involuntarily, until the judge decides whether the child can return to the parent or until the child is adopted. Temporary custody of your child may be granted to the state child-welfare agency by the court.

Placements with the child-welfare agency typically involve several steps. First, your family is assigned to a special worker to identify any major concerns. Second, a service plan is developed to address these concerns. Third, a social worker will provide you with ongoing support to meet the service plan objectives. If you are a parent with depression recently discharged from the hospital, the service plan might include objectives like "the parent will follow the hospital discharge treatment plan" and "the parent will take all medications as pre-scribed." The service plan is a road map for you to follow. It's important to understand that the service plan also contains the obligations and responsibilities of the child-welfare agency. Thus, you should be sure that the document contains all the necessary supports and services, your responsibilities, and the agency's obligations as well. For example, it might include items like, "the mother will drive the child to all counseling appointments," or "the child-welfare agency will provide a parent aide." It is extremely important that steps to be taken by each party for you to reunify with your children are clearly spelled out.

Foster parents are licensed, trained, and monitored by the child-welfare agency. They have some say in decisions affecting a child placed in their care. Foster parents can make emergency and routine medical decisions, though this can vary. They often treat the child as part of their own family, which might involve having the child attend church with the foster-care family, getting the child's hair cut, and letting a teenager have her ears pierced.

You can be an active participant in planning your child's placement in foster care. Be sure to talk with the social worker about how you will be involved in your child's care and how decisions will be made about your child. Ask for explanations if you don't understand decisions that are made. You should be engaged with the social worker in talking about what you want for your child. Let your social worker know your preferences about your child's daily routine, schooling, health care, and participation in religious activities. Be sure a realistic plan is in place for your children to be returned to your care and custody. The plan should clearly outline *who* has to do *what* by *when*. Responsibilities and deadlines should be agreed upon by everyone and documented in language everyone understands. Find out where to turn if you're not satisfied with the service planning process, your child's placement, or your treatment by the agency. Is there an agency ombudsman or a formal grievance procedure? If you feel over-whelmed, frightened, or intimidated by the process, ask a friend, relative, or an advocate to join you in meeting with agency representatives.

Typically, biological parents have the right to visit their children while they are in foster care, unless there are safety concerns. A visitation schedule is spelled out in the service plan and should include arrangements for supervision, if it is recommended, and transportation. Visitation is normally set up by the social worker; however, sometimes visitation is coordinated by the foster parents. If you are working to regain custody of your child, try to obtain as much visitation as possible. Be sure to attend visits regularly, as this is a factor the court will review to determine custody.

Legal Guardianship and Adoption

There are differences between legal guardianship and placing your children for adoption. A legal guardianship only temporarily suspends a parent's custo-dial rights, allowing you to continue to play a role in the child's life. Adoption may completely and permanently terminate your right to custody. Some of the differences between legal guardianship and adoption are outlined below.

Legal Guardianship

- Guardianship temporarily suspends rights and responsibilities of biological parents

- Guardian has sole rights to and control of the child

- Child has no inheritance rights from legal guardian

- Child is not considered a dependent of the legal guardian

- Child's birth name remains legal name

Adoption

- Terminates child's legal relationship with biological parents

- Adoptive parents have full legal, custody, parental, and financial responsibilities for the child

- Adopted child has inheritance rights from adoptive parents

- Adoptive parent can claim child as a dependent for income-tax purposes

- Child can take family name of adoptive parents

In a case where a person's parental rights might be terminated or where a parent feels it is best for his child to be placed in a permanent, alternative home, an "open" adoption can be suggested to the court. This can happen if continued contact with the biological parent is found by the court to be in the best interest of the child. Open adoptions allow for some degree of contact between the biological parents, the adoptive parents, and often the child, as well. Typically, adoptions are "closed"—the biological parents and the adoptive parents never know each other, and there is no contact between the biological parents and the child.

Standby Guardianship

Many states provide for what is called a "standby guardianship." This type of guardianship allows parents to choose a relative or friend to take care of their children in the event they become unable to care for them due to an illness or death. The standby guardian is pre-approved by the court, so when a crisis occurs, children are subjected to as little disruption as possible. Contact your state attorney bar association to find out if this option exists in your state.

If you are considering choosing someone as a guardian for your children, you may find the following questions helpful. You may wish to share these with potential candidates so they can see what a guardian's responsibilities actually involve.

$\checkmark$

Questions to Consider When Choosing a Legal Guardian

1. Is this person someone you trust and who already has a good relationship with your children? _____ Yes _____ No

2. Is this person aware of all the responsibilities of a legal guardian? _____ Yes _____ No

3. As a legal guardian, this person will receive funds to provide for your children (e.g., from you, Social Security, public assistance programs, welfare). Is this person aware that there may be financial demands that may require her to use her own money to raise your children (that funds for your children may not be sufficient or may run out)? _____ Yes _____ No

4. Has this person thought about how being a legal guardian might affect his own family, children, health, etc.? _____ Yes _____ No
   If "Yes," please list possible affects:
   _____

5. Does this person have the time and energy it takes to raise your children, especially if this person already has children? _____ Yes _____ No

6. What are some of the specific reasons you want this person to be a legal guardian for your children?

   _____

   _____

   _____

Preparing for Legal Outcomes

True

The legal system often sets parents against each other. The court's decision can make you feel like a "winner" or a "loser." What will you do if you are not satisfied with the outcome of your case? You may be so focused on "winning" that you are totally unprepared for your disappointment when things don't go your way. Even "winning" has its price. Think about how you will handle all the powerful emotions that are bound to surface.

1. What feelings might surface if you "lose"?

   _____

2. What effect will such emotions have on your illness?

   _____

3. Who can you talk to after the court makes its decision?

_____

The same holds true even when you are pleased with the outcome.

1. So, what feelings might surface if you "win"?

_____

2. Are you prepared to deal with all the responsibilities outlined in the court's decision?

_____

3. Will you feel you have to be a "super" parent now, to compensate for your mental illness?

_____

You may wish to explore these questions and others in more detail with your counselor, a trusted friend, or a supportive relative.

You May Be a Winner

Involvement in the legal system often takes on an adversarial tone, especially for people labeled with depression. Battles are fought, and won or lost, with a psychiatric diagnosis used as ammunition by one parent against the other. Often, children are the real losers, especially in divorce and custody situations. You can navigate, survive, and use the legal system, with the help of knowledge and good representation, to increase the likelihood of positive outcomes for your children and you. Prepare yourself, ask questions, and participate as actively as you can.

Chapter 11

When Your Children Are Living with Others

There are many reasons why you might be separated from your children—planned or unplanned, short-term, long-term, or permanently. You may be in the hospital because of your depression with no visits, or only occasional, hour-long visits with your children. If you were hospitalized in an emergency and had no other childcare resources, your children might be in foster care through the social-services agency (child welfare). You may be separated or divorced from their other parent and share custody, with the children moving back and forth regularly between his home and yours. Or your ex-partner may have custody, and the children may visit you on weekends or during school vacations. Perhaps your children are living with their grandparents or an aunt or uncle while you take a break from full-time parenting to work toward recovery. You may have had your parental rights terminated by the court.

These separations affect everyone. The impact varies with how the separations are handled. Visits may bring you and your children great joy and pain in the same moment, because along with time together, visits mean more goodbyes. If you haven't seen your children in a while, you may not know what toys to bring to a visit or what food to have on hand at home. While visits may be fun, time with children can also be stressful. You may ultimately have to make some tough decisions about how much time with and responsibility for your children you can manage successfully.

Your Feelings About Separations from Your Children

In the most positive of situations, you may be separated from your children in a voluntary, planned, time-limited fashion. We all take vacations from our children to maintain our well-being and to nurture our adult relationships—whether that planned break is at a health spa or a psychiatric facility. Ideally, relatives, friends, or baby-sitters care for your children in your absence. You provide lengthy instructions—lists of nap times and bed times, favorite foods and toys, and phone numbers where you can be reached in emergencies. You trust your carefully selected childcare provider, and they respect you as a parent. You return home at the time arranged, and your children are delighted to see you.

In the worst-case scenario, your separation is unplanned or involuntary. An emergency hospitalization may result in your children moving in the middle of the night to a relative's or friend's house, or a foster home, if no one else is available to care for them. You may be involved in a conflicted divorce situation, where your depression has been identified as an issue by your ex-partner and your capacity to care for your children has been called into question in court. Unfortunately, if your depression is severe, you may neglect your children, and someone, perhaps their classroom teacher, may notify the state social-services or child-welfare agency. Social services may insist that your children remain with relatives or live in a foster home while you take time to focus on your recovery.

You probably have a range of thoughts and feelings about being apart from your children. You may be relieved that they are well cared for by people you know and trust, so you can focus on taking care of yourself and dealing with your treatment issues. Or you may be furious that your authority as a parent has been undermined by an ex-partner, social worker, or judge. Many parents, depending on why and how the separation has occurred, feel one or more of the following:

- **It's my fault my children are not with me.** Not necessarily true. Others, including your children, may accuse you of not being well enough to care adequately for them. A diagnosis of a psychiatric disorder like depression can be "used against you" by others. Unfortunately, the stigma of mental illness is powerful, and family members, helping professionals, and even judges make decisions based on stereotypes and ignorance. In fact, there is as much variability in parenting skills among parents in general as there is among parents with depression. Parenting does not come "naturally" to anyone; it's a set of skills that develops over time with practice and feedback. Even when you're depressed, you may be quite capable of providing for your children. In your family, in fact, you may function as the primary caregiver. So, the separation from your children may not be your fault and, certainly, your depression is not your fault.

- **If I can't take care of my children twenty-four hours a day, I'm a failure.** Not true. There are many ways to be a parent and to be actively involved with your children. Caring for them full-time is only one way. Choosing to go to the hospital to attend to your recovery may be the right decision for you and your children. Creating a situation in which grandparents provide respite care may be healthy for everyone. In a divorce situation, allowing your children to have a primary residence with their other parent may be the best choice. Your success or failure as a parent is measured by the decisions you make for your children, with their well-being as your priority, and not by how many hours a day you are with them.

- **I don't deserve to be with my children because I have depression. I am a terrible role model for them.** This is not true. As one mother with depression put it, "I sometimes think we make the better parents because it is so hard to be like this, and we have to try twice as hard." You did not choose to be depressed, but you can choose to make efforts to manage your symptoms and focus on wellness and recovery. You can choose to seek the help you need to promote your recovery. You can focus on your successes rather than your failures. You may be, as a person actively coping with what can be a life-threatening illness, the most significant role model in your children's lives.

- **My husband (mother-in-law, social worker) is trying to steal my children away from me.** This may or may not be true, though if you are at all paranoid, these feelings can really grow out of proportion. Your husband actually may threaten to take the children away from you because of your depression. Your mother-in-law may seem to be working hard and even competing with you to be a "better mother" to your children than you are. The social worker is probably just trying to do what's right for your children, even though it may feel like she is undermining your functioning as a parent. It may be tricky to tease out "reality" in these relationships, but allow yourself the possibility of believing that others may have your family's best interests at heart.

- **My kids don't love me anymore. They will forget I am their mother.** Not likely. Most children love their parents through thick and thin, even in extreme situations when their parents are abusive or abandon them. They may be angry with you or angry about the situation if they are unable to live with you or see you when they want. Your child may scream and yell, "I hate you, Daddy," or even try to hit you. He doesn't really hate you—he's just angry and doesn't know how else to express it. Also remember that children never forget. Think about all the stories you have read in the newspaper about adopted children looking for their birth parents twenty, thirty, or forty years after their adoption. They may come to call another person "Mom" or "Dad," but you are never truly replaced by another.

Cathy talked about her grief at losing day-to-day contact with her child.

After the birth of a baby, we all plan to spend the majority of our lives with that child. So, when the time arrives that we are no longer permitted to be with our children, this produces a "grieving process." Grieving is a normal emotional experience that all human beings go through. Without grief, there can be no moving on in life—we become stuck. Becoming stuck can increase symptoms and, all too often, make us feel as if something is wrong with us.

So what do we do when we lose a significant part of our lives? We grieve. We feel sad, angry, go through denial, bargaining, acceptance, and feel generally overwhelmed. You might be saying to yourself, "How can I heal when I am in so much pain?" It's not easy, but I learned that we become stronger and more sensitive to ourselves and others if we grieve.

People diagnosed with a psychiatric disorder may experience the loss of many roles, including that of parent, worker, or healthy person. Simply becoming a parent often triggers the feeling of losing one's self in the overwhelming joy and unrelenting day-to-day demands of caring for a child you love more than life itself. Acknowledging these losses and developing a new identity as a healthy parent, with or without depression, with or without twenty-four-hour-a-day responsibility for childcare, is a challenge for all of us.

Evaluating the Situation and Understanding Your Feelings

How do you feel about your children's current living or visiting arrangement? What are your worries about being separated from them? Are there benefits in the current arrangement? How does it affect you? You may have negative and positive thoughts and feelings, some that may be distorted by your grief or anger. Answering the following questions will help you think more clearly about these issues. Record your answers on the lines provided. Use additional paper, if necessary, or write in your journal.

What is your children's living or visiting arrangement?

_____

_____

Are you with your children as often as you are able? Yes/No (circle one)

What was your role in determining this arrangement?

_____

_____

Were you an active participant in the decision-making process? Yes/No (circle one)

What are your worries about the current situation? What do you fear most?

_____

_____

Are you comfortable, overall, with the situation? Yes/No (circle one)

Describe your relationship with your children's other caregivers.

_____

_____

Are they generally positive relationships? Yes/No (circle one)

How do you spend your time with your children?

_____

_____

Do you usually have a good time together? Yes/No (circle one)

How do you spend your time when you are not with your children?

_____

_____

Are you able to focus on wellness and recovery? Yes/No (circle one)

What are the pros and cons of this living arrangement?

_____

_____

Do the benefits outweigh the disadvantages? Yes/No (circle one)

Review your answers. If you find you have circled more "Yes"s than "No"s, you may be satisfied with your arrangements with your children. Congratulations on negotiating the transition to a new parenting identity! If you have circled more "No"s than "Yes"s" the remainder of this chapter will guide you in improving the situation.

Understanding Your Children's Reactions to Separations from You

Many books have been written about helping children cope with divorce. Some of the advice in these books may apply to your separation from your children, whether it's temporary or permanent, the result of divorce or not. Children of different ages tend to respond in characteristic ways, regardless of the cause of the separation. Parents with depression tend to blame themselves and feel responsible for any signs of unhappiness or distress they see in their children. Or, they may think their children are trying to "hurt" them, on purpose, with their words or actions. It is important to understand that children's reactions, the ways they express themselves, are related to their ages and circumstances and are in no way related to your depression.

Depending on your children's ages or maturity levels, it may be difficult to know exactly how they are feeling about a separation from you or a new family situation. It's important to understand that children's feelings of anger and sadness are quite normal in these situations, and that these feelings need to be expressed. Unfortunately, *how* children express their feelings does not always lead you to understand *what* they are feeling. For example, babies or toddlers may have difficulty sleeping, may be cranky, or may be clingy and afraid to leave you. Slightly older children may have temper tantrums, possibly about seemingly irrelevant issues. They may regress to clinging to their "blankie" or a pacifier, or wetting their pants or the bed. School-age children may seem sad or withdrawn. They may complain of stomachaches and make daily visits to the school nurse. Or they may pick on other children on the playground. Preteens may be much more articulate in expressing their feelings, blaming you for everything that is wrong in their lives. Teens may withdraw into their own worlds, hanging out in their bedrooms, playing loud music, and avoiding you altogether. They may not want to share any information with you.

Remind yourself that these are the normal ways of coping for children of these ages. In fact, your children may act this way whether or not they have feelings about their family situation or separations from you. All you can do is open the door to communication, providing opportunities to talk and helping them label their feelings. You can do this by thinking about how you might feel and suggesting possibilities to them. And try not to respond to or judge their feelings too quickly. Don't rush to defend yourself or help them feel better right away. Just listen and give yourself some time to really hear and understand.

Children can say things that are painful, but try to understand that these statements reflect confusion or hurt your child feels. Ask yourself how you would feel if you had no control or say in a difficult situation. You may already know how this feels if you have been hospitalized or have lost day-to-day contact with or custody of your children. Your answer to this question can help you understand how your children might be feeling and help you deal with their verbal and nonverbal expressions of anger or frustration. Try to focus on the positive aspects of your children expressing their feelings, and do not let what they say make you more depressed.

Your Relationship with Alternative Caregivers

Your relationship with others who are caring for your children can be a source of great comfort and pride or anger and frustration. If you have negotiated a mutually supportive, respectful relationship with someone you trust—an ex-partner, family member, or foster parent—you can work together in the best interest of your children. This is something to be proud of. However, many parents who share caregiving responsibility with others feel vulnerable, as if they have failed. The other caregiver may be viewed as a competitor—either in the "who is a better parent contest," or in the "battle" for the children's affections. Your children may be caught in loyalty binds, torn between attachments to family members or caregivers.

In the best situations, people who share responsibility for children serve as resources to each other. Good communication is key, as successful management of schedules and relationships depends on an open flow of information back and forth. This may require informing and educating alternative caregivers about your depression to alleviate any fears or stigma that may exist. If you feel this is too daunting a task for you to take on yourself, enlist the assistance of a friend, advocate, helping professional, or member of an advocacy or support group like the National Alliance for the Mentally Ill. Advocacy groups often have educational information available, which you can obtain in doctors' offices, at local agencies, or on the Internet. There may be support groups available in your community for grandparents caring for grandchildren, or foster parents, that may offer education about psychiatric disorders.

People who successfully share the care of children also share information about children's needs and interests, joys and concerns. Ideally they are consistent about rules, limits, and behavior-management strategies. This sharing can be difficult to achieve, particularly if one parent feels undermined or disempowered by the other. On the other hand, some parents with depression report having very supportive, ongoing relationships with those individuals who provide respite or share custody. These individuals can be incredible resources, providing information about your children that can enhance your ability to care for them successfully.

One mother reported such an incident with her teenaged son and her ex-husband, who had custody. The boy lived at his father's during the school week and visited his mother on the weekends. Fortunately, she and her ex-husband spoke often. In a phone conversation, her son announced he wanted to go into the city on the train by himself for the first time during the coming weekend. While the mom's initial reaction was to be shocked and worried, she had the presence of mind to continue to talk with her son about his plans and to consult with his father. Dad felt the boy could manage the trip and worked with Mom and the son during the week to negotiate the plan for the weekend. The boy's father, in this instance, worked well together with his ex-wife to decide what would be best for their son.

There may be creative ways to solve other problems in shared parenting arrangements. Another mother we know was quite concerned when custody of her daughter was awarded by the court to her ex-husband during their divorce. While the mother was viewed as the less adequate parent because of her depression, she also knew that her ex-husband had never cared for their daughter on a day-to-day basis and could not even cook. This mother negotiated an agreement with her ex-husband that she would prepare and bring dinner to the house each evening, so she could be sure her daughter was eating healthy meals. This obviously was a great benefit to the father and daughter, also providing a meaningful way for the mother to be involved continuously in her daughter's life while she pursued her recovery. Ultimately, this pair of divorced parents agreed on a shared custody arrangement when Mom was well.

Emphasizing the Positive

While it may be difficult to totally conquer your fears and anxieties about being away from your children, it's important to attempt to focus on the positives for your children and yourself. If the negatives outweigh the positives, or if you have real concerns about your children's safety or well-being, it is essential to identify steps to shift the balance to the positive side of the equation.

Take the time to list below the positives and negatives in your relationship with other caregivers. If you have difficulty generating positives or negatives, ask a friend or support person to help you think this through. You could ask your children, though it may make them feel like they are caught in the middle between you and the other caregiver, which you should try to avoid. And if they came up with more positives than negatives about the other caregiver, your feelings might be hurt. However, you might think about what the positives and negatives are *from their perspectives*, if you can, to get a more complete, better understanding of the relationships involved. What might be a negative for you (like undermining your authority by allowing your daughter to get her ears pierced without your permission) might actually be perceived as a positive from your daughter's perspective!

Positives: (For example, my ex-husband supports our children's relationships with my parents and their grandparents, or the foster mother consults with me about selecting clothes for my children.)

Negatives: (For example, my ex-wife forgets to share information about school activities with me, or my sister-in-law let my teenage daughter stay out later than I would like.)

If the negatives in the relationships outweigh the positives, it may be time to take action to improve your relationship with your co-parent. First, run your lists by an objective third party—your advocate or helping professional, or a friend or someone who is not a family member. Make sure you're not just emphasizing the negatives because you are depressed. Decide on several things you would like to change. Try to be clear about your goals and motives and that the changes will benefit your children and you.

Specific things I would like to change: (For example, I would like to receive information about school activities in advance, so I can show my children I care by attending.)

Talk over ways to approach the other caregiver with an objective third party, like a good friend or relative, or an advocate. Role play with your friend or advocate a potential conversation that you might have with your co-parent. Practice asking for what you want or need to have happen and get feedback to maximize your likelihood of success. If you are unable to make changes on your own, you can always engage the services of a professional mediator or even an attorney. This course of action may be expensive, but may be your last resort if you are truly concerned or worried about conflict in your relationship and its impact on your children.

Planning for Visits

Making visits meaningful requires planning. Adding to this challenge is the fact that you may not be living at home right now, you may be in the hospital, or your visits may be supervised. The most important things about visits (and time with your children in general) are that they are consistent, dependable, and safe—both physically and emotionally. Children develop secure feelings about themselves and others if their lives are predictable and if they know they can count on you. If you're struggling with depression right now, it may be better to arrange for fewer, shorter visits that are manageable for you and are, therefore, positive experiences for your children. This strategy may work better than making promises for more frequent, longer visits that you can't keep or deal with successfully.

Your personal hygiene, dress, and behavior send messages to your children about how you're doing and also influence how your children react to you. If you can, make an effort to dress for the occasion. This will help you feel better, too. Do not drink alcohol or abuse substances on visits. Remember, your children's perceptions of how you are doing affect them greatly. A visit is an opportunity to model self-care and a healthy lifestyle for your children.

It's important to keep a positive attitude about visits, no matter how you feel about your situation or whether you are happy with the schedule. Many parents talk about visits as being painful reminders of what their lives might have been like. This is true for parents without depression who are separated from their children, as well as for those with depression. Leaving each other when the visit is over can be sad and painful. Having a schedule in place and knowing when you will visit again will make things easier for everyone and give you both something to look forward to.

Making a Calendar Together

Children benefit from knowing the schedule. You can work together to make a calendar for the next few months to plan for and keep track of visits, as well as to mark other events, activities, and holidays. Simply sketch out a calendar or print out a blank one from your computer. You can decorate the calendar with crayons and markers or stickers. Make two copies of the calendar—one for the children and one for you. Share the calendar with the other caregiver to be sure you agree on the dates, times, and locations of visits. This will prevent conflict that can occur when there is confusion about the schedule and disappointment for your children.

Current Interests and Favorite Activities

Your children's interests and preferences may be changing fast, depending on their stages of development. A child who loves a certain kind of cereal one week may hate it the next week. Favorite television shows come and go. These things are hard to keep track of even when you are spending twenty-four hours a day together and even more difficult to monitor when you're separated for any length of time. You need to know about your children's interests and activities to plan for successful visits. Sit down with your child and fill out the following checklist. Modify the categories to fit your child's age and stage. You may want to re-do this activity every few months. If you cannot sit together with your child for whatever reason, or she is too young to respond, you might talk over the checklist with the other caregiver.

Current Interests:

☐ Favorite music: _____

☐ Favorite television show(s): _____

☐ Favorite book(s): _____

☐ Favorite sport(s): _____

☐ Favorite subject(s) in school: _____

☐ Favorite color: _____

☐ Favorite food(s): _____

☐ Favorite friend(s): _____

☐ Other favorites (outfits, games, pets, teams): _____

_____

Current Activities:

☐ Favorite thing(s) to do for fun: _____

☐ Favorite thing(s) to do to relax: _____

☐ Favorite thing(s) to do for exercise: _____

☐ Favorite activities at school: _____

☐ Other favorites (collections, hobbies, video games): _____

_____

You may want to jot down your children's names and the dates on the checklists, and save these as a record of your children's growth and development over the years.

Tips for Visits

Having an idea about your children's interests and activities will go a long way toward helping you plan successful visits. Depending on your child, she may enjoy a trip to a park, playground, or zoo. Public libraries often offer free passes to local museums or can be a destination in themselves. Nature walks, fishing, baking cookies, drawing, and coloring are all examples of activities that can provide opportunities for talking with your children, exploring their interests or concerns, or simply spending quiet time together. Television and videos can help trigger discussions in a nonthreatening way and can provide a "common ground" for conversation. Try to provide for some "down time" as well as more active events. While some parents worry that their children watch television too much, watching television can be a convenient way for children to relax and cope with transitions.

Don't try to compensate for all the time you are not with your children in one visit. Too much activity can be overwhelming. Some parents end up spending too much money during visits. They may feel guilty for having an illness and for all the times they are not able to be with their children, or they may want to show how much they miss and love them. This is a dilemma faced by one divorced father with depression. During visits, he often spends large amounts of money on food and entertainment. Lunch at a fast-food restaurant and a trip to the Children's Museum or bowling may cost him close to $100. More than anything, this father wants his children to enjoy their visits and have a good time. But he realizes he can't afford to spend so much money during these visits.

This is an example, once again, of a situation in which you may have to let go of your own feelings to do the right thing for your children. The better choice, and the right thing for your children, is to plan for something affordable that does not stress you out and add to your depression.

Special Situations

The Hospital. Parents often wonder if children should visit them in the hospital. While some hospitals have rules and regulations regarding children's visits, others have no policies at all. The decision may be left to the discretion of the parent. Your decision should be based on the length of your separation from your children, their ages, how well you are feeling, and what the hospital facility is like. The longer you are apart from your children, the more important it is to arrange for visits. Separations are handled differently by children of different ages. You may have to judge by how each child is doing on an individual basis. Plan for a visit when you are feeling better, rather than worse. Try to be as upbeat as possible. Ask the person caring for them in your absence to bring along an activity—a coloring book or game you might play together. Explain that you think about and miss them very much, and that you will be back home when you are feeling well and ready. Children may wonder why you are in the hospital or may have been witnesses to suicide attempts. Explain that you are working toward recovery and are in the hospital to stay safe. Reassure them that, no matter what, your illness is not their fault. If the hospital has a visiting room, a sunroom, or a cafeteria, perhaps you could arrange to visit there. If you want to visit with your children but are worried about the impact of your illness or the visit on them, or are not sure how you will react, ask for help from your social worker or counselor. Remember, you can stay in touch by phone, cards, or letters if visits aren't a good idea.

Supervised Visits. There may be times when, for whatever reason, you may be required by the court to have someone supervise your visits with your children. Having a mutually agreed-upon supervisor can help eliminate conflict with your children's other parent and allow you to focus on your children. The supervisor may be a relative, friend, minister, or other community member. The supervisor may be appointed by the court.

You may find being supervised a stressful experience. Barbara offered some advice about how to make supervised visits less tense and more pleasant.

> *In my weekly visits with my daughter, we usually have a nice time because I always plan to do something special with her. For instance, I will bring nail polish and we will do each other's nails. We like to play games like cards, chess, checkers, solitaire, Chinese checkers, or tic-tac-toe. We draw pictures and there are times when we talk and tell jokes. One thing I've noticed is that when we talk about health and sex education, the supervisor sometimes gets upset. But these subjects are just what my daughter is learning in school. We also talk about roller skating, hobbies, or friendships. My daughter asks about family members and friends she misses, and I tell her what is happening.*
>
> *Honesty is best, even when the supervisor doesn't like it. Your children will know you are telling them what is good or bad and what the consequences are when they do something wrong. My daughter tells me what she does wrong, like skipping school or coming home late after curfew time. She doesn't feel shame and she tells me, even though she knows I will tell her to do better in the future. I am glad my child is able to talk to me about anything. Your children know you will always be there for them and will answer their questions truthfully.*

As difficult as supervised visits may be, they may be your only option. It's important to try to focus on your children in this situation, considering their needs and feelings. Your shame, humiliation, or anger at having your interactions monitored must be set aside during visit time to make the experience as pleasant as possible for your children. Find someone to debrief with between visits. This venting will help you cope with your feelings about visits, the supervisor, and being supervised.

Maintaining Balance During Visits

Many parents feel guilty about taking time during visits to focus on their own needs and interests, especially if they do not see their children often. Visits may be stressful, and you need to take care of yourself during these times. You can only meet your children's needs if your own are met. As a role model, it's important for you to demonstrate to your children that you have certain needs that have to be recognized even when children are around. The trick is to build supports in on a regular basis, ahead of time. The importance of having a balanced lifestyle extends beyond recognizing physical or emotional needs and often involves having extracurricular activities like hobbies or sports, other relationships, and work.

Peter explained how he meets his own needs when his children are with him.

> *To keep myself a whole person, I keep myself on a schedule. I do what I need to do for myself when the children are sleeping or out at school. I go to physical therapy or take a walk in the park. I keep a doctor's appointment or go shopping. I keep close to the people who mean a lot to me, even if it is just by phone.*

Meeting Your Needs

Below, try to identify three needs you have that may not be met during visits with your children. It may help to think of times during recent visits when you were most stressed. What was stressing you? What would have helped you feel better? Examples of unmet needs might include the need for more rest or contact with other adults your own age. You may have needed a "time-out." The solution may be as simple as a bubble bath, if you can leave your children safely to watch a video while you are in the tub. Write your three top needs on the lines below, along with action steps you can take to meet your needs.

Need #1: _____

Action Steps to Meet This Need (specify 2 or 3 possibilities):

_____

_____

Need #2: _____

Action Steps to Meet This Need (specify 2 or 3 possibilities):

_____

_____

Need #3: _____

Action Steps to Meet This Need (specify 2 or 3 possibilities):

_____

_____

Post this list on your refrigerator, so you can remind yourself on a daily basis to build these action steps into your everyday life. They will help you achieve wellness on a daily basis, and will serve as an example to your children of how to achieve a balanced lifestyle.

When Your Symptoms Interfere with Your Visits

What do you do when you have an important activity planned with your children and you begin to experience a flare-up of symptoms? This is when it's important to have a backup plan. Having a plan shows good judgment on your part and contributes to good parenting. As Carrie explained:

I think that, if a parent is not really feeling good themselves, they should have a backup plan in place. The plan would include a trusted friend or relative to call when your symptoms flare up and would allow you to remove yourself from your children for an hour or so. That way, you could go somewhere, speak with a friend, cry if you need to, or see your doctor or therapist if that's what you need. If you don't have a backup plan, the symptoms may negatively affect your child. Your children may blame themselves for your illness, cling to you, tell you they love you all day long, act like they are your parent, be overprotective of you, and focus on you instead of their childhood. My child used to say, "Mom, don't leave me. Are you always going to be there?" Our children depend on us to be there, so we must plan for times when our symptoms flare up. Your child also needs to know about your illness and be involved in creating your backup plan.

Take the following steps to develop your backup plan:

- Talk to someone you can trust and confide in about creating a backup plan. A friend, relative, minister, counselor, or advocate will do just fine. Have them help you identify your strengths, resources, and supports.

- Involve other supports for yourself and your children, such as a neighbor, school teacher, coach, or parent of a friend.

- Explain your symptoms to your children, and allow your children to ask questions and express their feelings about your symptoms. Think of this as explaining the "mental-health facts of life" to your children.

- Draft a written plan with people to contact and phone numbers. Review the plan with your support network and your children. Post the plan in a readily visible or accessible place for easy implementation if the need arises.

Coping Between Visits with Your Children

Steve talks about his experience in visiting his daughter.

> *It is painful when we have to let go of our children. I try to make sure my five-year-old daughter understands why I can't see her more often, and how I wish I could. It's important to also make sure my daughter knows that none of this is her fault. You deal with limits on custody by taking advantage of every opportunity to speak with or be with your child. Do not burden your child with your feelings of anger and sadness over not being able to see them more often. I also feel that, even if you're not going home with your child, it's very important that no one leaves a visit frustrated or angry. At the end of each visit I tell her, "God bless you, I love you, and I will see you next week." And we always hug and kiss.*

Determine strategies for coping that work for you when you are separated from your children. Here are some suggestions.

- Try to keep yourself busy. Have an activity or two planned in advance that you can do immediately after visiting or speaking on the telephone with your child. This won't eliminate the pain and sadness you may feel over not having more contact with your child, but it can help prevent you from slipping into a deeper level of depression and despair. Possible activities might include seeing a friend or two, exercising at the local gym, walking, jogging, or swimming.

- Keep duplicates of your child's favorite toys, books, and games on hand, along with a favorite blanket or special pillow. You can either bring some of these with you when you are visiting with your child or, if your child comes to your home, keep these items in a permanent place. This will accomplish two goals: helping you feel less lonely after visits and helping your child feel more comfortable during visits.

- Don't spend too much time alone, even if you are tempted to isolate yourself as protection against further disappointment or pain. Learning to trust others is not easy after losing contact with a child, but it is essential to healing and regaining control of your life. Go out with friends or talk with your counselor. Remember, you may be lonely, but you do not have to be alone.

- Stick to a regular schedule. Do whatever it is that you usually did before this crisis occurred. Get up early, take a shower, get dressed, and put some makeup on.

- Keep pictures or other mementoes of your experiences together in an album or scrapbook. If you have a video or cassette recorder, make tapes to play during your times apart. Make copies for your children to have, too. Having pictures of your children and displaying them proudly helps you feel better and lets your children know they are important in your life, and that you think about them when they are not around.

- Communicate with your children via some agreed-upon means: telephone, e-mail, or cards and letters. Be reliable—call or communicate when you say you will—and be upbeat. Your children need to know that you are all right when they're not around. It's okay to miss them, but reassure them that you take steps in their absence to maintain your health and well-being.

Planning for the Holidays

It may be especially difficult to cope during the holidays without your children. Holidays are traditionally the time when families are together. Expectations for warmth and closeness are high. You may feel particularly depressed without your children. If you are unable to arrange to see them or it's not your "turn" to have them for the holiday, make an active effort to keep yourself on an even keel. You may achieve some comfort by spending time with close friends or participating in activities organized by your church or social club. You may help out at the community shelter or food pantry by preparing or serving a meal. Rent your favorite movie. You may plan with your children to celebrate the holiday the next time you are together, making an effort to incorporate the best of your old family traditions or develop new ones together.

Think ahead to the next holiday. Where will your children be? What will you be doing? Make a concrete plan for activities and contacts with friends. Build in some relaxation time. Record your plan in your journal or on a piece of paper to refer to when the holiday arrives.

Is More Time with Your Children a Possibility?

Losing custody or contact with a child can leave you feeling overwhelmed and, oftentimes, in despair. Many parents with psychiatric disorders may feel that they don't stand a chance in court when it comes to seeking custody or increased visitation with their children. Even worse, they may feel that they do not deserve to have custody or increased visitation with their children. Feelings of unworthiness can be difficult to overcome without the support of a counselor, friends, or family. Try to work on maintaining a positive attitude. Easier said than done, right? Well, nothing truly worthwhile in life is ever easy. And, as with any overwhelming task in life, the easiest way to tackle it is by attacking the problem in pieces.

It is important to grieve and talk about not having your children with someone you trust. This is a very important task, because it can help you start to regain confidence in your ability to parent and help you to start planning for the future. Other pieces might involve enrolling in a parenting skills class (since we all could learn more about parenting well), taking steps to ensure that you take the time to take care of yourself (focus on your own wellness), and making a plan to take care of your children if and when you decide to seek custody.

It is also a good idea to think ahead of time about the possible outcomes of a custody or visitation dispute—win or lose. Oftentimes, parents put so much of their energy into the legal battle that they fail to plan for coping with the often overwhelming emotions which follow a judge's decision. It will help if you prepare for these pieces with a counselor, trusted friend, or family member. If you lose your legal dispute, try to learn from it by finding out what factors concerned the judge. That way, you can focus your energies on addressing these concerns and be even better prepared the next time. If you win in court, try to understand that the changes you think will be positive may be met with mixed reviews by others and may be very challenging to implement.

Determining the Best Living Situation for Your Children

What do you think is best for your child? Courts make custody decisions based on what they consider to be in the best interests of the child, which you may or may not agree with. Determining what's best for your children may depend on many factors, some of which may be beyond your control. Try to think ahead about your child's best interest and the factors the judge might be considering. Use this form to help you decide what you think is best for your child, and how best to handle feelings that you may be experiencing as a result. Space is provided for you to add factors that we have not listed. Try to get feedback on your ideas from a trusted friend, relative, or counselor.

My Child's Living Situation

Safety (What is the safest environment for my child to be raised in?)

_____

_____

Stability (Can I provide a stable home environment for my child?)

_____

_____

Cleanliness (Is my home clean and the surroundings pleasant?)

_____

_____

Stimulating (Can I provide stimulation for my child and a good learning environment?)

_____

_____

Time (Do I have the time to devote to all of my child's needs and meet my needs, too?)

_____

_____

Supportive (Can I provide a supportive environment for my child to grow and flourish?)

_____

_____

Other Factors to Consider

_____

_____

_____

Marcia describes how she thinks most parents feel about working to have custody of their children.

> I find that fear is the main thing in most parents. In meetings, it's important for the parent to try to remain calm and try to express their own feelings and thoughts. Do it politely, with respect for others, but firmly. And do not give up trying, even though it may be hard and discouraging. When one thing fails, look for another solution. When we've

shown the children how we persist in our efforts to get them back, it also serves to help them cope with future obstacles and difficulties they may face in life. It teaches them to always keep searching for new and different ideas and angles to overcome problems and to make the situation better for everyone involved. It helps to bring a friend with you to meetings and to court, not necessarily to talk for you, but to be there to give you support, courage, to help you decide how to express yourself, and to understand what happens afterwards.

You may decide on your own that your ability to care for your child twenty-four hours a day is limited. Regardless of whether or not you choose to seek custody or increased visitation with your children, remember to focus on enjoying whatever time you do have with them. Remind them that you are okay, and do not create any "loyalty conflicts" for them by saying bad things about your ex-partner, their legal guardian, or foster family. Visits are a time for you and your children to develop and maintain positive relationships, not to air your grievances.

Parenting Well Is a Lifelong Pursuit

Remember, whether you are with your children twenty-four hours a day, weekends or holidays, or less frequently, you can never be replaced by anyone in your children's hearts and minds. Find ways to give your children emotional support, even if you can't be with them. This is the kind of support that lets your children know that they are loved no matter what happens and that you are there for them whenever possible. Your emotional support has very positive effects on your children's sense of self-esteem and confidence. Your relationships with your children will be stronger for your efforts. Your recovery will be enhanced by the efforts you make to parent your children well.

Resources

Chapter 1

Organizations

(Check with these organizations to see if they have a state chapter in your state.)

For Depression

National Depressive and Manic-Depressive Association
730 N. Franklin Street, Suite 501
Chicago, Illinois 60610-7204
(800) 826-3632
(312) 642-0049
(312) 642-7243 (fax)
www.ndmda.org (Web site)
(They provide educational materials on mental illness and information on support groups in your state.)

National Foundation For Depressive Illness, Inc.
P.O. Box 2257
New York 10116
800-239-1265 *or* 800-248-4344
www.depression.org (Web site)
(They have information on mental illness and can provide referrals for state-specific resources.)

National Alliance for the Mentally Ill
Colonial Place Three
2107 Wilson Blvd., Suite 300
Arlington, VA 22201-3042
800-950-NAMI (6264)
703-524-9094 (fax)
703-516-7227 (TDD)
www.nami.org (Web site)

National Mental Health Association's National Consumer Supporter Technical
Assistance Center
1021 Prince Street
Alexandria, VA 22314-2971
800-969-NMHA (6642)
703-684-7722
703-684-5968 (fax)
800-433-5959 (TTY Line)
ConsumerTA@nmha.org (email)
www.nmha.org or www.ncstac.org (Web sites)
(They provide brochures and fact sheets on mental illness as well as referrals for state-specific resources.)

For Substance Abuse

Adult Children of Alcoholics
(ACA/ACoA)
P.O. Box 3216
Torrance, CA 90510
310-534-1815

Alcoholics Anonymous World Services
475 Riverside Drive
P.O. Box 459
New York 10163
212-647-1680 (U.S. meeting info.)
Internet: www.alcoholics-anonymous.org

Al-Anon and Alateen Family Group
Headquarters, Inc.
1600 Corporate Landing Parkway
Virginia Beach, VA 23454-5617
800-344-2666 (U.S. meeting info.)
Internet: www.al-anon.alateen.org
or www.alateen.org//alateen.html

Cocaine Anonymous
World Services Organization
3740 Overland Avenue, Suite C
Los Angeles, CA 90034-6337
310-559-5833
Internet: www.ca.org

Moderation Management Network, Inc.
P.O. Box 3055
point Pleasant, NJ 08742
732-295-0949
Email: moderation@moderation.org
Internet: www.moderation.org

Mothers Against Drunk Driving (MADD)
511 E. John Carpenter Freeway, Suite 700
Irving, TX 75062
Hotline: 1-800-GET-MADD (438-6233)
Internet: www.madd.org

Narcotics Anonymous
World Service Office
P.O. Box 9999
Van Nuys, CA 91409
818-773-9999
Internet: www.na.org/index.htm

National Institute on Drug Abuse
671 Executive Boulevard, Suire 5128
Bethesda, MD 20892
800-638-2045
301-443-4577
Internet: www.nida.nih.org

Toll-Free Information Numbers

1-800-ALCOHOL (252-6465)

National Drug & Alcohol Treatment Refereal Services
1-800-662-HELP

1-800-DRUGHELP (378-4435)

American Council on Alcoholism
1-800-527-5344

Centers for Disease Control and Prevention (CDC) National AIDS Hotline
1-800-342-AIDS (2437)
1-800-344-SIDA (7432) Spanish
1-800-AIDS-TTY (243-7889) TDD

Domestic Violence Hotline
1-800-572-7233

Higher Education Center for Alcohol and Other Drug Prevention
1-800-676-1730

Mothers Against Drunk Driving Victim Hotline
1-800-GET-MADD (438-6233)

National Child Abuse Hotline
1-800-422-4453

National Domestic Violence Hotline
1-800-799-SAFE (7233)

National Clearinghouse for Alcohol and Drug Information
1-800-729-6686 (1-800-487-4889 TDD)

National Council on Alcoholism and Drug Dependence, Inc.
1-800-NCA-CALL (622-2255)

National Institute on Drug Abuse (NIDA) Hotline
1-800-662-HELP (4357)

Partnership for a Drug Free America
1-800-624-0100

Internet Web Sites

AdCare Health System
"Self-Test to See if You Need Help for an Alcohol Problem"
www.adcare.com/problem.htm

American Academy of Child and Adolescent Psychiatry provides information on:
"Making Decisions About Substance Abuse Treatment for Your Child or Adolescent"
www.aacap.org/publications/factsfam/subabuse.htm
Suggests questions parents can ask to get the information they need to make good decisions about their child's or teenager's substance abuse treatment.

Check It! Web page (http://drugs.ort.org/home.htm)
"How Much Do You Know (About Drugs)"
http://drugs.ort.org/truef.htm

Cigarette Smoking Web Page
http://ash.org

Dealing with Adolescent Experimentation
www.cts.com/crash/habtsmrt/adol.html

Connecticut Clearinghouse—A Resource Center for Information About Alcohol,
Tobacco, and Other Drugs
www.ctclearinghouse.org/ccfact.htm

Consumer Information Center (www.pueblo.gsa.gov)
Pueblo, Colorado 81009
"Growing Up Drug Free: A Parent's Guide to Prevention"
www.pueblo.gsa.gov/cic_text/children/drgfree/drugfree.htm

Information on Alcoholics Anonymous (AA)
www.recovery.org/aa/pamphlet/aainfo.html

Internet Mental Health Web Page
www.mentalhealth.com

Intervention Center—Family Intervention Web page
"Helpful Guidelines for Planning an Intervention"
www.intervention.com/servs.html

John Hopkins Test for Alcoholism—20 Questions to Determine if You Are an
Alcoholic
www.public.usit.net/rfhale/hopkins.htm

National Center on Addiction and Substance Abuse (CASA) at Columbia University
www.casacolumbia.org

"National Directory of Drug Abuse & Alcoholism Treatment and Prevention Programs"
Provided by the Substance Abuse and Mental Health Service Administration
(SAMHSA)
http://findtreatment.samhsa.gov/facilitylocatordoc2.htm
*(The SAMHSA directory allows you to type in your city, state, and zip code and will
then provide you with a list of treatment facilities in your area. You do not need all three
identifiers [city, state, zip code]; any one will access the information.)*

Partnership for a Drug-Free America
http://drugfreeamerica.org

RU Aware? Alcohol Education Page
"The Affect of Alcohol on You"
www.runet.edu/~kcastleb/affect.html

Santa Barbara Alcohol and Drug Program (www.silcom.com/~sbadp)
"Alcohol and Other Drug Abuse Symptoms of Adolescents"
www.silcom.com/~sbadp/treatment/adoleschecklist.htm

Self-Help Magazine Website
"Should you be concerned about your drinking?"
www.shpm.com/articles/atd/alcques.html

Stories from People (personal accounts of how drug use affected their lives)
www.druguse.com/exp.html

"Teens: Alcohol and Other Drugs—Facts for Families"
http://www.aacap.org/publications/factsfam/teendrug.htm

Web of Addictions Web page (www.well.com/user/woa)
"Fact Sheet—Fetal Alcohol Syndrome"
www.well.com/user/woa/fsfas.htm

Whole Family Center Web page
www.wholefamily.com

Books

Depression

Carter, R., and S. K. Golant. 1998. *Helping Someone with Mental Illness: A Compassionate Guide for Family, Friends and Caregivers.* New York: Times Books.

Copeland, M. E. 1997. *Wellness Recovery Action Plan.* Brattleboro, VT: Peach Press.

———. 1994. *Living with Depression and Manic Depression: A Workbook for Maintaining Mood Stability.* Oakland, Calif.: New Harbinger Publications.

———. 1992. *The Depression Workbook: A Guide for Living with Depression and Manic Depression.* Oakland, Calif.: New Harbinger Publications.

U.S. Department of Health and Human Services. 1999. *Mental Health: A Report of the Surgeon General.* Rockville, MD: U.S. Department of Health and Human Services, Substance Abuse and Mental Health Services Administration, Center for Mental Health Services, National Institutes of Health, National Institute of Mental Health.

To order a copy of the full report (currently $51) call (202) 512-1800. To order the Mental Health: A Report of the Surgeon General—Executive Summary (a synopsis of the full report) call toll-free (877) 964-3258 or write to: Mental Health, Pueblo, CO 81009.

Substance Abuse

Banfield, S. 1998. *Inside Recovery: How the Twelve Step Program Can Work For You.* New York: Rosen Publishing Group.

Hatfield, A. B. 1992. *Dual Diagnosis: Substance Abuse and Mental Illness.* Arlington, VA.: National Alliance for the Mentally Ill.

Johnson, V. E. 1986. *Intervention: How to Help Someone Who Doesn't Want Help—A Step-By-Step Guide for Families and Friends of Chemically Dependent Persons.* Minneapolis: Johnson Institute Books.

Leite, E., and P. Espeland. 1987. *Different Like Me: A Book for Teens Who Worry About Their Parents' Use of Alcohol/Drugs.* Minneapolis: Johnson Institute Books.

Lerner, Katherine. 1988. *Something's Wrong in My House.* New York: Franklin Watts, Inc.
(Real stories from kids and teenagers on how alcohol affected their lives.)

Mooney, A. J., A. Eisenberg, and H. Eisenberg. 1992. *The Recovery Book.* New York: Workman Publishing Company.

Shuker-Haines, F. 1994. *Everything You Need to Know About a Drug Abusing Parent.* New York: Rosen Publishing Group.
(For children ages ten to eighteen who are dealing with a drug-abusing parent.)

Chapter 2

Organizations

National Association of Child Care Resource and Referral Agencies
1319 F Street, NW, Suite 500
Washington, DC 20004-1106
202-393-5501
202-393-1109 (fax)
Email: info@naccrra.org
Internet: www.naccrra.net
(To learn more about childcare financial assistance.)

Books

Bolles, R.N. 1999. Berkeley, CA: Ten Speed Press.

Cage, C.A. 1998. *Can You Start Monday? A 9-Step Job Search Guide.* Englewood, CO: Cage Consulting.

Douglas A. 1998. *The Unofficial Guide to Childcare.* Foster City, CA: Hungry Minds Inc.

Ehrich, M. 1999. *The Anxious Parents' Guide to Quality Child Care.* New York: Perigee.

Galinsky, E. 1999. *Ask the Children: What America's Children Really Think About Working Parents.* New York: William Morrow & Co.

Glassman, P., and T. Arnold. 1994. *My Working Mom.* New York: William Morrow & Co.

Hansen, K. 2000. *A Foot in the Door: Networking Your Way into the Hidden Job Market.* Berkeley, CA: Ten Speed Press.

Kennedy, D. 1998. *Balancing Acts: An Inspirational Guide for Working Mothers.* New York: Berkley Publishing Group.

Levine, J. A., and T. L. Pittinsky. 1998. *Working Fathers: New Strategies for Balancing Work and Family.* Ft. Washington, PA: Harvest Books.

Sale, J. S., K. Kollenberg, and E. Milinkoff. 1996. *The Working Parent's Handbook.* New York: Simon & Schuster.

Toll-Free Numbers

Child Care Aware hotline
800-424-2246
For information about local licensed child care providers and pre- and after-school programs.

Social Security Administration
800-772-1213
800-325-0778 (for the hearing impaired)

Web Sites

CareGuide
www.careguide.com
(This site offers a national network of care managers, a toll-free support center and Web site to provide families with everything they need to assess, plan, manage, and monitor the best care for their loved ones.)

Center for Psychiatric Rehabilitation, Sargent College of Health and Rehabilitation Sciences at Boston University
www.bu.edu/sarpsych/

Internal Revenue Service
www.irs.ustreas.gov

(You may be eligible for federal tax breaks; for free informative publications, call the IRS at 1-800-TAX-FORM, or go to their Web site.)

National Network for Child Care
www.nncc.org

Social Security Administration
www.ssa.gov

Chapter 3

Benefits and Entitlements

Cash Benefit Programs

Social Security Disability Insurance (SSDI). Federal assistance program for persons who have worked and paid Social Security taxes (FICA) for enough years to be covered. You must be considered medically disabled and expected to be disabled for at least twelve months. Persons should not be working or, if working, earning less than a certain income per month. You can obtain an application and receive additional information on eligibility requirements at your local Social Security office.

Supplemental Security Income (SSI). Federal assistance program for medically disabled individuals with little or no income or resources. The amount of payment you receive is based on any income you receive in a month, your living arrangements, and the state that you live in. You may be eligible for both SSI and SSDI. You can obtain an application and receive additional information on eligibility requirements at your local Social Security office.

Various State Programs. Emergency assistance programs for disabled persons, needy families with dependent children, women with young children, and women who are pregnant. Check with appropriate state or local agency for additional information and eligibility requirements. Each state has their own rules and guidelines.

Health Benefit Programs

Medicare. Federal health insurance program for persons over sixty-five years old or disabled. If you are on SSDI, you are automatically enrolled after receiving benefits for twenty-four months. Has PART A, which covers hospitalizations, and an optional PART B (which you must pay a premium for) that covers physician's services, outpatient services, therapist, diagnostic tests, and other services. Both parts have deductibles (out-of-pocket expenses) you are responsible for.

Medicaid. Federally funded program usually administered by the state. Provides funding for medical services for disabled persons, pregnant women, children, and low-income elderly. Eligibility is determined by your income in comparison to the poverty level and a higher level if you are pregnant.

Children's Medical Plan. Many states provide medical coverage for children (up to eighteen) who are from low-income families and who do not qualify for any of the above programs.

Food Programs

Food Stamps. Federally funded program administered by your state. These monies, supplied on an ATM type card, can only be used for food. Eligibility is determined by your income and, even though you have some income, you may be eligible if you have children and do not meet the maximum income level established. Many people must work or do community service in order to remain eligible for food stamps.

Special Supplemental Nutrition Program for Women, Infants and Children (WIC). Federal health and nutrition program for women who are pregnant, nursing, or have children under five years of age. You are automatically eligible for WIC if you currently receive food stamps.

Food Pantries and Soup Kitchens. Normally run by community-based agencies, charities, churches, or service agencies. Food pantries provide food for you to take home and prepare, whereas soup kitchens provide you a prepared meal. Contact you local United Way office for additional information or location.

Housing Programs

Various State and Local Programs. Many states, cities, and private agencies provide assistance for housing, utilities, and telephone expenses. Check in the white pages section of your phone book under "United States Government"; your state, "Government of"; your city (or county or town), "Government of"; or under a specific private agency for details. Your welfare department may be able to refer you to necessary resources. If you are involved in a program you can also ask your advocate for assistance.

Books

Bodnar, J. 1997. *Dr. Tightwad's Money-Smart Kids.* 2d ed. Washington, DC: The Kiplinger Washington Editors, Inc.

Domingues, J., and V. Robin. 1993. *Your Money or Your Life.* New York: Penguin Books USA.

Godfrey, N. S., and C. Edwards. 1994. *Money Doesn't Grow on Trees: A Parent's Guide to Raising Financially Responsible Children.* New York: Simon & Schuster.

Goodman, J. E. 1995. *Everyone's Money Book.* 2d ed. Chicago: Dearborn Financial Publishing, Inc.

Orman, S. 1997. *The 9 Steps to Financial Freedom: Practical & Spiritual Steps So You Can Stop Worrying.* New York: Crown Publishers, Inc.

Otfinoski, S. 1996. *The Kids Guide to Money: Earning It, Saving It, Spending It, Growing It, Sharing It.* New York: Scholastic Inc.

Chapter 4

USDA Food Guide Pyramids

U.S. Department of Agriculture
Center for Nutrition Policy and Promotion
1120 20th St., NW
Suite 200, North Lobby
Washington, DC 20036-3475
(202) 606-8000
http://www.usda.gov/cnpp (Web site)

A copy of the USDA's Food Guide Pyramid Booklet, updated 2000 (5th edition) can be obtained at the following Web address:
http://www.pueblo.gsa.gov/cic_text/food/ food-pyramid/main.htm (Web site)

A sixteen-page booklet, "Tips for Using the Food Guide Pyramid for Young Children 2 to 6 Years Old," includes the adapted pyramid graphic and accompanying information on good nutrition for children. The booklet is available to the public on USDA's Center for Nutrition Policy and Promotion Internet home page at http://www.usda.gov/cnpp or through the Government Printing Office by calling (202) 512-1800 and asking for stock number 001-00004665-9.

Childrens' Cook Books and Web Sites

Coyle, R., and P. Messing. 1987. *Baby Let's Eat!* New York: Workman Publishing.

Evers, C. L. 1995. *How to Teach Nutrition to Kids.* Tigard, OR: 24 Carrot Press.

Heyhoe, K. 1999. *Cooking with Kids for Dummies.* Foster City, CA: IDG Books Worldwide Inc.

Eating Disorders

Garner, D. M., and P. E. Garfinkel, eds. 1997. *Handbook of Treatment for Eating Disorders.* New York: Guilford Press.

Chapter 5

Books

Bilodiau, L. 1992. *The Anger Workbook.* Minneapolis: Compcare Publishers.

Davies, W. 2000. *Overcoming Anger and Irritability: A Self-Help Guide Using Cognitive Behavioral Techniques.* New York: New York University Press.

Davis, J., and Hyland T. L. 1999. *Angry Kids, Frustrated Parents: Practical Ways to Prevent and Reduce Aggression in Your Children.* Boys Town, NE: Boys Town Press.

Lachner, D. 1995. *Andrew's Angry Words.* New York: North South Books.

Moser, A., Ed.D. and D. Melton, III. 1994. *Don't Rant & Rave on Wednesdays.* Kansas City, MO: Landmark Editions, Inc.

Peurifoy, R. Z. 1999. *Anger: Taming the Beast.* Tokyo: Kodansha International.

Chapter 6

Books for Children

Denboer, H. 1993. *Please Don't Cry, Mom.* Minneapolis: Lerner Publishing Group.
(*Written for children ages six through twelve, this book aids in understanding a parent with depression, It could also be used for younger children, four through eight, if they were read to and shown the illustrations. It shows how a young boy reacts to a mother with depression. It explains depression, how a child and others in the family deal with this illness, and how one gets help. It introduces the reader to an antidepression medication, a psychiatrist, and how to cope during the recovery time.*)

Lashkin, P., and A. A. Moskowitz. 1991. *Wish Upon a Star: A Story for Children with a Parent Who Is Mentally Ill.* Washington, DC: American Psychological Association.
(*This book is written for children ages five through seven explaining how a young girl deals with her mother's hospitalization for a psychiatric disorder. It begins by discussing psychiatric disorders and covers building a support system for a child as well as the parent that requires treatment. This book also covers dealing with the time a parent is away while in the hospital and helps explain why they must be away.*)

Leite, E., and P. Espeland. 1987. *Different Like Me: A Book for Teens Who Worry About Their Parents' Use of Alcohol/Drugs.* Minneapolis: Johnson Institute Books.

Lerner, K. 1988. *Something's Wrong in My House*. New York: Franklin Watts, Inc.
   (Real stories from children and teenagers on how alcohol affected their lives.)
Sanford, D. E. 1993. *It Won't Last Forever: A Child's Book About Living with a Depressed Parent*. Grand Rapids, MI: Zondervan Publishing House.
   (Written for children, ages five through ten, this book shows how a young girl whose mother suffers from depression handles everyday life. It covers feelings a child will experience and explains hospitalizations and medications. Suicide is also discussed. In the back of the book there are guidelines to help a child cope with a parent who has depression and that encourages them to ask questions.)
Shuker-Haines, F. 1994. *Everything You Need to Know About a Drug Abusing Parent*. New York: Rosen Publishing Group.
   (For children, ages ten to eighteen, who are dealing with a drug-abusing parent.)

Books for Parents

Ames, L. B., F. L. Ilg, and S. M. Baker. 1988. *Your Ten- to Fourteen-Year Old*. New York: Dell Publishing.

Also in the same series:

Your One-Year-Old—Ames, Ilg, and Haber
Your Two-Year-Old—Ames and Ilg
Your Three-Year-Old—Ames and Ilg
Your Four-Year-Old—Ames and Ilg
Your Five-Year-Old—Ames and Ilg
Your Six-Year-Old—Ames and Ilg
Your Seven-Year-Old—Ames and Haber
Your Eight-Year-Old—Ames and Haber
Your Nine-Year-Old—Ames and Haber

Videos

Depression: Helping Families Cope (Parent Tape). 2000. 38 min. Produced by Innovative Training Systems, Newton, MA. Videocassette.
Depression: Helping Families Cope (Child Tape). 2000. 14 min. Produced by Innovative Training Systems, Newton, MA. Videocassette.

Both videotapes are part of a videotape series available from Innovative Training Systems for $49.95 plus S&H. Innovative Training Systems, 199 Wells Avenue, Suite 108, Newton, MA 02459, 617-332-6028 (telephone), 617-332-1820 (fax), www.itshomepage.com.

Chapter 7

Books

Bloomquist, Michael L. 1996. *Skills Training for Children with Behavior Disorders: A Parent and Therapist Guidebook.* New York: Guilford Press.

Caissy, G. A. 1994. *Early Adolescence: Understanding the 10 to 15 Year Old.* Cambridge, MA: Perseus Publishing.

Coburn, K. L., and M. L. Treeger. 1997. *Letting Go: A Parents' Guide to Understanding the College Years.* New York: HarperCollins Publishers.

Gurian, M. 1998. *A Fine Young Man: What Parents, Mentors and Educators Can Do to Shape Adolescent Boys into Exceptional Men.* New York: Penguin Putnam, Inc.

Nelsen, J., L. Lott, and R. Intner. 1995. Roseville, CA: Prima Communications, Inc.

Nelson, J., C. Erwin, and C. Delzer. 1999. *Positive Discipline for Single Parents.* Roseville, CA: Prima Communications, Inc.

Pipher, M. 1994. *Reviving Ophelia: Saving the Selves of Adolescent Girls.* New York: Ballentine Books.

Ross, P. A. 1995. *Practical Guide to Discipline and Behavior Management for Teachers and Parents.* Alexandria, VA: Newsletter Book Services.

Swihart, E. W., and P. Cotter. 1998. New York: Bantam Books, Inc.

Turecki, L. T. 2000. *The Difficult Child.* New York: Bantam Books, Inc.

Weinhaus, E., and K. Friedman. 1991. *Stop Struggling With Your Child: Quick-Tip Parenting Solutions That Work for You and Your Kids, Ages 4 to 12.* New York: HarperCollins Publishers.

Toll-Free Parenting Hotline

800-475-TALK (8255)

Internet Web Sites

www.fosterparents.com
(This site is for the purpose of sharing information with foster and adoptive families, prospective foster and adoptive families, and anyone involved in the field of working with at-risk children.)

www.parenting-qa.com
(This site offers expert answers to your parenting questions.)

www.parentsplace.com
(This site offers parenting advice and more.)

www.pueblo.gsa.gov/press/homework.htm
(Helping your child with homework for parents of elementary and junior-high-school aged children.)

www.wholefamily.com
(Whether you are a parent, teen, couple, or senior, this site provides the tools and advice you need to build strong, healthy, loving relationships. A team of experts and professionals offer real-life solutions to the toughest challenges facing you and your family today.)

Chapter 8

Books

Brazelton, T. B. 1998. *Touchpoints: Your Child's Emotional and Behavioral Development.* Reading, MA: Perseus Books.

Hickman, D., and V. Teurlay. 1992. *101 Great Ways to Keep Your Child Entertained While You Get Something Else Done: Creative and Stimulating Activities for Your Toddler or Pre-Schooler.* New York: St. Martin's Press.

Krueger, C. W. 1999. *1001 Things to Do With Your Kids.* New York: Galahad Books.

Leach, P. 1986. *Your Growing Child: From Babyhood Through Adolescence.* New York: Alfed A. Knopf.

Leach, P. 1997. *Your Baby and Child: From Birth to Age Five.* New York: Alfred A. Knopf.

MacGregor, C. 1999. *365 After-School Activities You Can Do with Your Child.* Holbrook, MA: Adams Media Corporation. (For ages five to ten).

Child-Friendly Web Sites

www.discovery.com
(Offers educational and entertainment information and activities for kids and parents.)

www.enchantedlearning.com
(Enchanted Learning.com produces children's educational Web sites and games that are designed to capture the imagination while maximizing creativity, learning, and enjoyment.)

www.kidsdomain.com
(Offers new children's software, shareware, freeware, and demos, along with new links, contests, and holiday pages. This site also offers an e-mail newsletter for children and an e-mail newsletter for grown-ups.)

www.nncc.org
(Offers information on childcare, child abuse, child development, and more.)

Chapter 9

Organizations

(Write to or call these organizations for information on support groups, organizations, services, and other resources available to you in your state.)

Depression & Related Affective Disorders Association (DRADA)
Meyer 3-181
600 N. Wolfe St.
Baltimore, MD 21287-7381
410-955-4647
Email: drada@jhmi.edu

National Association of Protection and Advocacy Systems (NAPAS)
900 2nd St. NE, Suite 211
Washington, DC 20002
(202) 408-9514
(202) 408-9520 (Fax)
(202) 408-9521 (TDD)
www.protectionandadvocacy.com (Web site)
(An association that represents federally mandated programs that protect the rights of persons with disabilities. They will refer you to the protection and advocacy agency in your state.)

National Association for Rights, Protection, and Advocacy (NARPA)
c/o Mental Health Association of Minnesota
2021 E. Hennepin, Suite 412
Minneapolis, MN 55413
(612) 331-6840
(800) 862-1799

National Empowerment Center
599 Canal Street, Suite 4E
Lawrence, MA 01843
1-800-POWER-2-U
Internet: www.power2u.org

National Institute of Mental Health
Depression Awareness, Recognition and Treatment (D/ART)
1-800-421-4211
(They provide information on depressive disorders, panic disorder, and anxiety/phobia disorders.)

National Mental Health Consumers' Self-Help Clearinghouse
1211 Chestnut Street, Suite 1207
Philadelphia, PA 19107
800-553-4KEY (4539)
info@mhselfhelp.org (e-mail)
www.mhselfhelp.org (Web site)
(A consumer-run, national technical assistance center serving the mental-health consumer movement. They help connect individuals to self-help and advocacy resources, and offer expertise to self-help groups and other peer-run services for mental-health consumers.)

U.S. Department of Education
Office of Special Education and Rehabilitation Services
A Guide to the Individualized Education Program (IEP)
www.ed.gov/offices/OSERS/OSEP/IEP_Guide/
(Each public school child who receives special education and related services must have an Individualized Education Program (IEP). This guide explains the IEP process, which is considered to be one of the most critical elements to ensure effective teaching, learning, and better results for all children with disabilities.)

Internet Resources

http://black.clarku.edu/~uway/hd100.html#LEGAL
(A confidential, twenty-four hour a day human services information and referral helpline for Massachusetts.)

Mental Health Net—Parenting Resources
www.mhnet.org/guide/parents.htm

Books

Advocacy & Self-Esteem Issues

Burns, D. 1989. *The Feeling Good Handbook.* New York: Penguin Books USA.

Copeland, M. E. 1994. *The Depression Workbook: A Guide for Living with Depression and Manic Depression.* Oakland, CA: New Harbinger Publications.

Garner, P., and S. Sandow, eds. 1995. *Advocacy, Self-Advocacy, and Special Needs.* Bristol, PA: Taylor & Francis, Inc.

Garson, S. 1986. *Out of Our Minds.* Buffalo, NY: Prometheus.

Ilardo, J. 1992. *Risk-Taking for Personal Growth: A Step-by-Step Workbook.* Oakland, CA: New Harbinger Publications.

McKay, M., M. Davis, and P. Fanning. 1981. *Thoughts and Feelings: The Art of Cognitive Stress Intervention.* Oakland, CA: New Harbinger Publications.

McKay, M., and P. Fanning. 1992. *Self-Esteem.* Oakland, CA: New Harbinger Publications.

National Mental Health Consumers' Self-Help Clearinghouse. April 2000 Pilot Version. *Self-Advocacy Technical Assistance Guide.* Philadelphia: National Mental Health Consumers' Self-Help Clearinghouse. *(Available by calling 800-553-4539, or online at www.mhselfhelp.org).*

Spaniol, L., and M. Koehler. 1994. *The Experience of Recovery.* Boston: Center for Psychosocial Rehabilitation.

Spaniol, L., M. Koehler, and D. Hutchinson. 1994. *The Recovery Workbook.* Boston: Center for Psychosocial Rehabilitation.

Assertiveness Skills

Bower, B., and G. Bower. 1976. *Asserting Yourself.* Reading, MA: Addison-Wesley.

Smith, M. J. 1975. *When I Say No, I Feel Guilty.* New York: The Dial Press.

Communication Skills

Fisher, R., and W. Ury. 1981. *Getting to Yes: Negotiating Agreement Without Giving In.* Boston: Houghton Mifflin.

Hopper, R., and J. Whitehead. 1979. *Communication Concepts and Skills.* New York: Van Nostrand Reinhold.

Lieberman, M., and M. Hardy. 1981. *Resolving Family and Other Conflicts: Everybody Wins.* Santa Cruz, CA: Unity Press.

Chapter 10

Publications

Boland, M. L., and B. A. Mooij. 1999. *Your Right to Child Custody, Visitation, and Support.* Naperville, IL: Sourcebooks, Inc.

Ward, D., and M. Shaw, Esq. 1995. *Helping Yourself through Family Court Proceedings: A Guide for Parents with Psychiatric Disabilities.* Albany, NY: The Mental Health Association in New York State.
(This guide is available online at www.mhanys.org, or by calling 518-434-0439 [ask for the Information Center], or by mailing your request to: MHA in New York State, 169 Central Avenue, Albany, NY 12206.)

Yarbrough, G. 1996. The legal rights of parents with mental illness. *Advisor* (Spring 1986):5-8.

———. 1997. The myths and realities of parents with mental illness. *Advisor* (Spring 1997):7-11.

Chapter 11

Books

Better Homes and Gardens Books. 1990. *Your Child: Living with Divorce.* Des Moines, IA: Meredith Corporation.

Jewett, C. L. 1982. *Helping Children Cope with Separation and Loss.* Harvard, MA: The Harvard Common Press.

Lansky, V. 1998. *It's Not Your Fault, Koko Bear.* Minnetonka, MN: Book Peddlers.

Schneider, M. F., and J. Zuckerberg, Ph. D. 1996. *Difficult Questions Kids Ask (and Are Too Afraid to Ask) About Divorce.* New York: Fireside.

Visher, E. B., and J. S. Visher. 1991. *How to Win as a Step-Family.* 2d ed. New York: Brunner/Mazel, Publishers.

References

American Psychiatric Association. 2000. *Practice Guidelines for the Treatment of Psychiatric Disorders: Compendium 2000.* Washington, DC: American Psychiatric Association.

American Psychiatric Association. 1994. *Diagnostic and Statistical Manual of Mental Disorders, 4th ed: DSM-IV.* Washington, DC: American Psychiatric Association.

Barnett, L. A. 1990. Developmental benefits of play. *Journal of Leisure Research* 22:138-153.

Becker, A. E., S. K. Grinspoon, A. Klibanski, and D. B. Herzog. 1999. Current concepts: Eating disorders. *New England Journal of Medicine,* 340(14):1092-1098.

Bourne, E. J. 1990. *The Anxiety & Phobia Workbook.* Oakland, Calif.: New Harbinger Publications.

Brazelton, T. B. 1998. *Touchpoints: Your Child's Emotional and Behavioral Development.* Reading, MA: Perseus Books.

Brennan, A. 1985. Participation and self-esteem: A test of six alternative patterns. *Adolescence* 4:385-400.

Budd, K. S., and M. J. Holdsworth. 1996. Issues in clinical assessment of minimal parenting competence. *Journal of Clinical Child Psychology* 25(1):2-14.

Burton, V. S. 1990. The consequences of official labels: A research note on rights lost by the mentally ill, mentally incompetent, and convicted felons. *Community Mental Health Journal* 26(3):267-276.

Chandler, B. E., ed. 1997. *The Essence of Play. A Child's Occupation.* Bethesda, MD: The American Occupational Therapy Association.

Coleman, D., and S.E. Iso-Ahola. 1993. Leisure and health: The role of social support and self determination. *Journal of Leisure Research* 25:111-128.

DeMarco, T., and K. Sidney. 1989. Enhancing children's participation in physical activity. *Journal of School Health* 59:337-340.

Downey, G., and J. Coyne. 1990. Children of depressed parents: An integrative review. *Psychological Bulletin* 108:50-76.

Feldman, M. J., and E. L. Gaier. 1980. Correlates of adolescent life satisfaction. *Youth and Society* 12:131-144.

Garner, D. M., and P. E. Garfinkel, eds. 1997. *Handbook of Treatment for Eating Disorders.* New York: Guilford Press.

Goodman, S. H., and H. E. Brumley. 1990. Schizophrenic and depressed mothers: Relational deficits in parenting. *Developmental Psychology* 26:31-39.

Grush, L. R., and L. S. Cohen. 1998. Treatment of depression during pregnancy: Balancing the risks. *Harvard Review of Psychiatry* 6(2):105-109.

Hammen, C. 1997. Children of depressed parents: The stress context. In S. Wolchik, ed. *Handbook of Children's Coping: Linking Theory and Intervention* (pp. 131-157). New York: Plenum Press.

Heyhoe, K. 1999. *Cooking with Kids for Dummies.* Foster City, Calif.: IDG Books Worldwide.

Jacobson, T., L. J. Miller, and K.P. Kirkwood. 1997. Assessing parenting competency in individuals with severe mental illness: A comprehensive service. *Journal of Mental Health Administration* 24(2):189-199.

Kaplan, H. I., and B. J. Sadock. 1998. *Synopsis of Psychiatry.* Baltimore: Williams & Wilkins.

Kaplan, H I., B. J. Sadock, and J. A. Grebb. 1994. *Kaplan and Sadock's Synopisis of Psychiatry: Clinical Psychiatry,* 7th ed. Baltimore: Williams & Wilkins.

Kessler, R. C., J. C. Anthony, D. G. Blazer, et al. 1997. The U.S. National Comorbidity Survey: Overview and Future Directions. *Epidemiologia e Psichiatria Sociale* 6:4-16.

Larson, R., and D. Kleiber. 1993. Daily experiences of adolescents. In P. H. Tolan and B. J. Coohler, eds. *Handbook of Clinical Research and Practice with Adolescents.* New York: Wiley. (pp. 125-145)

Leach, P. 1986. *Your Growing Child: From Babyhood Through Adolescence.* New York: Alfred A. Knopf.

———. 1997. *Your Baby and Child: From Birth to Age Five.* New York: Alfred A. Knopf.

Miller, K. 1985. *Ages and Stages: Developmental Descriptions and Activities, Birth through Eight Years.* Chelsea, MA: Telshare Publishing Co.

Mowbray, C. T., D. Oyserman, J. K. Zemencuk, and S. R. Ross. 1995. Motherhood for women with serious mental illness: Pregnancy, childbirth, and the postpartum period. *American Journal of Orthopsychiatric* 65(1):21-38.

Mueser, K. T., R. E. Drake, and G. R. Bond. 1997. Recent advances in psychiatric rehabilitation for patients with severe mental illness. *Harvard Review of Psychiatry* 5:123-137.

National Mental Health Consumers' Self-Help Clearinghouse. April 2000 Pilot Version. *Self-Advocacy Technical Assistance Guide*. Philadelphia: National Mental Health Consumers' Self-Help Clearinghouse.

Nulman, I., J. Rovet, D. E. Stewart, J. Wolpin, H. A. Gardner, J. G. W. Theis, N. Kulin, and G. Koren. 1997. Neurodevelopmental of children exposed in utero to antidepressant drugs. *The New England Journal of Medicine* 336(4):258-262.

Oyserman, D., C. T. Mowbray, P. A. Meares, and K. B. Firminger. 2000. Parenting among mothers with a serious mental illness. *American Journal of Orthopsychiatry* 70:296-315.

Rudorfer, M. V., M. E. Henry, and H. A. Sackeim. 1997. Electroconvulsive therapy. In A. Tasman, J. Kay, and J. Lieberman, eds. *Psychiatry*. Philadelphia: W. B. Saunders Co.

Savin-Williams, R. C. and T. J. Berndt. 1990. Friendships and peer relationships. In S. S. Feldman and G. R. Elliott, eds. *At the Threshold: The Developing Adolescent*. Cambridge, MA: Harvard University Press.

Steadman, H., E. P. Mulvey, J. Monahan, P. C. Robbins, P. S. Appelbaum, T. Grisso, L. Roth, and E. Silver. 1998. Violence by people discharged from acute psychiatric inpatient facilities and by others in the same neighborhoods. *Archives of General Psychiatry* 55:393-401.

Taylor, L., and R. E. Ingram. 1990. Cognitive reactivity and depressotypic information processing in children of depressed mothers. *Journal of Abnormal Psychology* 108:202-210.

Taylor, T. K., and A. Biglan. 1998. Behavioral family interventions for improving child-rearing: A review of the literature for clinicians and policy makers. *Clinical Child and Family Psychology Review* 1:41-60.

Tips for Using the Food Guide Pyramid for Young Children 2 to 6 Years Old. 1999. Washington, DC: U.S. Department of Agriculture, Center for Nutrition Policy and Promotion.

USDA's Food Guide Pyramid Booklet. 5th ed. 2000. Washington, DC: U.S. Department of Agriculture, Center for Nutrition Policy and Promotion.

U.S. Department of Health and Human Services. 1999. *Mental Health: A Report of the Surgeon General*. Rockville, MD: U.S. Department of Health and Human Services, Substance Abuse and Mental Health Services Administration, Center for Mental Health Services, National Institutes of Health, National Institute of Mental Health.

Van de Kooij, R. 1989. Research on children's play. *Play and Culture* 2:20-34.

Vicary, J. R., E. Smith, L. Caldwell, and J. D. Swisher. 1998. Relationship of changes in adolescents' leisure activities to alcohol use. *American Journal of Health Behavior* 22:276-282.

Ward, D., and M. Shaw, Esq. 1995. *Helping Yourself through Family Court Proceedings: A Guide for Parents with Psychiatric Disabilities*. Albany, NY: The Mental Health Association in New York State.

Webster's Ninth New Collegiate Dictionary. 1991. Springfield, MA: Merriam-Webster, Inc.

Williams, S., and R. McGee. 1991. Adolescents' self-perceptions of their strengths. *Journal of Youth and Adolescence* 20:325-337.

Wisner, K. L., A. J.Gelenberg, H. Leonard, D. Zarin, and E. Frank. 1999. Pharmacologic treatment of depression during pregnancy. *The Journal of the American Medical Association* 282(13):1264-1269.

Joanne Nicholson, Ph.D., has been a clinical and research psychologist for over twenty years. She is Associate Professor in Psychiatry and Family Medicine at the University of Massachusetts Medical School, and Associate Director of the UMMS Center for Mental Health Services Research, where she directs the Child and Family Research Core. Nicholson has established an active, client-based program of research on parents with mental illness and their families. She writes extensively on the challenges facing these families, and provides training and consultation to professional and consumer groups.

Alexis Henry, Sc.D., OTR/L, is Assistant Professor of Occupational Therapy at Sargent College of Health and Rehabilitation Sciences at Boston University, and Adjunct Research Assistant Professor of Psychiatry at the Center for Mental Health Services Research at the University of Massachusetts Medical School. Her research focuses on enhancing participation in valued life roles for people with psychiatric disabilities, and she collaborates actively with clients with psychiatric disabilities, service providers, and other stakeholders in the development of research related to these issues. Henry is a Fellow of the American Occupational Therapy Association, and is the 1998 recipient of the Early Career Research Award from the International Association of Psychosocial Rehabilitation Services.

Jonathan Clayfield, M.A., is a project coordinator at the Center for Mental Health Services Research at the University of Massachusetts Medical School. He is a licensed mental health counselor with considerable experience in community-based mental health treatment programs as well as in the psychiatric rehabilitation clubhouse environment. Clayfield provides technical assistance and consultation to agencies interested in establishing support programs for parents with psychiatric disabilities and has presented workshops on supporting parents with psychiatric disabilities at local and national conferences. He recently earned the designation of registered psychiatric rehabilitation practitioner from the International Association of Psychosocial Rehabilitation Services.

Susan Phillips, B.S., is a research coordinator at the Center for Mental Health Services Research at the University of Massachusetts Medical School. Phillips coordinates the NAMI Research Institute-funded Stanley Scholars and intern training programs at the Center. She has extensive experience training and supporting individuals with psychiatric disabilities to work as research assistants at the Center. She also coordinates the quarterly publication of the *Parent Link* newsletter, which provides updates on current research, programs, resources, and information that support parents with psychiatric disabilities and their families.

Some Other
New Harbinger Titles

Thinking Pregnant, Item TKPG $13.95

Pregnancy Stories, Item PS $14.95

The Co-Parenting Survival Guide, Item CPSG $14.95

Family Guide to Emotional Wellness, Item FGEW $24.95

How to Survive and Thrive in an Empty Nest, Item NEST $13.95

Children of the Self-Absorbed, Item CSAB $14.95

The Adoption Reunion Survival Guide, Item ARSG $13.95

Undefended Love, Item UNLO $13.95

Why Can't I Be the Parent I Want to Be?, Item PRNT $12.95

Kid Cooperation, Item COOP $14.95

Breathing Room: Creating Space to Be a Couple, Item BR $14.95

Why Children Misbehave and What to do About it, Item BEHV $14.95

Couple Skills, Item SKIL $14.95

The Power of Two, Item PWR $15.95

The Queer Parent's Primer, Item QPPM $14.95

Illuminating the Heart, Item LUM $13.95

Dr. Carl Robinson's Basic Baby Care, Item DRR $10.95

The Ten Things Every Parent Needs to Know, Item KNOW $12.95

Healthy Baby, Toxic World, Item BABY $15.95

Becoming a Wise Parent for Your Grown Child, Item WISE $12.95

Stepfamily Realities, Item STEP $16.95

Why are We Still Fighting?, Item FIGH $15.95

Call **toll free, 1-800-748-6273,** or log on to our online bookstore at **www.newharbinger.com** to order. Have your Visa or Mastercard number ready. Or send a check for the titles you want to New Harbinger Publications, Inc., 5674 Shattuck Ave., Oakland, CA 94609. Include $4.50 for the first book and 75¢ for each additional book, to cover shipping and handling. (California residents please include appropriate sales tax.) Allow two to five weeks for delivery.

Prices subject to change without notice.